C000301224

JAVELIN BOYS

JAVELIN BOYS

AIR DEFENCE FROM THE COLD WAR TO CONFRONTATION

STEVE BOND

GRUB STREET • LONDON

Published by
Grub Street
4 Rainham Close
London SW11 6SS

A CIP record for this title is available from the British Library

ISBN-13: 978-1-910690-40-6

Cover design by Daniele Roa

Printed and bound by Finidr, Czech Republic

DEDICATION

To my dear father Cyril Norman Bond who introduced me
to the wonderful world of aviation.

CONTENTS

PREFACE

GROUP CAPTAIN J K PALMER OBE FIMGT RAF (RETD)

Sixty years on, when apart and asunder, parted are those who are singing today. When you look back and forgetfully wonder, what you were like in your words and your play.[1]

I was recently invited to talk to a mixed Rotary audience in that lovely hazy after-dinner hour, about life as a professional aviator in the post-World War 2 era. Aware that I'd be facing some pretty switched-on, potentially critical folk, many with their own stories of life at university as budding surgeons, High Court judges and business barons, plus one ex-Tiller Girl, I planned my speech observing the Chatham House Rule and spent weeks titivating the English and trying to ensure that the form in which I would deliver my recollections would capture the splendour and elegance of the occasion.

On that memorable night I gulped down a precautionary brandy and courage as the president rose to introduce me, and looked out on the candlelit sophistication of dinner jackets and glamorous dresses to deliver my practiced blurb on 'The way we were'. But even as I framed the words to grab their attention and get them on my frequency, an inner voice told me to tell it as it was, and not as perhaps they wanted or expected to hear. Flamboyantly, I discarded my script, beamed a smile to all corners of the room and started with, "I actually joined the RAF by mistake".

As all octogenarians will know, the passing years play tricks on one's memory – some of our greatest stories are about things that never happened at all! But I was keen not to perpetuate the post-war film-makers' image of 'RAF types' as handsome moustached carefree chaps with one eye on a pretty girl and the other on Rita Hayworth, or the 'kick the tyres, light the fires', gung-ho arrogance of the little creep played by Tom Cruise in *Top Gun*. The boys and men in uniform that I worked or flew with post 1945 were a microcosm of British manhood, ranging from lads who just scraped through the 11-plus exam to university graduates, coming from 'poor as a church mouse' families, to the rich and titled.

Whatever the secret was in the Aircrew Selection and Training corridors, the mix of pilots and navigators/system operators arriving in fighter squadron crewrooms in the 1950s and 1960s were seamlessly glued by tradition, and as George Black wrote in Steve Bond's book *Meteor Boys*, 'There was great camaraderie, but if you didn't show a bit of spark and let yourself go occasionally, you weren't part of the fighter force.' I hasten to add that the bomber/strike, maritime 'Kipper fleet', and transport fraternities all had similar bonds and allegiances, but as a fighter boy you walked tall and carried your head high.

---

1. Adapted from the Harrow School song 'Forty Years On' by Edward Ernest Bowen and John Farmer.

Looking back to when the Javelin entered service some 60 years ago, it is worthwhile reflecting on how life was then for the lucky chaps who flew the new aircraft. The massive 1950s build-up of aircraft and crews to fight a conventional war, had seen the jet largely replace piston-engined aeroplanes. Many pilots serving on 8/12 year commissions had been lured to civil airlines. Many permanent overseas bases became staging posts, or were supplemented in times of tension by fighters of the new Tactical 38 Group, in-flight refuelled from the UK. At a time when missile technology, both air and ground launched, was really taking off, some poor souls even fell for the line that their best career path was to sit in a tent and press pretty buttons!

But no such cynicism blurred my vision back then, or spoilt the thousand hours I spent in the Javelin, wearing the famous colours of 23 Squadron at Coltishall and Leuchars, before the 'Red Eagles' converted to the 'Shiny silver pursuit ship' the Lightning Mk.3 in 1965. To be truthful, my colleagues and I knew little about the world's politics – or cared much! We were part of a proud, vibrant, dynamic force that faced a deadly serious enemy that confronted them from the Arctic Circle down to the Mediterranean.

RAF stations in the UK, and a great many overseas in Germany, the Med, Middle and Far East, were exciting places both in terms of the flying and the family life, with the vast majority of wives living on base, and the various messes the centres for a great social life. In the fighter world you might live anywhere from Lossiemouth in Scotland, down to the south coast of England, or overseas accompanied by families on any one of those many far-away bases, most with guaranteed sunshine, cheap cars and alcohol and a way of life that was so different from that in the UK. In 2017, the world has shrunk, and places like Hong Kong, Singapore, Calcutta, Bahrain, Aden and Cairo, with magic in their names and a unique appeal in lifestyle, culture, customs, dress and food, have lost their mystery and charm by becoming westernised. By 1962, fighter crews having spent most of their flying 'up and down in an hour', were routinely flying long-range single legs and full squadron detachments using in-flight refuelling.

Any aviator will tell you that being a part of this or that squadron, flying this or that aircraft, from this or that base, was the happiest most fulfilling period in their lives. In my 38 years I think that the '50s and '60s were the best for the thrilling mix of flying, social life and the promise that there was more to come as new aircraft, with undreamt of performance and reliability, entered service. On reflection, I can honestly say that I enjoyed flying whatever was put before me, even though when I returned from a US exchange tour, having flown the F-101 Voodoo and the early US Marines version of the F-4 Phantom, the Javelin was a bit of a let-down in performance and electronics capability. Like almost all British combat aircraft, the Javelin was too long in development and didn't reach anything like its full potential until the Mk.9 entered service. But – and as the RAF always did in my era – both engineers and aircrew got the very best out of what British industry was able to provide, and I remember 23 Squadron as a very happy outfit, immensely proud of its majestic beast.

Later in my career, when serving in MoD Operational Requirements and the defence industry, I was to realise – and even understand – why the RAF seldom if ever, got the performance and reliability that it had clearly specified and negotiated for. Planned in-service dates were seldom met, and stipulated minimum acceptable performance levels seldom achieved. Partly, that was because industry (both UK and US) had a knack in their extremely competitive world, of promising what they knew could never be achieved and, partly because the procurement agencies were not professionally acute, with most linked to politicians totally uninterested in the armed services.

For reasons now lost in the mists of time, there was a period when it seemed that whatever industry offered in a competition, it would find its way into service. The Hunter's chief rival, the Swift, proved useless as a fighter and not much better in its reconnaissance role. The Javelin was the RAF's choice as its night/all-weather fighter, allegedly having a greater development potential, leaving its rival the DH.110 to enter naval service as the Sea Vixen, whilst the medium bomber world had a mix of Valiant, Victor and Vulcan, where one type should have filled the role adequately.

But if procurement was in a pickle, the last to complain were us fighter jocks, who welcomed the mean-looking delta-wing Javelin as the RAF's first truly all-weather missile/guns armed fighter, with a big advance operationally on its much loved Meteor predecessor. It is easy, as we see all too often in today's media, to criticise things past. As professional aircrew, we knew from the RAF grapevine that the Javelin had a chequered upbringing, with delays to its intended in-service date. 'Undesirable flight characteristics when approaching the limits' were cited, ground crew complained it was awkward to work on, and critics assessing the USAF century-series fighters and the US Navy's F-4, said the Javelin was 'a day late and a dollar short'.

Nonetheless, when I arrived on 23 Squadron in 1962, with a famous new boss, Wg Cdr A J 'Red' Owen, DSO, DFC, AFC, the atmosphere and the spirit amongst the crews was exceptional. In-flight refuelling was commonplace by then, but on 23 we flew non-stop to Aden, and then the first full 12 aircraft squadron deployment to Singapore. Once en route from Karachi to Gan, we lost seven out of 12 who diverted due to a dodgy chicken curry working its way through our sensitive systems, and there were squeaky moments at 36,000 feet amidst Indian Ocean cu-nims, with only a dinghy diversion if you screwed up the basket connection! But we never lost or left behind a single aircraft. As befits a fighter squadron based in Scotland, to the Javelin I say "Better luv'd ye canna be".

INTRODUCTION and ACKNOWLEDGEMENTS

The Gloster Javelin was the United Kingdom's first line of night/all-weather air defence, both at home and in Royal Air Force Germany, from the mid-1950s when it began replacing the Meteor and Venom, until the advent of the Lightning in the early 1960s. Its primary role at that time was as a high-level bomber interceptor. It then continued to serve in Cyprus, from where a squadron was deployed to Zambia at the time of Rhodesia's Unilateral Declaration of Independence (UDI), and its swan song came in Singapore, particularly during the period of the Indonesian Confrontation, where the last squadron was disbanded in 1968.

A relatively modest 434 Javelins were built, which served in 18 different squadrons. The aircraft has attracted a lot of sometimes ill-informed criticism, and is often said to have been a bit of a lumbering beast. It had a number of nicknames attached to it including 'Flying Flat-iron' and 'Harmonious Dragmaster' (due to its curious engine note when taxiing, and a whining sound when airborne, aided by the airflow over the gun ports). However, lumbering is not the impression expressed by the aircrew who flew it. Yes, it had its aerodynamic quirks and could be dangerous if not handled correctly, but most express quite an affection for it, with one pilot saying it was his favourite out of all the many aircraft types he had flown in a lengthy career.

In the late 1940s, the RAF's air defence system consisted largely of early variants of the Meteor and Vampire day fighters, neither of which were fitted with air interception (AI) radar, leaving them heavily reliant on ground-controlled interception (GCI) techniques. The only airborne AI radar in service at that time, was fitted to the Mosquito NF.36 which still equipped five home and three overseas-based squadrons, and which was rapidly becoming outdated. Although work was already in hand to develop radar-equipped night-fighter versions of the Meteor, Vampire and later the Venom, it was clear that the comparatively modest performance increase they offered was unlikely to be a match for the Soviet Union's burgeoning nuclear-capable bomber force. Therefore, they were considered as very much a stop-gap measure until a night/all-weather fighter with a much higher performance could be developed and brought into service.

Thus the Javelin's origins can be traced back to Military Aircraft Specification F.4/48, which was issued on 10 June 1948 to the de Havilland and Gloster aircraft companies in response to the RAF's Operational Requirement (OR) 227. This requirement called for a fighter with a maximum speed at 40,000 feet of not less than 525 knots, with an endurance of two hours, and a rate of climb of not less than 1,000 feet per minute at 45,000 feet. This was specifically aimed at addressing the high-flying bomber threat to the UK's airspace. A crew of two was specified, as was the armament of four 20 or 30mm Aden guns with sufficient ammunition for ten seconds firing time.

De Havilland's response was the DH.110, which first flew from Hatfield on 26 September 1951. Gloster's P.280 design, under the leadership of R W 'Dick' Walker, was the subject of a contract to build five Armstrong Siddeley Sapphire-powered prototypes under the company's designation GA.5. The first of these, WD804, made its maiden flight from Moreton Valance in Gloucestershire on 26 November 1951, flown by Gloster's chief test pilot Sqn Ldr W A 'Bill' Waterton AFC. The RAF subsequently opted for the Gloster aircraft, with a production order coming on 7 July 1952, while the DH.110 went on to be developed into the Royal Navy's Sea Vixen carrier-borne fighter. The specification was re-issued on 23 July 1952 to cover the production Gloster aeroplane, now called the Javelin, in its F.1 version, although the designation was changed to fighter all-weather (FAW) in February 1954. The only significant change to the specification was to make provision for the carriage of at least two air-to-air rocket batteries, which were never fitted in operations.

Flight testing of the five prototypes at both the manufacturer's facilities and the Aeroplane and Armament Experimental Establishment (A&AEE) at Boscombe Down, exposed a number of issues with the design. On 29 June 1952, Bill Waterton was lucky to escape when he crash-landed the first prototype at Boscombe Down after the loss of both elevators, due to flutter at high speed. Almost exactly a year later, on 11 June 1953, the second prototype was lost after getting into a so-called 'super-stall'. This was a situation when, at high angles of attack and with low airspeed with flaps down, the nose was raised and a stall began which caused the wings to become self-stabilising. This resulted in a high rate of descent, from which recovery proved to be, in this case, impossible, test pilot Peter Lawrence losing his life. The other effect of the 'super-stall' was that the wings blanked off the airflow to the tailplane, again leading to loss of control. The solution decided upon, was to fit the wing with an artificial stall-warning device which sounded a buzzer to warn the pilot of the onset of a stall. In addition, it was decided that the Javelin could be too dangerous in such stall conditions, and on entry into service, both spinning and any manoeuvring in the vertical plane were strictly forbidden. The aircraft would tend to spin at the stall without warning, with flat spins usually developing with a high rate of rotation, which proved to be very difficult to recover from. A double-edged comment in a Boscombe Down test report stated 'It is unfortunate that the … work of the firm was not quicker and more comprehensive, because (with earlier elimination of the snags) it would have been an outstanding aircraft."[2]

Another major problem, and the cause of a number of accidents and close-calls, was a tendency for the Sapphire engines to self-destruct under certain conditions; a failure known as centre-line closure. If there was a sudden drop in air temperature when operating at high power settings, for example when flying through dense

2. Mason, Tim, *The Cold War years, Flight Testing at Boscombe Down 1945-1975*, Hikoki 2001.

cloud (especially in tropical cumulonimbus conditions), the engine compressor casings would rapidly cool and contract, causing the rotating compressor blades to come into contact with the casing and suffer instant, catastrophic failure and leading to the destruction of the engine. The engines were later modified by applying an abrasive coating to the inside of the casing, which was intended to allow the blade tips to grind themselves down rather than fail! However, centre-line closures continued to occur until the end of Javelin flying in Singapore. Blade shedding was also a problem with the Sapphire, which was fitted with a steel containment shroud to prevent shredded blades from entering the other engine.

A further issue for the squadrons to cope with was the prevalence of starter fires. Early marks were fitted with two 5-inch diameter starter cartridges for each engine which, when fired, fed cordite gas to the starter turbine to spin up the engine. Problems came on occasions when the starter motor failed to disengage and accelerated with the engine to self-destruction, or when both cartridges fired simultaneously, in either case a disastrous fire could be the result. The FAW.8 and FAW.9 had a different system, and used a small cordite cartridge to ignite AVPIN (isopropyl nitrate) liquid fuel in a starter chamber. It became standard practice for starter crews to leave the starter bay panel open to check for AVPIN leaks and fires, until both engines were running.

Much of this still lay ahead however, when the first of 40 production FAW.1s, XA544, made its maiden flight on 22 July 1954. Fitted with AI 17 radar, with an effective range at altitude of about 18 miles, this variant was fitted with Sapphire Sa.6 engines, each giving 8,300 lbs of static thrust. Its maximum permissible all-up weight was 36,500 lbs (a little over 16 tons) and it could carry 765 gallons of fuel.

The following month, August 1954, 46 Squadron was reformed at Odiham in Hampshire as a night-fighter unit, equipped with Meteor NF.12s and NF.14s. The Meteors were only destined to be on charge for a comparatively short period, while the squadron got into its stride, as it had been chosen to be the first unit to fly Javelins, and the first anywhere in the world to fly delta-winged aircraft. The first aircraft to arrive was XA570 on 24 February 1956, but sadly this aircraft was to become the first to be lost when it crashed on approach four months later, killing the squadron commander and his navigator.

At this time there were no dual-control Javelins available; the T.3 trainer variant was not to enter service for another three years, so new pilots' first flights were essentially solos. The squadron settled into what would become the Javelin force's stock-in-trade, with flying programmes largely consisting of practice interceptions (PIs), usually of Javelin v Javelin, but also of Javelins being vectored by ground control and their own radar to intercept high-flying aircraft such as Canberras, and later the V-bombers. Of these, the Vulcan proved particularly difficult to catch, as it tended to fly at the extreme edge of the fighter's altitude performance envelope. The Mk.1 was also the first Javelin variant to reach RAF Germany, when 87 Squadron received 46 Squadron's Mk.1s as the latter changed over to the Mk.2 in 1957.

Top: FAW.1 XA552 over Gloucestershire 1956. (Adrian Balch collection)
Bottom: FAW.5 XH691 E of 228 OCU's 137 Squadron, Leeming April 1961. (Adrian Balch collection)

Here they took over the immediate readiness role (previously the task of USAF units) under the code name 'Fabulous'.

Following completion and test flying as standard production aircraft, two Mk.1s became the only Javelins ever to fly with engines other than the Sapphire. In 1959 XA552 was sent to de Havilland at Hatfield for the installation of re-heated Gyron Junior engines, as a part of the test programme for the forthcoming Bristol Type 188 supersonic research aircraft. Later moving to Filton, the programme was completed in 1963 and the aircraft disposed of. The second engine test-bed was XA562, which was fitted with the Rolls-Royce Avon engine, a direct competitor to the Sapphire. Like '552 before it, initial conversion work was carried out by Napier at Luton, before the aircraft arrived at Rolls-Royce's flight test airfield at Hucknall near Derby, where it flew with the Avons (again equipped with reheat), from the summer of 1958 until early 1960. It too ended up as scrap.

Chronologically, the next variant to enter service was the FAW.4 (again with AI 17 radar), which, in later batches, introduced an all-flying tailplane to improve longitudinal control and stability, plus vortex generators on the upper wing surface to extend the high-speed buffet boundary. Produced by both Glosters and Armstrong-Whitworth at Bitteswell, first deliveries were made in October 1956. The RAF took delivery of 50 examples, which served with a total of eight squadrons at home and in Germany, 141 Squadron at Horsham St. Faith being the first, followed by 3, 11, 23, 41, 72, 87 and 96. Next came 63 FAW.5s beginning in March 1957, with Armstrong-Whitworth again joining in the production effort. This variant also had AI 17 radar, but began addressing the aircraft's duration issue by carrying an extra 250 gallons of internal fuel, raising the total to 1,015 gallons. It was also designed to carry four underwing Blue Jay (later renamed Firestreak) missiles, although this was not introduced into service until the Mk.7. However, the necessary pylon fit for the missiles also enabled the carriage of four droppable fuel tanks, each of 120 gallons capacity. Entering service with 151 Squadron at Turnhouse, a further four units followed including 72 at Church Fenton plus 5, 11 and 87 in Germany.

The FAW.2 (of which there were 31), was fitted with the US-designed AI Mk.21/22 (APQ43) radar and followed on into service in April 1957, reaching 46, 85 and 89 Squadrons. A second radar was selected for a number of reasons, not all connected with seeking improved performance. The thinking was that two sources of radar supply were probably more sensible than relying on just one, and additionally, this would give any potential aggressor more frequencies to try and jam. Presumably therefore, a substantial airspace incursion might see both radar types amongst the airborne response, and by example, between them the squadrons based in Germany did have a mixed radar fleet. All Javelins fitted with the AI 22 radar could be identified by having a noticeably shorter nose, with the radar being behind a hinged radome rather than a removable one in those marks fitted with AI 17. Although the main armament still remained the four 30mm cannons, in 1958 a single FAW.2 was also the first Javelin to actually carry Firestreak missiles for trials, although none were fired at that time.

During conversations with many pilots, and especially navigators, the issue of having two radars, and getting to grips with their operational and performance differences and characteristics, was frequently raised. The views expressed have been included a number of times throughout these pages, but it is worth so doing to illustrate just how much this was in the forefront of their minds, not least because the radar was undoubtedly the principal tool in the Javelin's armoury.

Five squadrons received the FAW.6 with AI 22 (33 built) starting in September 1957 when 89 Squadron at Stradishall gave up its Venom NF.3s, quickly followed by 29 Squadron at Acklington who previously flew the Meteor NF.11. Nos. 41, 85 and 89 Squadrons also received Mk.6s as did 46 Squadron, which disbanded at Waterbeach in June 1961, by which time the Javelin force was already coming down from its peak numbers. That status had been reached the previous year, when no fewer than 14 squadrons were equipped with the type. The Mk.6 had the same increased internal fuel capacity as the Mk.5, only differing by having the US radar.

A major change in the design came with the AI 17-equipped FAW.7, with no fewer than 142 being built by Glosters and Armstrong-Whitworth. This took advantage of the uprated Sapphire Sa.7 engines, which offered a 32% increase in power over the Sa.6 fitted to the earlier marks, giving a thrust of 11,000 lbs. The Mk.7 was also able to carry four Firestreaks, had yaw dampers to reduce the so-called 'Dutch roll' yawing oscillations, and a fully-powered rudder. Deliveries began in March 1958, and by that summer 33 Squadron at Leeming was receiving Javelins to replace the Meteor NF.14s that it had flown for just a year. This unit was followed by 23, 25 and 64 Squadrons plus 228 Operational Conversion Unit (OCU), also at Leeming, whose increasing tasking led to the displacement of 33 Squadron to Middleton St. George (now Durham Tees Valley airport).

Almost in parallel with the FAW.7 came the FAW.8, which was fitted with AI 22 radar. However a significant major change for this final major new-production mark, was the fitting of a reheat system to the Sapphires, which became the Sa.7R

FAW.8 XH966 during Firestreak jettison trials. (Adrian Balch collection)

and offered a marked increase in performance, especially at altitude. Static thrust for each engine was 10,500 lbs dry, but increased to 12,300 with reheat. Only 47 Mk.8s were built (with 13 more being cancelled during final assembly and dismantled for spares), serving with just two squadrons (41 and 85) from November 1959.

The start of the new decade saw a major escalation of the Cold War with four principal triggers occurring within the first three years. The first was the shooting down of Gary Powers' Lockheed U-2 reconnaissance aircraft over the Soviet Union on 1 May 1960. Next came the abortive 'Bay of Pigs' invasion of Cuba, by exiles from that country who set out from the coast of the US in April 1961. The consequent, inevitable rapid heightening of tension between East and West resulted in an increased state of readiness for RAF squadrons in Germany. Over the ensuing two years, a number of home-based Javelin squadrons were sent to Germany to strengthen the incumbent fighter force, with aircraft being maintained on constant Battle Flight alert. The third trigger was the construction of the Berlin Wall in 1961, and the threat of a blockade of the air corridor to the city from the west. In the following year the Russians were found to be positioning long-range ballistic missiles in Cuba, bringing the world perilously close to a nuclear war. The Javelin force was thus at the forefront of air defence in central Europe at one of the tensest periods of the entire Cold War.

The FAW.8's improved performance led to a decision to modify the still being built FAW.7 fleet, to a similar reheat-equipped standard (while retaining the AI 17 radar), this resulting in the ultimate Javelin, the FAW.9. The Mk.9 became by far the most numerous Javelin in service, with 118 being converted, some being modified whilst still on the production line. By now the aircraft's maximum permissible all-up weight had risen to 44,700 lbs, just under 20 tons, an almost 35% increase over the FAW.1. Entry into service was only a month after the Mk.8

in December 1959, with the first aircraft going to 25 Squadron at Waterbeach, followed by 5 and 11 Squadrons in Germany, 23, 29, 33 Squadrons in the UK and finally, 60 and 64 Squadrons in Singapore, the only Javelin units to be permanently based in the Far East Air Force (FEAF). Once in service, successful in-flight refuelling trials led to many of the fleet being fitted with a fixed, and very ungainly, 20 feet long flight refuelling probe on the starboard fuselage. Most of those so fitted were later modified by Armstrong-Whitworth at Bitteswell to allow the carriage of four 230-gallon drop tanks, thus becoming the FAW.9R.

Top: T.3 XH395 Z 46 Squadron, Waterbeach September 1960. (Adrian Balch collection)
Bottom: AW.9 XH715 M 228 OCU, Leuchars July 1966. (Adrian Balch collection)

It was in these later years that the Javelin again came to the fore in two troubled areas of the world, far removed from the Cold War. In 1964 there were signs that Indonesia was engaged in a major build-up of its forces in opposition to the establishment of the Federation of Malaysia, which had come into being the previous year. For the next two years the so-called Indonesian Confrontation continued, with both air and land incursions. Again, air power played a major part, with Javelins of 60 and 64 Squadrons operating in the theatre from 1961 to 1968.

Then in November 1965, Rhodesia declared its UDI from the United Kingdom, and there were fears that neighbouring Zambia might be under threat. The air defence of Cyprus was the responsibility of 29 Squadron's Javelin 9s, which were deployed to Zambia to protect both their airspace and incoming oil-carrying transport aircraft. The squadron finally returned to Cyprus in the summer of 1966.

To complete the story of the development of the Javelin, there is one remaining variant of the aircraft to be mentioned, the T.3 dual-control trainer, built in response to Specification T.118/D. Featuring a slightly raised rear cockpit for improved visibility, it had a 1,115 gallons fuel capacity, but was not fitted with radar as it was purely used for pilot training. The first prototype, although built by Glosters, was assembled by Air Service Training (AST) at Hamble in Hampshire. It was flown for the first time by 'Dicky' Martin from Brockworth on 20 August 1956, but it would be early 1959 before the first of the 22 production models (five more being cancelled), started reaching the squadrons. Most units had one or two on strength, while others went to the OCU.

A further radical, higher-performance development of the Javelin was proposed, but was destined not to come to fruition. For the 1953 Specification F.153D, Gloster's P.370 response was a new variant referred to as the Super Javelin, or the thin-wing Javelin, to be powered by Bristol Olympus engines and to have a Mach 1.6 performance in level flight. Intended to carry Red Dean or Blue Jay missiles, 18 prototype and pre-production examples were ordered in 1955. Construction of the resulting G.50 model prototype aircraft had started, when the government cancelled the project in July 1956, this being a precursor to the notorious Duncan Sandys defence review decision the following year, which maintained that no more manned fighter aircraft would be required after the Lightning.

The operational Javelin fleet declined markedly throughout the 1960s, both as the overall RAF fighter force continued to shrink, and as the replacement Lightning came to the fore. Even so, it was not until 1 May 1968 that the last unit, 60 Squadron at Tengah, Singapore, was disbanded. The event was marked by an impressive formation flypast, after which most of the aircraft were unceremoniously scrapped on site. Just one Javelin flew on at Boscombe Down, until it too was retired on 24 January 1975 and flown to Duxford – itself a former Javelin station – for preservation by the Imperial War Museum. Today, just ten complete examples survive as museum pieces to remind us of what was, for the much of the Cold War, our first line of air defence.

Putting this book together has only been possible with the help of all the following Javelin Boys who have so enthusiastically allowed me into their homes, endured many lengthy telephone calls, answered interminable questions and granted access to their precious log books and private photograph collections.

Cpl John Augoustis, Laurie Bean, SAC Ken Beere, Sgt Ken Brereton, Air Cdre Jack Broughton OBE, Mike Bryant, Sqn Ldr Brian Bullock, Sqn Ldr Don Chapman, Chf Tech David Curnock, Flt Lt Derek 'Moose' Davies, Wg Cdr Peter Day, Wg Cdr Ed Durham, J/T Cliff Edwards, Cpl Bryan Elliott, Sgt Malcolm Elliott, Gp Capt Mel Evans, Sgt Roy Evans, Sqn Ldr Jim Froud, Wg Cdr Piers Gardiner, Sqn Ldr Mike Gill, Flt Lt Bill Hustwayte, Sgt Terry Jackson, Wg Cdr George Lee, Cpl Doug Mansfield, Flt Lt Eric Marsh, Wg Cdr Peter Masterman, Flt Lt Alan Mudge, Gp Capt Kel 'Johnny' Palmer, Wg Cdr Forbes Pearson, Sqn Ldr Bill Ragg, Sgt Mick Speake, Flt Lt Norman Spence, Flt Lt Pete Wallington. Gentlemen, I thank and salute you all.

In addition, I must also say a big 'thank you' to many others who have helped along the way. If I have forgotten anybody please accept my humble apologies.

Richard Andrews, Alec Audley, Adrian Balch, Gp Capt Dougie Barr 46 Squadron Association, Gp Capt Chris Christie, Rick Cooke 60 (R) Squadron Shawbury, the late Colin Fair, Martin Fenner, Richard Forder, David Ketcher, Flt Lt Alistair McFarland 41 Squadron Association, the late Geoff Mann, John Mounce, Michael Napier, Dr Ray Neve, the late Dave Paterson, Sqn Ldr Mike Sayer. I must once again express my gratitude to John Davies and all the crew at Grub Street for their continued support and encouragement. Finally, my thanks and love to my darling wife Heather, who has been a great help sense-reading and proof-reading my manuscripts and giving me endless advice.

I have endeavoured wherever possible to correctly credit the origins of all photographs and other material I have used. It has to be said that in the Internet age the true source of some material is not always possible to identify with certainty, so if I have inadvertently omitted anyone, please accept my apologies.

Dr Steve Bond

CHAPTER ONE

'WE RISE TO CONQUER'[3] – 46 SQUADRON

THE BOYS

Sqn Ldr Don Chapman
Pilot. 39 Squadron Mosquito. Aide-de-camp to AOC Iraq. CFS Little Rissington, Meteor. 46 Squadron Javelin. Fighter Command ground tour. Left the RAF and went to de Havilland as a flight test observer.

Flt Lt Eric Marsh
Pilot, joined in 1952. Trained on Tiger Moth, Chipmunk, Oxford and Meteor. 153 and 85 Squadrons Meteor NF.12/14. 46, 60, 23 Squadrons and Fighter Command Ferry Squadron Javelin. Lightning Flt Simulator. Manby Jet Provost. CFS and Nottingham University Air Squadron (UAS) Chipmunk. Left the RAF in 1968 and flew for BOAC.

Flt Lt Pete Wallington
Navigator, joined in 1952. Trained on Brigand and Meteor NF.11. 46 Squadron Meteor NF.11 and Javelin. 139 and 213 Squadrons Canberra. Radar Research Flying Unit Pershore. 13 Squadron Canberra. Met Research Flt Canberra and Hercules. Left the RAF in 1999.

INTO SERVICE

In October 1955, two Javelins on Ministry of Supply charge were flown to Coltishall in Norfolk to take part in the annual air defence Exercise Beware. Operating alongside the resident Venom NF.3s of 23 and 141 Squadrons, the Javelins proved to be very impressive in action against high-flying Canberras, with Wg Cdr Edward Crew and his navigator Sqn Ldr Jim Walton claiming eight 'kills', duly painted on the side of their aircraft in time-honoured fashion. The other two crews involved were Wg Cdr Richard 'Dicky' Martin with Flight Lieutenant (Flt Lt) Williamson and Sqn Ldr Peter Scott with Flt Lt R E Jeffries.

Wg Cdr Crew had a distinguished wartime career as a Beaufighter and Mosquito night fighter pilot and at the time of the Javelin trials was the commanding officer of the Central Fighter Establishment (CFE). Sqn Ldr Walton went on to command 25 Squadron during its Javelin era. Wg Cdr Martin flew Hurricanes and Tomahawks during the war, became an instructor at the Empire Test Pilots' School (ETPS) and joined Glosters in 1953. Sqn Ldr Scott had flown the F-84 Thunderjet in Korea during an exchange posting to the United States Air Force (USAF). The year after Exercise 'Beware', Flt Lt Jeffries survived an involuntary ejection from his Javelin following a mid-air collision with a Hunter (see Appendix Three).

The first Javelin to be handed over to the RAF was XA566 which arrived at the All Weather Wing of the CFE at West Raynham, Norfolk on 3 January 1956, followed two days later by XA565. The task was to develop the operational deployment strategy for the type and a third example XA568 was added on 2 March.

It had been decided to reform a squadron to take the first operational aircraft, rather than converting an existing unit. 46 Squadron had enjoyed a distinguished history as a fighter unit from 1916 until late 1944 when it suddenly found itself flying Stirlings and Dakotas on transport duties until it disbanded in February 1950. It was chosen as the first Javelin squadron and reformed on 15 August 1954 at Odiham in Hampshire which was a day fighter station with two squadrons of Meteor F.8s. To enable the new crews to have time to gel in anticipation of the first Javelins arriving, it received a mixed-bag of Meteor night fighters.

"The early days were affected by shortages of manpower and equipment; although training began almost immediately, it took until the end of October for the squadron to reach a strength of 12 NF.12/14s and one Meteor T.7 for training and categorisation. By March 1955 when Wg Cdr Frank Birchfield took over as CO from Sqn Ldr David Ross, the manpower situation was improving, but Mechanical Transport (MT) shortages caused problems for the squadron, whose dispersal was on the opposite side of the airfield to the rest of the station. By June 1955, it was recorded that the squadron had received some Meteor F(TT).8s for target towing, and that its strength had reached 48 officers and 110 NCO/airmen."[4]

Pete Wallington was fresh out of navigator training and among the first to arrive at Odiham.

> "My first tour was on Meteors, fresh out of training. I started in September 1952, when I joined from school. I graduated from nav school in December 1953 – Hullavington. I then went to Colerne for navigator training. Somebody had to, so I did the Brigand and did my night-fighter AI training. Basically it was a single pilot aeroplane; he had to get in first, and then we pushed his seat back up first, with its armour-plated back-plate, and behind him they had made two seats, sideways, along the port side of the cabin. The AI was on the starboard side, two sets, and the instructor sat on the left-hand seat with the student nav on the right-hand one. You shoved your head inside a big rubber mask and looked at the screens and you attempted to follow the blip in front. Every time you said turn left, to port, you went backwards; every time you turned to starboard, you tilted forwards. When you said go up you went to the right and when down you tilted left so you were 90 degrees out in all your senses. Behind that was a little rumble seat and behind

3. The motto of 46 Squadron who flew Javelins from February 1956 to June 1961.

4. 46 Squadron Association.

that the fuel tanks so there was a stench of petrol all the time, with your head stuck inside the rubber mask and all your senses 90 degrees out.

"It was absolutely revolting and actually the instructor said that if you could get through this course without being airsick you'd never be airsick in anything and I wasn't. I was never airsick in all those years of flying. That was it. From there I went to Leeming where I converted on to the Meteor NF.11. I was crewed with a pilot. They had more pilots than navs because the washout rate of navs was quite high. The instructor said that either you'd got it or you hadn't. It wasn't something you could teach. They could show you what they meant but you had one screen that showed the blip in the horizontal plane, ahead left or right of you, and another screen that showed it above or below and you had to correlate the two, side by side, and convert that into a 3-D picture in your own mind. You had to decide which way you wanted to go to intercept it. This was something that you either cottoned on to, soon, or you never did. It was an AI Mk.10 radar. I crewed up with a guy called Evan Wright who was a single-seat pilot from the war. He was old; I was 18 but he was 30-something and he christened me 'Junior'. Apparently I was at that time the youngest nav in Fighter Command, because I'd come through the mill so quickly. I was at Colerne in February '54 and then I went to Leeming in August and straight on to a squadron there.

"The Meteor was totally different. A bit rapid, you know, but it was great fun. I do remember very well the first trip I did with Evan; his name was Evan but everyone called him Wilbur! This was immediately after I'd been told 'This is your pilot; go and fly with him'. We got airborne and it was literally just a general handling flight with me in the back to get used to the aeroplane. It had been bashed into us at nav ground school that you've just got to keep telling the pilots where they are: 'pigeons to base, pigeons to base'. Distance and bearing from where you are to base. So we were airborne at altitude, above 8/8ths cloud, and I thought it was about time I told him where we were so I gave him the pigeons to base figures but he started descending and just gave a sort of sniff. I explained what the phrase meant but he just said, 'I know. We're over Linton-on-Ouse' and we were! That's a typical single-seat pilot and he'd been so for about ten years at that stage, or more, and he taught me an awful lot. I got on very well with him. We were posted to Odiham, 46 Squadron and when we converted on to the Javelin in '56 Wilbur converted with me and I was with him for about eight months and then he was grounded and put on to air traffic, largely I think because of his age. I then crewed with another night fighter pilot from Mosquitoes. We had no training Javelins at that time. The Handling Squadron at Boscombe Down had two Javelins, two of the prototypes, which did the release-for-service work."

Top: Javelin No.1 Course at Gloster's, Moreton Valance December 1955. (via Pete Wallington)
Bottom: 46 Squadron FAW.1 XA623 G flying over the south coast of England. (46 Squadron Association)

Initially, two 46 Squadron pilots were sent to Boscombe Down to convert to type and then train other pilots at Odiham. Each pilot had to pass a detailed written examination before being taken aloft in the back seat of a Javelin. Following this he flew one with his navigator in the back and the crew then had to complete a total of twelve trips, half at night, before they were declared operational. **Pete Wallington:**

> "Our boss was Wg Cdr Frank Birchfield and the squadron commander when we reformed was David Ross but he reverted to senior flight commander when Frank Birchfield arrived. The two of them went to Boscombe and basically the Javelin test pilot there got in the front and Frank Birchfield got in the back. When they got airborne, the test pilot gave Frank a set of speeds and altitudes to fly and when they got back they simply swapped seats and repeated the flight. That was Frank's conversion and then he did the same thing with David Ross."

Thereafter, conversion courses were run by Glosters at Moreton Valance, with the first one taking place in December 1955 for ten crews, of which the following members have been identified: Bob Bragg, Malcolm Cresswell, David 'Dickie' Dawes, Alan Elphik, Howard Fitzer, 'Jock' Fraser, Joe Lyons, Eddie Scott, Pat Street, Danny Sullivan and Pete Wallington.

Wg Cdr Birchfield had served on several Spitfire squadrons during the war and commanded two of them, 92 and 234. Awarded the Air Force Cross (AFC) in 1941, he completed his night-fighter course at 228 OCU in January 1955 before being posted to Odiham. On 2 January 1956 he was attached to Handling Squadron at Boscombe Down to convert to the Javelin. **Pete Wallington** continues:

> "When we formed the squadron with Meteors we had NF.14s with the AI 21 so we had to learn the new one. Fortunately the crews had come from all sorts of different squadrons but when we formed the squadron there were just five of us. A fellow called Flt Lt 'Jock' Fraser came by himself and then there was myself (and Wilbur) and another called Ken Nicholls and his nav called Colin Gower. We were the first five to arrive at Odiham, waltzed into the wing commander's office on day one and he said, 'Oh God, not five more people to look after'. He looked at the three pilots and asked whether they were with 54 or 247 Squadron, which were two Meteor F.8 squadrons then. Then he looked at us and assumed we were simply station navs. We told him we were from 46 Squadron. He was quite unaware of a 46 Squadron but then remembered that someone had mentioned that they might be getting a third squadron at Odiham so he told us that we could take over an empty hangar on the other side of the airfield and that was it.
>
> "We had no aeroplanes at that point just the five of us. Gradually other guys and aeroplanes stated arriving and on 27 August 1954 Jock Fraser and I did the very first flight (an air test after acceptance) of the reformed 46 Squadron in Meteor NF.12 WS692, which is now in the Newark Air Museum. That was the first flight of the reformed 46 Squadron. Again, the Javelin FAW.1s we converted to were equipped with AI 17s, an updated AI 10, whereas we were all familiar with the AI 21s, so they took all our '12s and '14s away and gave us 12 old Meteor NF.11s to refresh ourselves on and a letter came down setting out the form of the refresher training. All the navs had to go through this but it didn't matter to the pilots because a Meteor was a Meteor was a Meteor but then the Javelins came along. It was all very *ad hoc* in those days.
>
> "The Javelin was another world. It went faster, it climbed better, it went higher. It didn't fly any longer than the Meteor because we converted on to the Mk.1, which didn't even have drop tanks when we got it, so it gave us about 35 or 40 minutes at the most. It had 765 gallons of fuel, and all the first trips were very short. I last flew a Meteor 11 on 28 March 1956 after a Javelin familiarisation with Sqn Ldr Ross on Javelin XA570 on 13 March 1956 for 40 minutes. That aircraft crashed when Frank Birchfield was flying it. He crashed on approach to Odiham with his nav Brian Chambers during a ground controlled approach (GCA) – both of them were killed. It was the only fatality we had on the squadron during the time I was on it. He crashed on a night trip when he was turning finals and hit a hill on 12 June 1956."

The crew had successfully completed a night-time practice interception (PI) and just before midnight they commenced their let-down back into Odiham. At around two miles out the pilot advised that he had the runway in sight, but almost immediately the aircraft struck a wooded hillside 1½ miles from the threshold. Wg Cdr Birchfield's military funeral was held at Odiham on 15 June. In addition to suffering this tragic loss, the squadron found itself having to replace all the Javelins' engines with modified versions, and there were issues with starter cartridge defects, both of which seriously impacted the flying programme.

On 2 July 1956, the first press day was held at Odiham attended by 82 press representatives from both local and national papers. The squadron's operations record book (ORB), recorded the event in some detail.

> "During the morning, under a grey sky and in a fine drizzle, five Javelins, lined up in front of the squadron hangar, offered ample opportunity for the press to photograph and film Javelins and to interview the crews. Despite the rain, great enthusiasm was shown and within minutes excited reporters were all filming and photographing the aircraft from various angles and positions, not unlike cameramen shooting a scene for a film.

A 46 Squadron FAW.1 XA628 R taxiing for the press on 2 July 1956. (46 Squadron Association)

FAW.1 XA628 R of 46 Squadron at Odiham's press day 2 July 1956. (46 Squadron Association)

"Soon afterwards the five Javelins, led by Sqn Ldr J L W [John] Towler, started up simultaneously and taxied out to fly in a formation of four over the airfield. This enabled the reporters to capture some excellent ground-to-air shots of the Javelin, first flying past slowly with wheels and flaps down and then very low and fast. Meanwhile, the fifth Javelin piloted by Sqn Ldr P D C [Pat] Street DFC, having taken off last, did an individual display showing the docility of the aircraft at high and low speeds and in general aerobatics [!] particularly impressive being a short take-off run followed by a very steep angle of climb. The climax of this display by the Javelins was a stream landing, viewed by reporters from an advantageous position at the end of the runway.

"After lunch, the five Javelins took off once again. This time the reporters climbed aboard a Blackburn Beverley supplied by 47 Squadron [from Abingdon] who were also engaged on extensive flying trials. The rear end of the [cargo] deck of the Beverley was exposed, enabling a large number of photographers to take air-to-air shots at the same time.

"Once again, four Javelins, led by Sqn Ldr Towler, flew towards the Beverley from the rear, in various formations, while Sqn Ldr Street in the fifth aircraft, diverted from the formation, provided the opportunity for some remarkably close air-to-air shots. To quote one newspaper, 'the smaller aircraft gradually nosed until even the chevrons could be clearly defined on the shoulders of the pilot'."

The following month it was the turn of King Faisal II of Iraq to be hosted. The afternoon's flying display included a Hunter and Valiant flypast, an aerobatic team display by 111 Squadron Hunters and a formation flypast by eight Hunters and four Javelins of the Odiham Wing.

More modifications continued to have a detrimental effect on the fleet. During July all fuel inlet pipes had to be replaced due to cracking and the flaps had to be modified following an incident with an aircraft at Moreton Valance. Other early issues included airbrake malfunctions, nose-wheel shimmy and double-starter cartridge firing. Nonetheless, by this time, **Pete Wallington** and the other crews were getting used to the aeroplane and beginning to settle into a routine.

> "In the beginning our trips were all handling trips and we were getting to know the aeroplane and how it worked. What sort of turning circle could we use for an interception? How far ahead did you need your target to be? We were having to work it out empirically by trying it all out. We always flew in pairs with the GCI, basically over Bournemouth and the Channel area. That was our patch. West Malling had the patch from Southampton eastwards and we did south of Southampton and westwards. We rarely flew north of the A4.
>
> "I thought it was a marvellous aeroplane; I thoroughly enjoyed it. The pilots weren't quite so enamoured of it because it wasn't as agile as a Meteor. It was a hefty old aeroplane, about 17 tons of it. You couldn't aerobat it at all, certainly the Mk.1 because it had a solid tailplane, with elevators on it, and if you got too nose-up, it blanked off the elevators and it stalled: it fell like a falling leaf. One of the Boscombe ones did exactly that: in the Handling Squadron they put a tail parachute on it for spinning trials. He went up to 40,000 feet and deliberately stalled it and it started doing this falling leaf spin but when he popped the parachute nothing happened. It just sat vertically above the aeroplane, just floating down, and at about 8,000 feet he banged out and the Javelin made an arrow-shaped splodge on Salisbury Plain."

On 8 December 1955 Sqn Ldr David Dick was carrying out a test flight from A&AEE Boscombe Down in FAW.1 XA561 when he was forced to abandon the aircraft after it had entered a flat spin from which, despite deploying an ineffective anti-spin parachute, he was unable to recover. The aircraft actually crashed near the village of Ashey on the Isle of Wight. **Peter Wallington** again:

> "We were banned from any manoeuvres in the looping plane. That was written in stone, because of the problem with the tailplane. Something happened in the first couple of months, however. Normally we went up in pairs and were sent off on a cross-country or just a handling flight and we were over the Channel at about 40,000 feet and Wilbur said we'd go back home and that he'd roll it over on its back and pull through. I told him we were not supposed to do anything in the looping plane but he pointed out that that would not be in the looping plane so he rolled it and pulled through

A run-in and break for 46 Squadron FAW.1s XA572 D, XA623 G, XA627 B and XA626 Q. (via Pete Wallington)

and I've never seen an altimeter unwind so bloody fast in all my life. There was a lot of cursing from the front and a lot of heaving and pushing and eventually he fought it level at 2,000 feet over the Channel. It just fell, upside down, and I was calling out the altitude all the way down because Wilbur had said 'Call the height, call the height' but it never occurred to me at any time to bang out. He was controlling the thing and as long as he was staying with it so would I.

"The other time it perhaps frightened me a bit was on the second or third trip with Wilbur. We got airborne into fairly low cloud but then the two alternators failed and his flight instruments froze. The next thing he said was that he could see a light gap and he began a descent but I shouted 'Climb, climb, climb' and he did. We popped out the top and then we could reset the altimeters and we got it all back. He was grateful that I shouted out because all he could see was a light patch; he had no idea what was underneath it. It was just an instant reaction to go for the light patch.

"After that we did the acceptance trials. We needed to do 1,000 hours with eight aeroplanes in eight weeks. We couldn't change aeroplanes; eight were allocated from the 12 we had. During that period, two of them were Cat.2'd [repair category] but the squadron made it with a day to spare."

The Intensive Flying Trial (IFT) had a target of 480 flying hours per month and was intended to both increase crews' familiarisation with the aircraft and to identify and, hopefully iron out, any problems with it. The programme saw two aircraft taking off every 30 minutes between 0830 and 2230 hours and the ORB made particular mention of 20 July '56 when between 0830 and 1600 hours, B Flight managed 20 sorties with only five crews. On 4 October the trial ended after four Javelins took off for a formation flypast during which the target was passed, the final total being 1,000 hours and 13 minutes. The ORB reported:

> "Sorties were divided between high level cross-countries and PIs at 45,000 feet. Some air-to-sea firing was attempted on the night of Wednesday 3 October, high level air-to-sea firing was attempted at altitudes between 24,000 feet and 48,000 feet on the range south of the Isle of Wight. Ventnor GCI station and a search aircraft from the squadron cleared the range for the firing aircraft. Pilots immediately noticed the brilliant gun flash from their four wing-mounted cannon, and deduced that a pilot would need to have a firm visual on his target since his night vision might be impaired by the gun flash.
>
> "On Friday 5 October, two formations of Javelins flew over the Gloster Aircraft Co. at Moreton Valance and Brockworth to celebrate the completion of Phase B [of the IFT]. The squadron had hoped to be allowed to flypast over Fighter Command Headquarters and 11 Group Headquarters on the same day, but this could not be arranged for reasons of flight safety in the London Control Zone."

Although the flying hours target had been achieved, two problems still remained, icing up of the air brakes at high altitude and the explosion of starter cartridges. The second of these continued to be an issue throughout the service of the FAW.1 to 6. **Pete Wallington** continues:

> "Frank Birchfield had been succeeded by Wg Cdr Harry White DFC AFC as the new boss [in June 1956]. He was a hard man, a wonderful guy [White's wartime service included flying Beaufighters with 141 Squadron]. The squadron would have followed that guy straight into a mountain if he'd asked them to, if he was leading a formation. He took the squadron by the scruff of the neck and told us what we were going to do. On that first day he had all the squadron in, day flight and night flight, and on the blackboard his navigator, a guy called Bob Franks, drew a set of figures. He said these would be the minimums we would achieve, pilots and navs, and that he would fly with every nav on the squadron to check that he could achieve those minimums and Bob Franks would fly with every pilot on the squadron, before the squadron could be declared operational. If we couldn't hack it, we would be posted. He then proceeded over the next few weeks to do exactly what he said, proving that we could do everything he had put up on the board. Anyway, when he was chatting away to us that day there was

one crew missing, two guys called Tony Walmer and Mark Hatton. They were airborne on an air test that day and we were using the short runway at Odiham because they were resurfacing the main one. They came in and were doing the usual run and break and Harry said 'Hang on, hold everything, I'd just like to see my first squadron landing' and, as he watched out of the window, Tony did a landing and the nose wheel collapsed. That was it; what an arrival for the squadron! So we did the hours in the period and away we went.

"Halfway through my second tour on the squadron, we converted to the Mk.2 (my first trip was in August 1957), which took us back to the AI 22. There was a big difference because of the presentation. The AI 10 and 17 was a rectangle and the bottom of the azimuth screen was you. With the AI 21 and 22 there was a wig-wag system and you were at the centre of the screen. If the blip was to the left of you then the aircraft you were looking for really was to the left of you. It was a much easier system to interpret, if you like. You still had no screen with the vertical displacement on it. It had a longer range. With the AI 10 it had to be a rather large aircraft, something like a Hastings in those days, to be able to get a 10-mile range on it. In a Meteor you were lucky to see seven or eight miles but in the Javelin you could almost double those ranges.

"The number of visits we had to the squadron was considerable because we were the only squadron with the Javelin. We were displaying them at all the air displays and all the Battle of Britain displays with a static one; we couldn't do aerobatics. My pilot Pete Hood and I were involved in the big Javelin flypast at Farnborough in 1958 with just about every Javelin in the RAF."

The formation consisted of 45 aircraft led by Wg Cdr Freddie Sowrey who had taken over as CO of 46 Squadron in May 1958, with the remainder coming from 29, 89 and 151 Squadrons. Operating out of Tangmere in West Sussex, it was flown on each of the three public display days and was followed by a second formation of 45 Hunters. As the leading Javelin squadron, 46 was much in demand for

Tangmere in September 1958 and 46 Squadron leads out the Javelin pack for a flypast at Farnborough. (46 Squadron Association)

public appearances, with four leading a formation of 12 Hunters for the visit of King Faisal of Iraq to Odiham in July 1956. One aircraft was added to a formation of three Spitfire PR.19s and a Hunter, flown from Biggin Hill in 1957 to mark the retirement of the Spitfires, which had been flown by the THUM (Temperature and Humidity) meteorological unit at Woodvale, Lancashire. **Pete Wallington** again:

Pete Hood and Pete Wallington over Farnborough 1957. (Pete Wallington)

"Queen Elizabeth did a royal visit to Leuchars, presenting a standard to 43 Squadron on 4 June 1957. Our squadron did a flypast for them and we went up to RAF Turnhouse, which is now Edinburgh airport, for a couple of weeks or so for practising but we studiously avoided flying over the city of Edinburgh. On the flypast morning, Harry White phoned up the Lord Provost of Edinburgh to thank him for their hospitality, to tell him about the flypast at Leuchars for Queen Elizabeth the second of England and the first of Scotland and to ask if he would agree to our flying in formation over Edinburgh afterwards, as a thank-you gesture. We came in from the east, over Edinburgh, and flew down Princes Street. Evan and I were No.3 and, honest to God, I was looking *up* at Edinburgh Castle. We stopped the traffic. Whenever we did a flypast we always deliberately used to set the rpm to give the blue note.

"Harry White instituted what he called the 'Squadron Break'. He said that when any of his aircraft arrived at an airfield they would arrive either with a radar approach, if the weather was bad, or if it was acceptable they would arrive with the Squadron Break, which involved 'all fours': 400 feet, 400 knots, 4g to pull! Sounds good, doesn't it, but then one day the squadron was asked to provide a target aircraft for the Central Fighter Establishment at West Raynham. It was to fly a couple of times during the day so Harry White called in me and a guy called Pete Hood. He told us to take an aeroplane up to West Raynham the next morning and when we got there to do whatever they asked. It was a lovely day so we scorched into the

Former 87 Sqn FAW.1 XA624 J awaits its fate after retirement at St. Athan in September 1961. [Adrian Balch collection]

airfield with 'all fours' and it was a level break, not a climbing one. We landed and, as we taxied in, air traffic said when you get here will you please report to the wing commander flying. We went to see him, expecting to be told what he wanted us to do that day, but instead walked straight into a bollocking, for doing a dangerous arrival. Anyway, the following day we flew in the morning and the afternoon but on each of those it was a radar approach and then we flew home.

"When we got back Harry was waiting for us and he asked us whether we'd had any problems. We said no so he told us he'd had a call from the Wg Cdr Flying at West Raynham, blowing in his ear about our arrival. What did we do? We said we'd done an 'all fours, sir'. Harry told us that they wanted another aircraft tomorrow and that we were going! He asked us what we were going to do when we got there and we said 'all fours, sir'. He said 'right on'. When we got there we were once again instructed to see the Wg Cdr Flying and he once again blew his top when he realised it was us again so we simply said 'well would you mind phoning our boss, sir' and I do not know what happened after that.

"I left the squadron in 1958 and went on to Canberras, first at Binbrook on 139 Squadron, but only for about six months, because the squadron then disbanded and became a Victor squadron. I then went on to Thor missiles for four years. From there I went to Germany, once again in Canberras, B(I).6s, 213 Squadron from 1963 to '66."

By the autumn of 1958 46 Squadron had changed over to the FAW.2, the earlier aircraft largely being passed on to 87 Squadron at Brüggen in Germany. FAW.6s arrived at Odiham in 1958 and these flew alongside the Mk.2s until the squadron disbanded at Waterbeach in the summer of 1961, having moved to the Cambridgeshire station in late 1959.

Eric Marsh had previously flown his first tour on Meteor night fighters at West Malling for three years before being posted to 46 Squadron in October 1957. He had another lengthy tour, remaining with the unit until disbandment.

"I was called up to do national service in 1951 when I was 21 years old, having had a reserved occupation with English Electric on Canberra design at Warton.

I went for an interview for the RAF and was given the option, on joining, to train as a waiter in the officers' mess (tongue-in-cheek), or as a pilot. No brainer – start flying. I started my flying on Tiger Moths, then Chipmunks, followed by twin-engine conversion on Oxfords when I gained my wings.

"I went to 209 AFS (Advanced Flying School) at Weston Zoyland to fly Meteors. I was sent on a cross-country up to Middleton St. George to land there, refuel and then fly back. When I got up there it was 8/8ths stratus and at the time when I should have been arriving my radio became unserviceable. I wondered if they would send somebody up to guide me in so I waited and waited and all the time I was going up and down I realised that if I went north-east I would be going over the sea and I'd be able to descend. Eventually that is what I decided to do, because I was getting very low on fuel. I stopped one engine to conserve fuel, came down and sure enough I came out of cloud about a mile from the shoreline at very low level. I jumped over a cliff and there was an airfield. I did just one circuit and there seemed to be no-one around so I landed and the other engine flamed out as I turned off at the end of the runway. I put the brakes on and a Land Rover came out and asked what I was doing there. I asked him where I was and he said I was about 15 miles from where I should have been. I asked if he could get me filled up from a tanker and he said yes so I asked him what sort of place it was. He said it was normally open only at weekends, for the RAuxAF (Royal Auxiliary Air Force) squadrons around Newcastle. They kept a duty crew there, just to keep things going, and they saw me come in. A couple of hours later they had me refuelled and rectified the radio problem. I went off to the airfield I should have been going to and then back to Weston Zoyland.

"There was then a hold-up in converting to Meteor night-fighter training, so I went to 64 Group Communications Flight at Rufforth. It was just over a year before further training on 228 OCU at Leeming on Meteor NF.12 night fighters and then I was posted to West Malling on 85 Squadron. Then they brought in 153 Squadron, at West Malling, so I just went down the road to help re-establish 153 and stayed there for four years before going to Odiham in October 1957 to join 46 Squadron on Javelins; they had just changed over from the FAW.1 to the FAW.2. We still had a Meteor T.7 because there was no dual-control Javelin T.3 until about some time later, so my first trip was in the back seat in the rad/nav's position. Harry White was the squadron commander when I joined."

His first Javelin flight was on 20 November 1957 in the back seat of XA814, flown by Flt Lt P C Gifkins, (who had a lucky escape earlier in the year when his Javelin got into a spin at 25,000 feet – he was able to recover from it at 15,000 feet). Two days later, Eric got airborne from the front seat in the same aeroplane, with his nav

Sgt Mason. They flew twice more that day (in XA811) with the first trip being 'Exercise 2 sonic boom' and the second 'Exercise 3 GCA and turns'. They completed their conversion on the 26th with 'Exercise 4 single engine overshoots and landing' (XA812) and 'Exercise 5 high level cross-country' (XA814). The next day they began an almost endless round of PIs. **Eric Marsh** continues:

> "I had a mid-air collision at night, when I collided with a target Javelin after my radar became unserviceable. We'd gone up to do PIs and the other one was the target. We were getting a bit short of fuel to get back down to Odiham. He said he was returning to base so he turned towards base and I was on the interception at the time. I got to about two miles on the curve and my radar went unserviceable. The target aircraft decelerated and descended through my flight path (without lights because he was the target). I didn't know it at the time, but he put his speed brakes out and came down so he went straight through my flight path. Of course, he'd reduced his speed as well so I had a very rapid overtake; it must have been three or four hundred miles an hour but the first thing I saw was his silhouette, which just about blanked the sky out. I pushed the nose down and I bumped into him. I knew I'd collided with him so I told the other pilot that I'd just hit him and he said 'Oh no, just slipstream' and he just turned on to his new course. I put a lot of negative g on by pushing forward and then it went off the scale at +12g when I pulled up and it didn't fly very well! He said his aircraft was flying normally. Our flight commander was OC night flying in the tower so I called up and told them my condition. I told him my aeroplane was very difficult to fly so he asked me to do a stall check. I found it was almost uncontrollable at about 160 or 170 knots, as opposed to its normal figure of about 110 knots. He told me to fly it in at 170 which I did and just about burned out the brakes in stopping. I wasn't used to high-speed landings.
>
> "What had happened was that, as I dived down, the right-hand half of my tailplane had hit his port wing inboard, just between the aileron and the fuselage. My nav described part of the right tailplane as missing and it looked all twisted and, sure enough, when we got out and looked there was a lot missing and it was all twisted and wrinkled. The skin was torn away but luckily the hydraulics were still intact; there was no leakage at all.
>
> "I received a reprimand because I was the aircraft behind. What was really at fault of course was the SOPs, the standard operating procedures: you should switch your lights on if you are the target and state your level and speed until the other one has identified where you are. A simple thing but never done, until that incident. Subsequently, the SOPs were changed to ensure a re-occurrence would not happen."

The collision was on 14 April 1958. Eric's aircraft was FAW.2 XA809 T which was repaired and stayed with 46 Squadron for a further three years. **Eric Marsh** again:

"The Javelin was nice to fly, a good platform for instrument flying and had adequate power. It was a great aeroplane; it had artificial feel put in. There were two switches on the right which were wired off, but if they accidently broke the aeroplane flew like a day fighter and that was glorious. It really was a beautiful aeroplane, very lively, but you could over-stress it and that's why they put the artificial feel in. Later Mks had better radar with a longer detection range, and it was easier to assess the target's heading and height.

"It wasn't a lumbering beast; it was perfect for the job it was built for, which was a night all-weather fighter, so you don't need something that has a rapid rate of roll. You just fly it almost like an airliner, sedate and on the instructions from your rad/nav, but it was a very nice aeroplane to fly. It was even better when (on a later squadron) we got the FAW.9s with reheat. People who converted from the Mk.1 to the 2 all said they preferred the Mk.1 to handle. It was a lighter aeroplane, seemed to have more power and had the belly tank.

"We did lots of PIs, normally one versus one but occasionally a Canberra squadron used to get involved. 43,000 feet was a common intercept altitude for PIs. It handled quite well at that height. My back-seater was Sgt Mason; he was a great chap. We flew No.2 in a formation with a Spitfire when it was presented to the Americans. We also did a flypast for the opening of the Empire Games at Cardiff Arms Park on 26 July 1958; three formations each of four aircraft. There was a big Javelin flypast at Farnborough in September 1958, but I wasn't there; 46 Squadron was leading them because they had the first Javelins; all the other squadrons followed behind.

"I had the occasional trip in a Vampire T.11 for aerial gunnery at Sylt for armament practice camp (APC). You were lucky if you got an APC because they used to distribute the camps amongst the squadrons. I went there only once and I think that was the only time the squadron went while I was there. We did an exchange with the French with their Vautour

46 Squadron leads a Hunter formation over Cardiff on 26 July 1958 for the opening of the Empire Games. (46 Squadron Association)

night fighters. I didn't get down there as only six Javelins went, but we did some PIs against the Vautours and they had a very similar performance."

The Spitfire Eric mentioned was a Battle of Britain Flight Mk.16 TE330, which, much to the chagrin of the RAF, was the one chosen to be presented to the United States. It had only just been restored to a fully-representative example including all the armament and equipment. It was flown to Odiham where the presentation was made on 2 July 1958, Eric flying overhead in XA773. During the APC, Eric flew 13 sorties, the first three being for cine only on the towed flag, followed by ten gun-firing sorties. His best score came on the eighth trip when he achieved 14% on target, which actually beat the score achieved by the pilot of the Vampire he flew in, who was demonstrating how to do it! The squadron exchange was with Escadrille (Esc).1/30 of the French air force, based at Tours and took place in April 1959, with Eric flying three PIs against them at 43,000 feet. He continues:

"There was one incident at Waterbeach. We were on standby at the end of the runway, the usual thing, and we were scrambled for a target over the North Sea. We turned on to the runway, opened up the power and did a controls check but the stick was stuck over to the right. We were already moving so I did a quick shutdown, went back to the apron and we found a screwdriver. The aircraft had just come back from full servicing and the screwdriver had jammed the controls. In fact, I still have that screwdriver; it has a bent blade!

"The Javelin T.3 performed much the same as the night fighter, perhaps a little bit lighter, because you didn't have all that fuel on board. But we were forbidden from manoeuvring in the vertical plane or to loop the aeroplane. The Javelin was transonic and the only way the aircraft would go supersonic was to put it on its back and pull through. I don't recall if the handling changed; it would be very, very steep in dives. There would be no consideration of controlling the aircraft by aileron control, so it meant one was most concerned to pull out of the dive."

After leaving 46 Squadron, Eric was posted to more Javelin flying on 60 Squadron in Singapore, followed by a return to the UK to join 23 Squadron at Leuchars for its final few months with the type.

Don Chapman was a former Mosquito NF.36 pilot and following a ground tour, an instructor on Meteors at Odiham, came to 46 Squadron in the later stages of its Javelin operations, in 1959.

"I had been flying Mosquitoes in this country but then I was due for an overseas tour. I continued flying them at Fayid but I was then posted to Iraq, doing a ground job as aide de camp to the AOC (air officer commanding), George Beamish. When I came back I went to CFS (Central Flying School). A lot of people who came back from the Middle East were sent to CFS and I converted to Meteors at Little Rissington. I then went on to teach people to fly Meteors at Odiham. After that, well, people didn't often do more than two years then, so I did two years on 46 Squadron from 1959 to 1961. It started off at Odiham and we went to Waterbeach when we were doing 24-hour standbys. Originally we had the Javelin FAW.1 but then we got the FAW.2.

"Those who flew the Javelin liked it, it didn't have the best of reputations because of losing the CO [see page 22]. When I joined the squadron there weren't any dual-control Javelins. You did one trip as a passenger in the navigator's seat so you didn't actually handle the controls while you were shown how to fly the thing. Then, on the same day, ideally, you got into the front seat and tried to remember what the instructor had told you. Anyway, it worked all right for me. I had an engine failure on my first take-off, which I didn't immediately recognise because I hadn't experienced the aeroplane before, under my own control. I wasn't used to the acceleration on take-off so the only way I knew about it was from the engine instruments; one of them had wound down to zero. The drive shaft between the turbine and the compressor had sheared and because this was my first flight the AOC was very interested and, in fact, came down to see me. Anyway, at that time, because the Javelin didn't have a good name everywhere, my experience with it helped to improve its reputation. Engine failure was not a drama because the engines were so close together. If you have engines out on the wings and one fails you feel it but if they're close together you hardly feel it at all. You can do all sorts of things on one engine in a Javelin which you couldn't do in a Mosquito.

"I liked the Javelin, I enjoyed it. It had loads of power and it would take you up to 40,000 feet. In fact I got up to 48,000 feet one day, but the last couple of thousand feet took quite a long time. I was probably doing an air test or something. I wanted to see just how high it would go, but normally we wouldn't do anything above 45,000 feet.

"In those days the air force maintained a couple of aircraft at immediate readiness (that's five minutes take-off warning) throughout 24 hours. The day-fighter squadron did it by day and we took over at sunset. It was done at Waterbeach because it was nearer the east coast and we were controlled by a radar station not very far from there. Everybody went to Waterbeach in those days. I think there were six Javelin squadrons in Fighter Command at the time and we took it in turns to go there to do this 24-hour standby.

"We only got scrambled for practice. I was never scrambled for what might have been the real thing. It happened occasionally, but not very often.

Our routine on the squadron was PIs time, after time, after time. You took off as a pair, in quick succession, and climbed up rapidly to about 40,000 feet and then carried on from there. Before we had the under-fuselage tank fitted our duration was only 50 minutes, so we got one interception each before we had to make our way back to base. With the under-fuselage tanks you could stay up for an hour and 20 minutes. The Javelin was generally reliable and engine failures were very rare indeed. In fact, I don't think we had another one on the squadron, during the couple of years I was there. They were Sapphire engines – very reliable normally.

"The radar we had was the AI 17 in the FAW.1 and the AI 21 in the FAW.2. The FAW.1 required quite a long and pointed nose but the FAW.2, because the radar was different, had a slightly shorter nose. Most people wouldn't notice the difference but we did. I think their pickup range was about the same for both but their behaviour was different because on the AI 17 you couldn't lock on to the target. With the AI 21, and in all the other marques, you could lock on to the target, once the navigator had found it. He would get things set up and press a button. It would lock on to the target and then the pilot would get a picture of where the target was, inside his windscreen. The effective range depended on the size of the target, but I suppose about ten miles. If you got ten miles that was pretty good, but the ground radar would take you to inside that distance. Hopefully they would line you up perpendicular to the target's track and then you could start your turn, under the navigator's control, when he had it in the right position on his own screen.

"We used to go up to Acklington, ideally annually, for APC. We also used to do detachments to the continent. I think it was Lübeck we used to go to, for two weeks at a time. I didn't have any really scary moments with the Javelin, but sometimes you would get caught out by weather. That was the only serious service failure I had, on the first trip. When I finished my tour I got a ground job at Fighter Command, largely because as a Sqn Ldr you'd normally expect to get only one flying job in that rank. There weren't that many flying jobs going. So 46 Squadron was my last *proper* flying tour."

Despite its substantial advance in performance over the previous night fighters and its somewhat challenging handling properties in some areas of the flight envelope, 46 Squadron had shown the Javelin to be a basically sound and valuable aeroplane. In a little over five years with the type, the sad loss of their first CO and his navigator was the only fatal accident suffered, although two more aircraft were damaged beyond economical repair in incidents; certainly not a bad safety record. There were however, quite a number of less serious incidents recorded in the squadron's ORB; for example in 1956 it noted the following.

"Flt Lt Tritton and navigator Flying Officer (Fg Off) D Roberts on 17 July, lost the starboard side of the canopy soon after take-off at a speed of 420 knots. The reason for this remains unknown, as does the whereabouts of the remains of the canopy, the loss of which was advertised in a local newspaper. Fortunately the crew were uninjured even though the navigator had his helmet visor shattered. Meanwhile the inevitable modification has come in as the result. This calls for larger inspection holes in the canopy for easier pre-flight inspections.

"A heavy landing in very gusty conditions at night did minor damage to the nose-wheel assembly on XA625 and on 15 August XA571 suffered Cat.3 damage on starting, hot gases from the starter cartridges burning a sizeable hole in the servicing bay floor.

"During the night flying period on Tuesday 4 September, Flt Lt R H Bragg with navigator Fg Off D Roberts in XA626, ran off the end of the runway after landing in poor weather conditions. The aircraft damage was assessed as Cat.3 [repairable]. On Wednesday 26 September, shortly after take-off, Flt Lt J Fraser in XA628 struck a flock of birds. The starboard intake fairing was smashed, and the inlet guide vanes and first row of compressor blades on the starboard engine were damaged, necessitating an engine change. The port side of the tail unit was also damaged, requiring a complete tail-plane unit change.

"In another incident on XA619 on 21 September, an explosion was caused by the discharge of hot gases into the servicing bay, due to misalignment of the port starter exhaust pipe with the outlet at the bottom of the fuselage, and the internal pressure set up collapsed the engine intakes inwards."

This had been the squadron's last hurrah as a fighter unit. It reformed one more time in September 1966 and spent the next ten years flying Andover transports from Abingdon and Thorney Island.

CHAPTER TWO

THE JAVELIN FORCE GROWS

THE BOYS

Air Cdre Jack Broughton OBE
Nav/radar. National serviceman, joined in 1952. 125 Squadron Venom NF.3. 89/85 Squadron Stradishall. AWFCS CFE West Raynham. Junior Command and Staff School, Ternhill. XI Squadron Javelin Geilenkirchen. Left RAF 1980. Went into air traffic development at NATS.

Sqn Ldr Brian Bullock
Nav/radar. 141 Squadron Meteor NF.11, Venom NF.3 and Javelin. 25, 11 and 29 Squadrons Javelin. A&AEE Javelin. Moved to air traffic control. Left RAF in 1987.

Sqn Ldr Mike Gill
Pilot. Joined 1945. Halton apprentice. Switched to aircrew and trained on Prentice and Harvard. 205 AFS. 226 OCU. 64 Squadron Meteor. CFS. 209 AFS. 7 FTS. CFS. 228 OCU. 41 Squadron Javelin '58-'60. Leuchars. Exchange tour RCAF Cold Lake, Bagotville, North Bay CF-100, CF-101B. HQ Fighter Command. Ternhill. RAF Germany Staff '66-'68. Retired and became a VAT inspector.

Flt Lt Bill Hustwayte
Nav/radar. Enlisted for national service 1951. Trained 5 ANS. 236 OCU, 220 and 224 Squadrons Shackleton. 238 OCU. 141 Squadron Venom. 141/41 and 25 Squadrons Javelin. 2 ANS. 242 OCU and 48 Squadron Hastings. Left RAF in 1967.

Wg Cdr George Lee
Joined in 1957, trained as radio observer. 1 ANS, 228 OCU, 89/85 Squadron Javelin. Retrained pilot '62/'63. 2 Squadron Hunter, CFS QFI Jet Provost, Hunter, Meteor, Vampire, Gnat. 79 Squadron Hunter, Meteor. MOD Jaguar, Hawk. Retired 1989. BAe 146 captain '90-'04.

Wg Cdr Forbes Pearson
Nav/radar. 85 and 29 Squadrons Javelin. 6 Squadron Phantom Coningsby. Phantoms at Wildenrath, Wattisham and Falklands. Exchange tour with Royal Navy. USAF 3rd AF commander's staff Mildenhall. Retired 1984. SHAPE.

Sgt Terry Jackson
Nav/radar. 228 OCU '57-'58. 151 Squadron Javelin Leuchars '58-'59. Left the RAF and became a flight test engineer with Blackburn Aircraft/Hawker Siddeley test flying Buccaneer and Phantom. Air traffic control in Australia from 1970. Director of aviation services and flying displays to the Australian International Airshow.

CREW TRAINING

As the Javelin began to settle into service and more aircraft arrived, so the force began to expand. In February 1957, 141 Squadron at Horsham St. Faith (now Norwich airport), began to change over from Venom NF.3s to Javelin FAW.4s, followed in March by 23 Squadron at the same station. Both units moved up the road to Coltishall at the end of May.

In order to facilitate the conversion process in the squadrons designated to receive Javelins, 228 OCU at Leeming – the night fighter OCU – established the Javelin Mobile Conversion Unit (JMCU) at the start of 1957. This 'travelling circus' was sent out to each new Javelin station to train both ground and air crew, the latter having the use of a simple cockpit procedures simulator. The JMCU also used a Valetta T.4 'flying classroom' for the navigators, fitted with AI 17 radar to fly practice PIs against their second Valetta which they used to ferry between stations. The navigators then had to undertake 13 sorties in a Javelin to complete their conversion, while the pilots were required to fly six daytime and one night sortie, using their own squadron aircraft. Meanwhile back at Leeming, 228 OCU had received some Mk.5s and courses for new pilots and navigators were soon in full swing.

Each pilots' course at Leeming lasted 15 weeks. In the early years, all had already completed at least one operational tour on either the Meteor or Venom night fighter. It was not until sometime later that pilots began to arrive at Leeming direct from a flying training school (FTS). Navigators had to do an initial ten-week course on a variety of aircraft including Valetta T.4s and Meteor NF.11s (these being replaced later by Canberra T.11s fitted with AI 17. Instruction was also provided on AI 22. During their 15 weeks together, the new crews flew approximately 75 hours by day and night.

COLTISHALL and WATTISHAM – 141/41 SQUADRON

The first Javelin to be delivered to 141 Squadron, FAW.4 XA637, arrived at Horsham St. Faith on 8 February 1957. 141 Squadron had always flown fighters since first being formed in 1918 with Sopwith Dolphins. During the Second World War it flew a variety of types including the Gladiator, Blenheim, Defiant, Beaufighter and finally the Mosquito, which it continued to fly post-war. After replacing these with Meteor NF.11s, it then re-equipped with the Venom NF.3 prior to the Javelins arriving. It was renumbered as 41 Squadron on 1 February 1958 after just one year with Javelins and thereafter had a brief resurgence as a Bloodhound missile unit at Dunholme Lodge in Lincolnshire from 1959 to 1964.

Early formation of 141 Squadron FAW.4s from Coltishall. (Brian Bullock)

Unusually, **Brian Bullock** had flown both the Meteor NF.11 and the Venom NF.3 operationally on 141 Squadron prior to getting his hands on the Javelin, a type he was to fly with several other squadrons. He clearly did not think too highly of the Venom night fighters that preceded it.

> "I followed the well-trodden path to a nav/rad seat in the Javelin. In my case, nav training in Canada, some months of stagnation on the ground awaiting on OCU allocation, and ab initio nav/rad training on AI 10 in the dreaded Brigands – smelly beasts – at RAF Colerne. This was followed by the OCU at Leeming in Meteor NF.11s. I arrived at Coltishall with my pilot in April 1955 to join 141 Squadron. During July '55, the Brigand circus arrived for the nav/rads conversion to the Mk.21 radar fitted to the Venom NF.3, which started arriving from August onwards. Roughly 18 months later, the navs were converting to AI 17 fitted to a visiting Valetta (this actually came to Horsham St. Faith because the runway at Coltishall was at that time being resurfaced). My first Javelin conversion flight was on 12 March 1957. 141 Squadron was the second to convert to Javelins and the first to receive the FAW.4.
>
> "For many reasons, most of the aircrew were delighted and relieved to say farewell to the Venom NF.3. The cockpit space was very crowded with the nav/rad sitting beside the pilot and on the starboard side, slightly canted to the rear. More importantly, there were serious design faults, leading to numerous major incidents. 141 Squadron had two crashes resulting in serious injuries but no fatalities. Our sister squadron at Coltishall, 23, also equipped with Venoms, lost a flight commander, an American exchange

crew and had numerous major incidents. One critical problem arose when one wingtip fuel tank became detached; usually, this was on take-off when it was full. There was insufficient rudder to counteract the aerodynamic forces, so the aircraft would bank uncontrollably and fly into the ground.

"After the large number of serious incidents, a signal from higher authority was distributed to the squadrons, noting the concerns of aircrew and suggesting that ejection seats could possibly be fitted. However, our wonderful nav aid GEE Mk.3 [radio navigation] would have to be removed – which option would we like? Everyone plumped for the ejection seat option, but we were subsequently informed that the GEE would not be removed and therefore ejection seats could not be fitted. Meanwhile, back in the Royal Navy, also flying a variant of the Venom NF.3 (the Sea Venom), they managed to convince the Admiralty that ejection seats and GEE Mk.3 must be fitted – they got their way.

"Another frequent issue was the number of wet (false) engine starts. Repeat starts usually resulted in a huge ball of flame from the jet-pipe, and the wooden tailplane and parts of the fuselage often caught fire. In a couple of extreme cases, the aircraft were burnt out. A clever, simple modification – an asbestos blanket thrown over the tailplane – proved to be quite an effective countermeasure. The Venom NF.3 was fitted with an American Mk.21 radar. Its presentation, PPI (plan position indicator) and contact range, were superior to those obtained on the Meteor's Mk.10, which was not surprising as this was the same equipment as fitted to the Mosquito NF.36. When the nose-mounted guns were fired, it often caused sufficient vibration in the nose for the radar to fail.

"The Javelin dwarfed the Venom, and was the first fighter aircraft to have ergonomically designed cockpits, lots of space for the crew, large, clear hoods and superior equipment with well-placed controls. Last but not least, ejection seats. The nav/rad sat in relative comfort, and the British-made AI 17, derived from the Mk.10 in the Meteor, reverted to B and C scopes and with a lock-on facility. This made controlled closures behind an evading target to the ident and simulated gun-firing phase so much easier; so much better than continually operating switches to change the AI radar coverage area to keep contact with the target. Average ranges of target pick-ups were good by contemporary standards; Javelin to Javelin 12-15

A moody shot of a 141 Squadron FAW.4 at Coltishall. (via Brian Bullock)

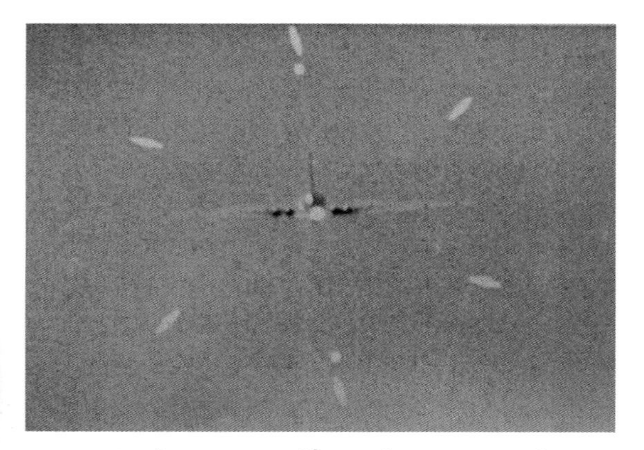

'Gotcha' – 25 Squadron's Mike Gawtree and Brian Bullock successfully intercept a Vulcan at 42,000 feet on 1 October 1962. (Brian Bullock)

miles, larger aircraft 15-20 miles. Following lock-on and closure to the visual ranges, a collimator provided target position information on the pilot's gun-sight, and the nav then only gave range info. We often did PIs up to 45,000 feet, and this led to some very interesting encounters with Vulcans. Surprising for us, this huge triangle of metal, much bigger than ours, was very manoeuvrable and up to around 40-45,000 feet. Surprise, surprise, when we were closing in for the kill they would very often throw us off. The Javelin was cleared to 50,000 feet and we wore pressure-breathing jerkins to stop our lungs collapsing if we suffered an explosive decompression, and leggings that inflated under heavy g forces to prevent the blood from draining to our feet.

"During one AIDEX (air defence exercise) in the UK, we closed in on one target for 10-15 minutes, finally coming to a situation where the range stabilised at well over a mile, and this was 99% vertical development – we were then at around 50,000 feet. This was reported to the GCI and after some delay we were instructed to break away immediately and 'phone the controller as soon as possible after landing. We were told the target was on a secret mission and we were not to discuss this incident with anyone. Years later it transpired that this target was almost certainly a Lockheed U-2.

"The squadron was detached to Tangmere for the annual SBAC flypast at the beginning of September. It was very hard work for the pilots and a jolly for the navs, unless you were leading the formation. After three days we went back to Coltishall and flew to Geilenkirchen on detachment to take part in Exercise Counterpunch. Plenty of targets, Canberras, F-84Fs and F-100s all at around 40,000 feet. Whilst we were at Geilenkirchen, the RAF Swifts were grounded. There was a Swift squadron detached to Geilers at that time and there were some very long faces among their pilots in the mess that day.

"Soon after we converted to Javelins at Horsham St. Faith, we were involved in Exercise Vigilant and enjoyed plenty of trade over the 3 or 4 days during the last week of May 1957; Canberras at 45,000 feet, Meteor F.8s, F-84Fs and Banshees [Royal Canadian Navy] all at around 40,000 feet. On 25 May I arrived at the shared squadron ASP (aircraft servicing platform) at Horsham just after the well-known 'Horsham incident' and I just saw the remains of the 23 Squadron Javelin on the taxiway."

On that day Javelin FAW.4 XA632 was taxiing for take-off when the front catch failed on one of the ventral fuel tanks which partially detached, dragged on the ground and caught fire. An unclear fire warning message from air traffic control (ATC) "Get out, you're on fire!" led to the pilots of two Hunters F.4s of 74 Squadron incorrectly reacting to it. One abandoned take-off and overshot the runway into an adjacent field, and the other was hurried into a hard landing during which the pilot ejected, the aircraft finishing up embedded in the wall of one of the airmens' blocks. The Javelin was burnt out and the pilot, John Wilkinson, was endlessly ribbed about it afterwards and told he should go for the 100 yards at the Olympics because he was running when he hit the ground! **Brian Bullock** continues:

> "On 1 February 1958 141 Squadron became 41 Squadron and the following five months were quite busy. The whole of March was devoted to our first air-to-air gunnery exercises, firing on banners towed by Meteors at around 20,000 feet. The results were very disappointing compared to those obtained on the Meteor and Venom, one point being that the Javelin guns were mounted in the wings and they were not as easy to harmonise as those fitted in the nose. During air-to-air gunnery exercises many of the nav/rads didn't like the harsh manoeuvres and g-forces that were inevitable when leaving the 'perch' position, establishing the correct gun-firing range, firing the guns, and breaking away to return to the perch. Some of the pilots were harsher on the controls than others. However, I was lucky enough to have a high air-sickness threshold. During an APC detachment to Sylt in October '62, my usual pilot Sqn Ldr Mike 'Hitto' King flew very smooth patterns, and this resulted in well above average scores. I remember 23%, 19% and on one occasion, the banner being shot off the tow-rope. Very often you were caught with the duty of attaching the banner to the tug. I hated that, you had to get underneath the Meteor at the end of the runway, crawl under and put the banner cable on the hook in the correct way so that the damn thing didn't fall off. It was noisy and drafty.
>
> "Out of Coltishall doing PIs high level about 100 miles out over the North Sea in the early days, 1958, my pilot reported two steady hydraulic warning lights. Pilot's Notes advised the controls would lock at any time and ejection advised. We decided to stay with the aircraft as long as possible and I put us on the extended centre-line of Marham's longer runway, while the pilot made control inputs that were very minimal and gentle – at the first sign of the controls stiffening we would eject. With a good headwind, we kissed onto the threshold at Marham and my pilot, who had often practised the nose-high aerodynamic brake, used this to the full. We came to a halt on the upwind ORP (operational readiness platform) after the slightest touch of braking. Ground crew opened the servicing hatch to be cascaded with oil and what was left in the system was only just measurable. We were lucky boys.

FAW.5 XA667 41 Squadron Wattisham. (41 Squadron Association)

"In the first week of April we were detached to Waterbeach for QRA which was called 'Fabulous' in the UK. The Javelins covered the night period and Hunters covered the day period. We alternated between two minutes' readiness in the cockpit on the ORP for an hour at a time, and ten minutes' readiness in the crewroom. It was very boring and very cold in the winter (there was no cockpit heating). There were few scrambles and most of those were practice against friendly targets. At the end of May we detached to Stradishall for formation practices and a flypast over Buckingham Palace on the 21st. Three weeks in June brought more air-to-air gunnery with results being a slight improvement compared to previously.

"On 3 July 1958 the squadron was posted to Wattisham. Almost immediately there were more formation practices prior to a flypast on the 12th over Baginton airport Coventry, where the King's Cup air race was being held. More rehearsals at the end of August and into September in preparation for Farnborough again."

At the end of his tour on 41 Squadron, Brian moved on to continue his Javelin flying with 11 Squadron in RAF Germany (see Chapter Four).

Having started his RAF career as a national serviceman, **Bill Hustwayte** completed his first tour as a navigator on Shackletons with 224 Squadron in Gibraltar. He then found himself retraining for the night-fighter force.

"I was a navigator on a four-year commission. I was on national service so was actually fortunate to be commissioned, which was quite unusual. When I got my wings I realised that I was never going to do an operational tour, but then because I got a commission, I could. I passed out and was posted to St. Mawgan, the School of Maritime Reconnaissance, and the aircraft were Lancasters. I finished there and then went up to Kinloss – that's a long journey by train. I thought I was crewed up, but the rest of the crew went somewhere else, and I went out to Gibraltar to 224 Squadron.

"In February 1957 I was posted to 141 Squadron on Venom NF.3s. They had this piddling little engine and the amazing thing was, every other start was a wet start, so they had to put an asbestos blanket over the tailplane to protect it from the ensuing fireball when the engine finally lit. You'd get some new squadron LAC [leading aircraftman] going up the line and he would see this and bravely rush up and pull the blanket off, 'No, no, that's just to protect the aeroplane'.

41 Squadron four-ship of newly delivered FAW.4s in 1958. (via Bill Hustwayte)

"In March '57 we converted to Javelins. There was no OCU, about four or five engineers came up from Glosters and we converted on the squadron. They came into the crew-room bringing models of the hydraulic system. On the Javelin everything was done by hydraulics, the right engine had two hydraulic lines and the left engine had two, but they didn't cross over. It was a very different aeroplane from the Venom in performance, and it had 'bang' seats! Because of that, Martin-Baker came up with a ground rig and we all had to sit on this thing and do about three dummy ejections I think.

"On our fifth trip we flew a Mk.4 supersonic in a dive – the maximum speed was Mach 1.08. We got up to about 40,000 feet, tightened all our straps, headed down and Terry [Dixon] shouted out '95..96..97..98' boom-boom-boom-boom – through – '1.08', air brakes out. I was amazed how little buffeting there was.

"I only had one exciting moment in a Javelin, when the hood came off. Both hoods slid back independently and the first check you did when you got in, was to look at the little yellow bars on either side to see that they were locked down. Obviously the one I was on was not properly locked. We were climbing up (as far as I remember we were at about 15,000 feet) and all of a sudden there was a tremendous bang and the hood came off – whoof! – just like that.

"We used to go out to Nicosia to do our QRA [quick reaction alert] there. We came back in a Mk.4 and halfway across we had two hydraulic pumps fail on the same side, which meant the aircraft didn't have any brakes, didn't have any nose-wheel steering and didn't have any flaps. That was it, but

FAW.5 41 Squadron Wattisham. (41 Squadron Association)

we still had full flying controls. So all four aircraft landed at El Adem in Libya. There was a concrete runway with sand either side, so we landed at the lowest possible speed, but it was still quite fast of course without flaps or air brakes. We started running down the runway and the aircraft naturally slowed because of the weight of it on the ground. Terry said 'We're going to get out', so we both stood up and put our ejection seat pins back in and stood up on the seats. As the aircraft got to the end of the runway, the nose wheel just canted slightly to the right. We ran off the runway, did this great big circle in the sand, came back and finally stopped. By then we were sat on the side of the cockpit, because we were going to run down the fuselage and slide off the back, where we'd only have been a few feet off the ground.

"We once flew some high-level PIs against Hunters. They were our targets that day, instead of having another Javelin, a Canberra, or a Vulcan or whatever it was. The Hunters might have had new pilots coming on, or they were just getting their hours in or something. Later on when we first got the Firestreaks, during PIs these would light up when we found the target, but we never got to fire one for real.

"In those early days, day and night crews sitting in the cockpit at readiness was always done at just one or two stations; the night one was always Waterbeach for some reason. I've no idea why it wasn't Coltishall which was closer to the coast, but eventually you did it from your own stations. It was a bind in winter, an hour and a quarter was the maximum we did and it was very, very cold in the aircraft; there was no means of heating it at all. I was on the night fighter force for seven years and I never had a 'Beep! Beep! Waterbeach...one Javelin... vector three five zero...flight level three six zero... squawking seven six three two...SCRAMBLE!' Yet some people had only been on the squadron for ten minutes and got a bloomin' scramble!"

A notable member of the squadron in 1958 was Ft Lt Nicky Varanand who, as the squadron members were to discover, was a Thai prince and a member of the Siamese royal family and a cousin of Prince Bira, the well-known racing driver of that era. He did not boast about this or the fact that he was enormously wealthy. The only clue to his background was his personal car number plates, which were unknown during this time. Nicky had five – NV1, NV2, NV3, NV4 and NV5, this last one being a Vespa scooter on which he rode to the squadron; the remainder were expensive vehicles in the 'Roller' (Rolls-Royce) class. He joined the RAF in 1942 and his seniority enabled him and his wife, Pamela, to move directly into a married quarter. During Christmas 1958 he invited the night standby crews to lunch at his home. Upon knocking, the door was opened by his butler, who had come from the family home in Surrey especially to serve drinks and canapés![5]

Mike Gill, previously a Meteor day fighter pilot, was also flying with 41 Squadron when he was forced to abandon his Javelin during a PI sortie out of Wattisham in early 1960.

> "I had to eject from an almost brand new Mk.8 which had only flown about eight hours. We had taken off for a PI and climbed up to 40,000 feet. We had already flipped as target and fighter, when I lost all generated electrical power. The battery only lasted for about three and a half minutes because it was trying to power the radar, we weren't quick enough getting it off. So it didn't last very long, but it was a pretty small battery anyway; it relied entirely on the generators – that's where the fault was.
>
> "I'd gone up through 30,000 feet of cloud and when I was up there, I remembered from met briefing that day that the top half of the country was clearer. I couldn't go down through the cloud without any instruments, so I wanted a hole to go down. I flew what I thought was north on the E2 compass, but what I didn't realise was that the compass, which is magnetic, swings about 20 degrees when the electricity alters. It's not all verified by electricity, but it is swung with the engines running.
>
> "I came down through a hole and found I was the wrong side of the Pennines; I was on the Carlisle side. I thought I was going to be over Newcastle or that bit of coast, with Acklington and a couple of other airfields. So I was on the wrong side of the Pennines and I couldn't get through, so I bailed out just south of Carlisle, at 1,000 feet. I didn't have long to play around, it had nose down trim on, so as soon as I let go of the stick to pull the face blind on the seat, it was going to nose-dive into the deck. It was open country, several miles south of Carlisle. The aircraft landed in a field and sort of splintered into pieces.
>
> "I didn't injure myself; I had a small back pain for a couple of days; that was all. I was clever, I bailed the nav out first. I had to shout to him because there was no intercom. I had to give the story and I said 'When I say 'go!' you pull that blind or you'll be talking to yourself'. He was all right; he waved at

5. 41 Squadron Association.

me from the ground. I went round in a circle in fact fairly near him and then I pulled mine at 1,000 feet. But I could see him waving at me, or to me.

"When we ejected, an hour and a half was nearly up. The fuel gauges weren't working, so I was working on time more than anything. A usual trip was about an hour and a quarter, so I'd already exceeded it and I know I was wondering when the engines were going to stop. I'd already stopped one, I was just flying on one. It was better to have slightly more power on one than to have two on idle."

This accident took place on 9 March 1960 and the aircraft was XH988 X, which came down at Crownstone Farm, near the small village of Durdar in Cumberland. Mike's navigator was Sgt Bob Lydall. Mike later went on to Canada to fly the similar performance CF-100 and then the CF-101B Voodoo, which he enjoyed a great deal, not least because it was truly supersonic.

Meanwhile, 41 Squadron continued to fly Javelins until disbandment came on the last day of 1963. It too became a Bloodhound missile unit, at West Raynham between 1965 and 1970, but was reformed at Coningsby on 1 April 1972 to fly Phantoms, which it did until 1976 when it switched to Jaguars at Coltishall. In April 2006 41 became a reserve squadron at Coningsby to operate Tornado and Typhoon aircraft as an operational evaluation unit, a role which continues to the present.

LEUCHARS – 151 SQUADRON

A fourth UK-based unit was created in June 1957, when 151 Squadron at Turnhouse (now Edinburgh airport) relinquished its Venom NF.3s in favour of the Javelin FAW.5 before moving to Leuchars five months later. First formed in 1918 for home defence, the squadron had always been a fighter unit; the owl on its badge signifying night fighting.

Terry Jackson joined the squadron as a navigator in early 1958.

"I was on 194 All Weather Course at 228 OCU from December 1957 until April 1958 when I was posted to Javelin FAW.5s on 151 Squadron at Leuchars, having trained with my pilot Flt Lt Stan Pomfret. The squadron was split into two flights, one doing night intercept training and the other on day shift carrying out nav exercises, air tests and day intercepts. Stan and I did most of the air tests due to my previous apprenticeship with the de Havilland engine company.

"Intercepts were carried out with a pair of aircraft flying together, both turning away at 90 degrees to set up separation, then alternately acting as target and interceptor. We also had the V-bomber force flying a circuit of the British Isles with each night fighter squadron launching aircraft for intercepts. Most of our operational intercepts were between 40,000 and

FAW.5 XA694 T from 151 Squadron Leuchars, at Biggin Hill 16 September 1961. (Steve Bond)

45,000 feet, although on one intercept Stan and I tried to catch a Vulcan and got to 48,000 feet. The old Jav was not happy at that altitude and the slightest control input would lose us 5,000 feet. Incidentally, the Vulcan turned out to be at 52,000 feet, but we were unable to pull up to complete the exercise.

"Intercepts, with practice 'enemy' targets were set up by a fighter control unit, and at the time a few 'new' ideas were being explored. One of them was the loiter technique. This consisted of each aircraft being given a loiter point to orbit at the end of a ten-mile-wide corridor orientated towards the enemy. Once a bandit was picked up on radar and it fell into your loiter corridor, you headed straight out trying to pick it up (radar range was not brilliant, at best 17 to 20 miles). As soon as a radar return was seen you kicked hard right or left depending on the bandit's offset, pulling around in a turn attempting to keep radar contact and, if lucky, roll out behind it. It did not prove very practical as there were a number of head-on near misses. The squadron abandoned the practice when our flight leader and his nav had a Canberra pass directly overhead, missing each other by about 50 feet with the nav not having seen a thing on radar!

"About twice a year the squadron did a week of air-to-air firing. A Meteor was used to tow the banner, which was metallised to show up on the aircraft's radar. Two out of the four of the Javelin's 30mm cannons were loaded with shells which had a coloured wax on the nose. If the target was pierced the shell left a coloured ring around the hole. Each pilot knew his own colour and therefore could count his hits when the banner was dropped back at base. The procedure was to sit up on the 'perch' position (about 500 yards out and above the banner) turn in, obtain a lock on radar, call range info to the pilot who adjusted his attack angle and fired. The breakaway was a hard climbing turn away from the flag with a quick reversal back up to the perch position ready for another go. The trouble was Stan only let fly with very short bursts so would do, usually, over ten runs. One of our NCO [non-commissioned officer] pilots used to fire as soon as he got the lock and was renowned for only doing a couple of runs. It was quite a violent exercise and it was one of the few times some of the navs were airsick.

"Aircrew teams took turns in attaching the banner to the Meatbox at the end of the runway. It was a tricky take-off procedure as the tow had to be run out carefully and the lift-off acceleration quite gradual as any hard snatch on the tow rope could snap it. We did have a bit of a scare on one occasion when just after lift-off the tow snapped and the banner plus tow line fell across the main north-south railway line; there was a big scramble to clear the line before the express came through. It was not unusual for someone to hit the balance weight at the bottom of the banner's spreader-pole and blow it apart, which started the banner spinning. It had to be jettisoned out at sea which meant any hits could not be counted.

"I was married and lived off base just outside St. Andrews. We had our own caravan in the corner of a field on a farmer's property. He had a herd of Jersey cows that were always sheltered in a huge barn during the winter. During the summer he had a lot of holiday people in caravans at the site and would clean out the upper floor of the barn, which normally was full of hay for the cattle to see them through the winter. There, on a Saturday night, he would have a true Scottish band and have an old-fashioned dance night – really great fun. The squadron had a couple of owls in a cage at the end of one of the hangars (owls were on our crest). I was in the shooting team and also had a good air gun so used to shoot the pigeons nesting in the roof of hangars to feed the owls. The pigeons were a nuisance as they messed all over the aircraft.

"There was an unfortunate incident with one of the Javelins which had been parked with one main wheel on an inspection pit overnight. The timber cover gave way in the early hours with the aircraft dropping in and landing on its wing, twisting the fuselage.

"During the winter we got roped in to the University of St. Andrews fledgling radio telescope project. Flying at night at high altitude the aurora borealis often displayed. We would radio back with a bearing and elevation for the telescope operators to get a radio spectrum. The Scottish weather was quite unpredictable. While night flying we had a number of local recalls when we all scooted for base before a heavy sea mist rolled in. Usually some crews did not make it and had to divert to other stations. Our main runway approach from the east was directly over the Bell Rock lighthouse, 14 miles in line to the runway. The Javelins were fitted with GEE Mk.3 and as a coincidence, one of the GEE lines ran down our runway, so the navs practised GEE let-downs just in case the GCA was unserviceable.

On quite a number of occasions a Russian fishing trawler factory ship used to anchor just outside the 20-mile limit. It was right under our approach path and it bristled with all sorts of aerials and was obviously monitoring all our radio, radar and traffic action.

"Winter was interesting. Doing a pre-flight on a cold and frosty night the pilots opted to do the run-around at ground level, we did the checks above. Flying boots were like roller skates on the Javelin's upper wing surface when it was nicely covered in ice, and checking pitot covers etc. was akin to competing for an Olympics ice skating medal. The only airborne incident I can remember was as flying in pairs for AI practice we were just joining our partner aircraft from slightly lower on the port side, when his slipper tank 'fell off' and shot passed us. Luckily both navs got a GEE fix and a ground team actually found it out in the Scottish highlands.

"The squadron did get involved in exercises and the following ones were gleaned from my logbook – 'Ciano', 'Kingpin', 'Sunbeam'. We did go on QRA stand-by for a short period during some concern over the Suez. We spent two hours in the aircraft, two in the crewroom on readiness, four hours in the mess, then eight hours at home (married aircrew) then rotated. Stan and I were just ending our two hours in the aircraft when we were scrambled to intercept a trawler that, according to the spooks, was suspicious. I think the bugger had caught too much fish and was low in the water struggling for port – all very exciting.

"I left the squadron in April 1959 to start the commission course to remuster as an air electronics officer (AEO) on V-bombers, but gave it all away and went back to the real world. I was amongst the last of the senior NCO aircrew and did not take very well to being an 'officer and gentleman' in the peacetime service – too much protocol for me. We had one master pilot and flight sergeant pilots plus some sergeant back-seaters in 151 Squadron and we were a dying breed.

"I later spent ten years as flight test engineer with Blackburn Aircraft/Hawker Siddeley at Holme-on-Spalding-Moor flying the Buccaneer S.1 and 2, the South African Buccaneer Mk.50 variant (rocket assisted) and the Phantom F-4K and M."

The squadron continued flying their FAW.5s from Leuchars until it was disbanded on 19 September 1961. It reformed on 1 January 1962 as the Signals Development Squadron at Watton, Norfolk, but this time flying a mixed fleet of Canberras, Hastings, Lincolns and Varsities, a far cry from its illustrious night-fighter role. Disbanded yet again in May 1963 it briefly re-emerged in September 1981 as a shadow squadron at 2 Tactical Weapons Unit (TWU) Chivenor in Devon flying the Hawk T.1 and T.1A until it faded away once more in 1992.

STRADISHALL AND WEST MALLING – 89/85 SQUADRON

In September 1957, the next Javelin unit to appear was 89 Squadron at Stradishall, Suffolk; another unit to cast off the Venom NF.3 in favour of a mixture of Javelin FAW.2s and 6s. This squadron had flown Beaufighters and Mosquitoes in North Africa and the Far East during the war and had been disbanded in May 1946, re-appearing to fly Venoms in December 1955. On 30 November 1958 it was re-numbered 85 Squadron, moving to West Malling in Kent the following year where by early 1960 it had switched to the FAW.8.

Jack Broughton, a former Venom night-fighter man, had joined the squadron in the early days, two months after it got its first Javelins.

> "During my night-fighter career I flew the Meteor NF.11 then Venom NF.3 and finally the Javelin. I joined the night all-weather force in 1955 having trained as a national service navigator and after two years I applied for a regular commission. When I was holding at Hullavington, I met a chap who persuaded me that night fighters was the way to go and so I did. I did 12 years on night fighters, it was the best time of my life. The beauty of it was, without bragging, I was good at it. It was a difficult job to do – you could either do it or you couldn't. For example, when I went to Gannets I was flying with very senior people who'd been doing it for years, and I could see changes in the background on the radar where a target was emerging, when these people couldn't see it. I just had that ability, it was just inbred, nothing clever.
>
> "I joined 125 Squadron at Stradishall, now High Point prison, in September 1955 flying the Meteor NF.11 for around six months before the squadron re-equipped with the Venom NF.3. There were two types of Venom night fighter: the Mk.2 and Mk.3. The NF.3 had American AI 21/22 radar originally fitted to the USAF F-89 Scorpion and subsequently it was fitted to the Javelin Mk.2, 6 and 8. I trained on the American radar but I also spent a short time with the Mk.10, a war-time version, fitted to the Meteor NF.11.
>
> "By the end of my national service I was already a qualified navigator and commissioned so after I decided to remain in the RAF and it took some three months to complete a refresher course. I then went on to fly in the Brigand T.5, the ab initio training aircraft for navigators joining the night-fighter force. I completed advanced training on to the Meteor NF.12 at Leeming before joining my first squadron, 125 on Meteor NF.11s and this squadron was re-equipped with the Venom NF.3 at the beginning of 1956. The Venom NF.3 was quite a nice aeroplane, much better than the Meteor and like a large Vampire with a wooden cockpit based on the Mosquito fitted with AI 21 radar. This utilised a PPI display whereas the British

radars used the B Scope and C Scope principle. The B Scope displayed an angle-off each side of the nose and a distance marker and the navigator then had to interpret the track of the incoming aeroplane by trigonometry. The AI 21 radar utilised a PPI displaying the actual track of a target. Navigator/radars tended to prefer one system or the other and sometimes when you changed squadrons you had a change of radar.

"I flew with No. 125 Venom NF.3 squadron for about 15 months before the defence minister Duncan Sandys wielded his axe in the 1957 Defence Review when half of the fighter squadrons were disbanded overnight. No. 125 was one of the squadrons disbanded and the younger crews went to 89 Squadron, a sister night fighter squadron on the same station, Stradishall. Later that year the squadron re-equipped with the Javelin Mk.2 and 6. I then flew the Javelin continuously from November '57 through to early 1966. In the middle of '59 the squadron moved en bloc to West Malling, which had been refurbished with a new runway. Unfortunately the squadron only stayed there for about 18 months, despite all the money that had been spent on it, essentially because the locals didn't like the noisy Javelins.

"We did exercises where we were patrolling for about 120 miles out to sea to have a chance of defending the coast from the latest Russian bombers. Whilst the Javelin was defending the UK, there was a high-level threat all the time. That only changed in about 1964 when it was said that the Russians were going to come in low. That's when the V-bombers had to change the style of their work to low level and got painted in camouflage rather than white.

"We got the posh Javelins, the Mk.6s and then we got the 8s. The 8 was a lovely aeroplane; it is the only aeroplane I've ever flown in where the separate scanner did the lock-while-scan. The Mk.8 was similar to the 9 but it had a better radar in my view. The extra push from the reheat was always worth having. People used to laugh about it because you used to get a decrease in speed if you put it in below about 10,000 feet. But, if you put the afterburner in at about 10,000 feet, you came out of the cloud at an angle of about 80 degrees that you were climbing at – it was very impressive. I always think of the 8 as being a very smooth aeroplane and a little bit of extra time aloft. You could do an hour and 45 minutes if you were lucky. One of the best aerodynamic characteristics of the Javelin was the air brakes. You would come overhead West Raynham at 40,000 feet. As a navigator in the back, watching the altimeter unwind and just about half a mile finals you'd pull out, put the gear down and land – it was exciting stuff. The Mk.7 was good, but it was all artificial. It carried Firestreak dummies, but it could never work because the pylons were not activated. They had dummy pylons and wooden Firestreaks. I did a Firestreak course at de Havilland's – they only did two. I then went back to CFE to lecture

85 Squadron FAW.8 XJ119 A getting airborne at West Raynham. (Ed Durham)

about it on the AWFCS (All Weather Fighter Combat School) course.

"I went once to Malta with the Battle of Britain pilot Gp Capt Foxley-Norris. He arrived at Stradishall where 85 Squadron was, on posting from Fighter Command, knowing that he'd only be there for about six months because we were on our way to West Malling and that was where he wanted to be. We had to go out to Malta for Maltex which always took place around about October. He came into the crewroom one day and I was slow getting out – 'You'. So I had to go with him. We get in this Javelin, we take off and we land at Orange in the South of France. As we're pulling in to the ORP, this Maigret-type Citroën came snaking up to the aeroplane, and stopped. Foxley-Norris comes down, 'Monsieur Foxley-Norris? The commandant invites you to lunch.' So he said to me 'You Jack, do the necessary, oxygen, fuel…' We had these big cartridges and they were as heavy as lead. They were in two tubes, and you had to put them in and screw them into position. The only way you could reach them was to stand on a chock.

"An hour and a half later I'm just finishing all this lot and Foxley-Norris comes back, 'We've had a lovely lunch'. I hadn't had a drink or anything, and he said 'Are we ready?', 'Yes sir, we're ready'. He sits in the cockpit, 'LP cock on, HP cock on', presses to start and the two engines wound up and wound down again – he hadn't put the LP cock on. So we now had to change the cartridges. You had to wear asbestos gloves, unscrew them both, let them onto the ground as they had to cool for a while, they were red hot. Then put two fresh ones up, then pick the old ones up and put them in the stowage which we called the bomb bay in the middle underneath. Then you had to button up the panel. We then started successfully.

"There were no steps at Orange, so you went to the back and at the bottom of the wing there was a pull-down step, so you step on that, step on the wing, crawl up the wing, by which time he was nearly taxiing. I get into the cockpit, I strap myself in, plug my R/T lead in. We're nearly at the end of the runway and he suddenly says 'What's the first heading nav?' I said 'Well I haven't been able to get any met', 'What have you been doing then?' 'I've been sorting the aeroplane out.' He said, 'Ah well, never mind, we'll go off south-east, it's in that general direction.' Off we went; of course on the radar you could pick up Sardinia, Corsica, the toe of Italy and Sicily, so you were reasonably safe."

Christopher Foxley-Norris flew Lysanders with 13 Squadron during the Fall of France and after volunteering for Fighter Command, flew Hurricanes with 3 Squadron during the Battle of Britain, before moving on to 615 Squadron, again with Hurricanes. He later flew Beaufighters and Mosquitoes and after the war had a long and distinguished career, finally retiring in 1974 as an air chief marshal. **Jack Broughton** continues:

"They say that more aircrew have been killed in celebrating the Battle of Britain than lost their lives during the battle itself. This reminds me how near I came to being part of those statistics when over one such weekend I witnessed at least six aircrew and ground crew perishing when practising for or flying in, Battle of Britain displays.

"It happened in September 1958. Night/all-weather aircrew worked a week flying during the day followed by a week on nights with extra duties on top: the most unpopular of these extra duties for nav/rads was flying with pilots working up their flying patterns for flying displays such as the Battle of Britain. At that time the squadron display pilot was Flt Lt Derek Kenney a popular, mature pilot who flew with Fg Off 'Randy' Lewis as his nav/rad. The squadron was tasked with providing an aircraft for a static and flying display at Syerston on Saturday 20 September, a day on which Randy was already committed to attending a family wedding in Wales. I was the next in line for this duty and was duly tasked with flying a sortie with Derek Kenney before the wing commander flying who was to authorise the limits of the display.

"Although I was on nights that week, at the appointed hour on Friday afternoon 19 September, I arrived in the squadron locker room to change into my flying kit to be told that the practice had been brought forward to that morning. It transpired that Derek and Randy had both tragically lost their lives [in FAW.2 XA779 M] carrying out a tight turning manoeuvre at slow speed with flaps and undercarriage selected when the Javelin stalled, crashed into the runway undershoot and burned out.

"It was decided that along with my pilot Jock Sneddon, I would ferry a Javelin up to Syerston on Saturday morning for a static only display and return to base in the evening. The event went without incident until late in the flying display, the highlight of which was a downwind flypast of a Rolls-Royce engine test-bed Vulcan. Painted all white, this impressive aircraft was not a familiar sight in September 1958. As it approached the airfield all eyes were focussed on the Vulcan which, as it came onto the airfield, appeared to start to shed pieces of its skin – it looked as if white soap flakes in ever increasing numbers and size were peeling off the wing until – no longer able to sustain flight – it reared and fell in a flat spin onto the ATC runway caravan. Three Avro and one RAF aircrew died in the crash along with three Syerston ATC personnel stationed in the caravan.

"Despite the crash, in his wisdom, the OC Syerston authorised that the traditional cocktail party should continue that evening in the officers' mess, much to the chagrin of the daily papers. Those visiting aircrew who were stuck at Syerston in flying kit and unable to fly out because of the crash site were allowed a few drinks behind the scenes, and it was a bleary pair who travelled by the Harwich milk train back to base to arrive in good time for Monday morning's flying programme!

"On a recent visit to the National Memorial Arboretum at Alrewas I was able to locate the names of my fallen colleagues and I presume the names of the others who lost their lives on that fateful weekend are also included."

The Vulcan was VX770, the first prototype and the crew comprised three from Avro plus an RAF navigator; it had flown over from Hucknall near Derby, where it was being used on Conway engine tests for Rolls-Royce. The cause was believed to have been a fatigue failure of part of the front lower wing attachment forging which led to the starboard leading edge peeling away, causing the wing to disintegrate.

The RAF was still learning how best to take advantage of the Javelin's capabilities and to pick up on the experience of the crews already flying it. Thus, after about two years on the squadron, Jack was pulled off to do some more advanced navigator training at the CFE at West Raynham. He continues:

"One of the major problems with crews on the night-fighter force was that there was no postgraduate training for navigators. Basically you went to a squadron and stayed there, as a result 89/85 was basically the same people for the best part of five years.

"Before 1958 fighter pilots could advance their ability by becoming a gunnery instructor on the pilot attack instructor's (PAI) course at Leconfield. Eventually this was expanded to become the day fighter leaders (DFL) course based at CFE. This was further extended to include night fighter pilots and nav/rads to form the Fighter Combat School featuring two elements: day and night/all-weather fighter crews. In late 1959 I attended the AWFCS (All Weather Fighter Combat School) course, which comprised advanced tactics, gunnery, cine, leadership and was posted back on the staff there in June 1960. I had been at West Malling for only a year and thereafter stayed with AWFCS for three years. It was quite an interesting outfit because we had a new course intake every four months of the best crews from the night/all-weather squadrons, who then went back to their squadrons to pass on the latest tactical knowledge.

"AWFCS was what made my career. I had a very good pilot called Mike Haggerty, who subsequently left the air force and went to fly for Court Line. He found out about development tactics for the F-102 from the extensive library which they had at CFE. We developed new tactics for the Javelin from that, which made it far more efficient. One of the things you got when you were training to be a navigator was, when you turn inside a target, when does it look right? You can't tell people when it looks right, but if you can spell it out in terms of angles-off and so on, then you can make progress. There are people who have done more time on the Javelin than me, because a lot of my CFE time at AWFCS was only 30-minute sorties. The main character from those days was Mike Miller. He'd been around for a long time, he started his Javelin days at Coltishall on the All Weather Development Squadron (AWDS), and subsequently was around Javelins until the end.

"We flew the Javelin Mk.4s and 5s equipped with the Mk.17 radar. I also flew with 85 Squadron equipped with the Mk.8 fitted with AI 21/22 that had moved to West Raynham. In 1962, AWFCS was tasked to convert new squadron and flight commanders joining the Javelin force. It was estimated that the unit had five years to run on as the Javelin Operational Conversion Squadron (JOCS). It was basically the same unit, taking in the wing commanders and squadron leaders who were assuming command of Javelin squadrons. AWFCS had about six Javelins, enough regularly to fly a formation of four. On completion of my tour I attended the Junior Command Staff School and was subsequently posted as deputy nav leader to 11 Squadron in Germany in March 1963 flying the Javelin Mk.9 with AI 17. The AWFCS team influence on Javelin tactics was outstanding so that by the time I arrived on 11 Squadron, the crews were much more professional.

"The Javelin world at one stage was remarkably close, most people knew each other. A lot of people spent a lot of time together, so that for the first five years on my squadron they were virtually the same people, although my first pilot was eased out as a result of the Sandys defence review because he was a lot older. I mostly only flew with two pilots during that time."

George Lee arrived on 89 Squadron fresh from training on 228 OCU at Leeming as a radio/observer, a year after Jack was posted to 89 Squadron.

"My path to the Javelin started in 1956 when, at 17, I was working as a technical clerk for an electrical engineering firm having left grammar school a year earlier. Like all boys of my generation I was facing conscription for two years national service on my 18th birthday. Conventional wisdom held that if you waited to be called-up it was most likely to be the army. I had always been eager to fly so I volunteered for the RAF before my birthday.

"In the mid '50s the defence minister had been influenced by some questionable scientific/engineering persuasion that guided missiles would dominate the future of aerial combat, and thus manned aircraft were an unnecessary expense. Large parts of the RAF fast jet force had been disbanded and much of the aircrew training programme severely cut back.

George Lee boarding 85 Squadron Javelin FAW.8 XJ118 D. (George Lee)

However, in 1957/58 the new Gloster Javelin was scheduled to enter service replacing the ageing Meteor/Vampire/Venom night/all-weather fighters which were no longer equal to the task. Somewhere in the system a belated realisation occurred that curtailment of flight training had been unwise and crews for the new Javelins, particularly nav/rads (radar navigators), were not going to be available in sufficient numbers. The short term answer was a reintroduction of NCO radio observers (ROs), a branch originally trained during WW2 as AI radar operators in Beaufighters.

"Having volunteered for aircrew training in the RAF, in late '56 I attended the Officer and Aircrew Selection Centre (OASC) at Hornchurch precisely at this critical moment in time. It seems that anyone with detectable aptitude whatever was offered training as an RO – I was. The RAF took approximately 100 youngsters for this requirement over a short period and I quickly found myself in a batch of 500 or so national servicemen undergoing initial recruit training (square bashing) at Bridgnorth. The whole intake were graded as AC2s with some four or five potential ROs scattered around. At the end of square bashing 12 student ROs were gathered together and sent to No. 1 Air Navigation School (ANS) at Topcliffe with the rank/description 'aircrew cadet' (somewhat lower than a snake's belly in a wheel rut). We underwent the standard basic navigator training syllabus for seven months up to the start of astro training (not much use in a Javelin) and then the seven survivors were presented with an RO brevet and promoted to sergeant. Unfortunately the Javelin OCU was jammed, so six of us were sent to the Meteor night-fighter OCU at North Luffenham for three months, to be introduced to basic airborne interception radar techniques. This consisted of 25 hours in the back of a rather smelly old Brigand, sitting sideways on a bench seat alongside a nav/rad instructor in a dark compartment. We were taught basic interception control giving directions to the pilot by assessing the target returns on the AI radar. An old single-piston Balliol trainer was used as the target.

"This three-month interval allowed time for space to open at the Javelin OCU and gave us an introduction to our future role. It did not prove to be an easy or smooth path. Several of our colleagues could not grasp the basic technique and were suspended from training. One point of interest subsequently emerged. Several RO students chopped for failing to meet AI training standards, were often sent back to nav school (where they had progressed to a satisfactory standard) and allowed to complete the full navigator syllabus. They also gained a commission. Needless to say, word of this development soon filtered back to those of us still undergoing RO training and I have little doubt that the subsequent rise in the RO suspension rate was, in many instances, self-induced. As a consequence of these events, only a small proportion of those originally selected for RO training actually reached operational Javelin squadrons in the role of nav/rad.

"With space now available at Leeming (the Javelin OCU) three ROs joined with a Fleet Air Arm lieutenant observer and four pilots destined to emerge as four Javelin crews. Initially, the student navs flew with a staff pilot and the student pilots took a staff nav in the rear. There was no directive or pressure for the students to crew up. It was left to us to arrange matters ourselves. Amazingly it all seemed to work out naturally and I crewed up with an experienced Flt Lt Cecil Jonklaas, who had already had a tour on Sabres (day-fighter role) and had just completed a tour on Vampires as an advanced instructor. I considered myself very fortunate. Crewing up occurred about one third into the course and for the remainder we mostly flew exclusively as a crew, practising all aspects of night/all-weather controlled interceptions. No further suspensions occurred and all four crews successfully completed the course.

"I recall only one noteworthy incident at this time, and it concerned the only potential safety problem that I experienced during my three-plus years in the back seat. Towards the final stage of the course, Cecil and I returned at daybreak from a late interception practice when the aircraft brakes decided to give up. The early morning was fine with a light 10-knot wind down the runway. We orbited to allow all other aircraft to land first (only one runway and we might block it), while senior 'wheels' contemplated all aspects in the tower. I understand from later discussion that the possibility of ejection for the nav/rad was even considered. Happily no one transmitted such a possibility because with only brake failure and 2,500 yards of runway, not to mention vast areas of flat grass, I was not about to join the 'Martin-Baker club'. Fuel was getting low and Cecil was unhappy with the lack of advice/orders from the tower. He briefed me that at our low weight we would touch down at the threshold at 135 knots and maintain directional control using the rudder as speed reduced. Just prior to losing rudder effectiveness he would steer off the side onto the grass for final roll out. It all went off exactly as planned and the soft grass brought us to a gentle halt with scarcely a bump. As far as I know the 'wheels' were still arguing the outcome in the tower.

"In the summer of 1958 Cecil and I were posted to 89 Squadron as a constituted crew. The squadron was part of a standard fighter wing comprising two Hunter squadrons (day-fighter role) and one night/all-weather squadron with Javelins, based at Stradishall south-east of Cambridge. On arrival I found that I was the only NCO amongst 80-90 pilots and navigators on the wing. My appearance in the sergeants' mess was not exactly greeted with much enthusiasm. The next youngest mess member was over 30 and all had undertaken many years of hard service before promotion to senior NCO level had given them mess membership. I could easily understand how a 19-year-old RO was not likely to be shown the welcome mat.

"Alternatively, Cecil and I were warmly welcomed by the boys of 89 Squadron (which changed its number to 85 Squadron three months later), and we immediately joined normal squadron activity in order to reach operational status as soon as possible. Our Javelins were Mks.2 and 6, the only difference being that the latter carried more fuel and could undertake longer endurance/range sortie profiles. We used to get a 50-minute sortie out of the Mk.2, and an hour and a half for the Mk.6. The two types of radar fitted to the Javelin both had a similar performance, but presented target information to the nav/rad in a different format. At the OCU we had been trained on the Mk.17, but 85 Squadron had the American equipment. In practice it was not difficult to operate with either set. We were declared operational after a short period and then took part in all exercises and detachments. Perhaps the most significant was holding QRA, fully armed, at two minutes' readiness overnight, a task which was rotated through all UK-based units.

"Standard routine on the squadron was to have one flight operating by day and the other flight took over when the sun went down. Each week the flights changed over giving all crews the constant opportunity of 24-hour operation. In general, we flew as pairs with one Javelin acting as the target and the other as fighter. Initial guidance was provided by ground control and reporting units who set up the geometry of the interception. When the fighter achieved a good position and the fighter nav/rad was confident of completing a successful interception, final control was taken by the intercepting aircraft until visual contact was gained by the pilot. This pattern worked well until one of the pair encountered a technical problem and had to return to base early leaving his playmate with little in the way of practice. We normally operated with Bawdsey, Patrington or Boulmer and occasionally, the ground radar unit would offer an unplanned target which happened to enter our area and this gave the chance to practice on an unknown aircraft until achieving a close visual on the stranger. We had to be careful with these opportunity targets as sometimes the odd airliner wandered through our operating sector and our civilian colleagues were not very happy to have a Javelin creeping up their backside! It was never really anything interesting. Originally, as I recall, we weren't allowed to creep up on Valiants and things like that because they had some funny electronics inside that played jamming games with the radar.

89 Squadron FAW.6 nearest camera, with 41 and 23 Squadron aircraft, West Malling 1957-58. (George Lee)

"Towards the end of 1958 another RO joined the squadron which made life a little more friendly when off duty. After one year on 85, Cecil was selected for an advance course at the CFE and we separated as a crew. Coincidentally, the squadron was relocated to West Malling in Kent and an NCO pilot, Master Pilot Tam Kirk, joined without a nav/rad. It was logical for us to crew up and we became, for a while, the only Javelin NCO crew. Over the next year ('59-'60) two more ROs and three ex-wartime NCO navigators arrived which gave the squadron a less one-sided nature. From April to June 1960 our early model aircraft were progressively replaced by new Mk.8s and the older Javelins were flown to Shawbury for storage."

Shawbury in Shropshire was the home of 27 Maintenance Unit (MU) which was responsible for holding Javelins surplus to immediate needs. It also prepared aircraft for re-issue and in the last few years of the Javelin's service, many of them were flown to Shawbury for disposal and scrapping. Other centres for Javelin maintenance and storage were 19 MU at St. Athan in South Wales, 23 MU at Aldergrove, Northern Ireland, 33 MU at Lyneham, Wiltshire, 103 MU at Akrotiri, Cyprus and 390 MU at Seletar, Singapore. **George Lee** again:

"The Mk.8 was a later development featuring an improved performance envelope thanks to the embodiment of reheat on the engines. However, engaging reheat was only effective above 20,000 feet as the increase in thrust required a major increase in fuel flow and the fuel pumps could not achieve the higher flow rate to support reheat at lower altitudes. Nevertheless, at high altitude the improvement in performance was quite impressive. The radar was improved because it had an automatic lock-on facility, not completely automatic because you had to operate it, but it would hold quite well. It had roughly the same amount of fuel as the Mk.6 and we carried Firestreak, as well as the four guns. It was considered to be a very much more capable aircraft. You didn't notice it so much from an aircrew point of view, other than the improvements in the radar system. Up at height it went better and we used to operate at 40 to 50,000 feet. West Malling was not an ideal location for a Javelin squadron, being only a few miles east of Heathrow and under the London Control Area. Our activities were often in conflict with civil traffic. Every month, every crew had to do a practice diversion to Heathrow and, because we were supposed to be low on fuel they pushed all the airliners out of the way. Before long, people were beginning to get a bit upset, with the result that the squadron was moved again in the autumn of 1960 to West Raynham in Norfolk. Tam had become close friends with one of the other NCO nav/rads and they opted to fly together. I had no objection as Don Walker, an experienced flight lieutenant, had asked me to be his nav/rad, and for my last year on the squadron we flew as a crew.

"Almost all ROs were serving on short-term engagements of five or nine years, and the end of my term was approaching. Most ROs were offered immediate commissions as a navigator, but I was still determined, if at all possible, to retrain as a pilot. Towards the end of 1961 the RAF tried an experiment by offering a limited number of NCO pilot and navigator courses to serving airmen. The opportunity was very short lived and I only just scraped in. Being an experienced nav/rad I was under some pressure to accept full retraining as a navigator, with the subtle hint that a commission could be included, but I was not interested. Fortunately my aptitude was appropriate for the front seat and I was delighted to be offered an NCO pilot's course.

"Several events now occurred (Aug '61) within a few days. Don left to join the transport force, my three-year tour was complete and I was expecting an immediate departure for pilot training. The latter happy event was rudely interrupted when the East Germans and Soviets decided to physically partition East and West Berlin and started erecting the infamous Berlin Wall. East-West tension rose and the squadron was deployed at very short notice to Laarbruch in West Germany as reinforcement for NATO forces. I became a spare nav/rad flying with other spare pilots within the detachment and feeling somewhat frustrated. The detachment lasted from September to November (for me), as my posting to flight training had arrived back at West Raynham in late October but had not been forwarded to Germany. Consequently, the training system was chasing after me, and I was hauled out of the back seat at Laarbruch on 28 November '61 (my

Scramble departure by 85 Squadron FAW.8s at Sylt April 1961. XJ124 K nearest the camera. (George Lee)

last trip) and rapidly returned to the UK. My logbook records 696 hours in the back seat of the Javelin as a nav/rad.

"Two years later, as a newly trained pilot, I was awaiting posting to an OCU and speculating on whether I would return to the Javelin but this time in the front seat, with the idle thought that, if so, I might be considered a full crew by myself. No such development transpired and I found myself back in the training world as a first-tour instructor. After completing this tour I was threatened with a tour as a Lightning pilot teaching AI techniques and set handling to new Lightning pilots at 226 OCU Coltishall. The prospect of more AI activity was a little too much and the system took a sympathetic approach to my protest, granting me my long hoped for path to the Hunter."

Forbes Pearson was another navigator on 85 Squadron, joining the unit in 1959. Later in his career he was forced to eject from his 6 Squadron Phantom when it suffered hydraulic failure in July 1969, thus becoming the first loss of an RAF Phantom.

"When I joined 85 Squadron at West Malling on my first tour with John Davies I was introduced to the wretched navigators' union. I went on drinking sessions in downtown Maidstone and discussed the crimes of our pilots. We had a loo seat on the crewroom wall into which the black outline of the head of the pilot of the month was displayed. He was voted for by the navigators as having committed the most heinous crime against us. All new pilots had to sit for modelling sessions against a shadow board. I learnt that pilots who erred consistently had to do gunnery on their own with the back seats empty. I don't know how they got radar lock-on; amazing now of course.

"85 Squadron was a law unto itself. As both John Davies and myself were first tourists, the CO had us in and told us that we would of course, be posted immediately. He told us that he only had master greens [the highest possible instrument rating] on his squadron – but he failed to get his way. Shortly after the squadron arrived at West Raynham I was on the desk when Ops Wing rang me for the pilots' ratings. I announced they were all master greens except mine which was now green. We had a master pilot and master navigator who always flew as a crew with a combined age of 106. The only items always carefully briefed prior to every one of our endless high-level PI sorties were that the pilots and navs should 'wear different-coloured Mae West life jackets and carry a torch –everything else is SOP – any questions?' The coloured Mae Wests referred to the frequency of individual SARBE search-and-rescue emergency locator beacons.

"I had been posted to 85 Squadron as a result of having trained on AI 17 and come top of my course at Leeming. I was selected for 85 which had AI 21 – deemed too space-age for ordinary mortals. My nav leader told me on arrival that the radar was a bit different but there was no special training available. 'Just give it a go and come and see me in six months' time if you have any problems.' I loved AI 21 which was a modified ASV [air-to-surface vessel] radar. After we moved to West Raynham, he took me on a visit to the USAF base at Sculthorpe (then a large B-66 wing) on a Friday which was their gambling night. I lost my month's pay in seconds and went back to base and swore never to gamble again. To my intense satisfaction I met my nav leader at breakfast the next morning and he was rather quiet about the previous night. Apparently he had been taken to the cleaners by the Americans for a lot more money."

85 Squadron was yet another illustrious fighter unit, particularly in the night-fighter role with Hurricanes, Havocs and Mosquitoes during the war and Meteors in the early 1950s. The motto 'We hunt by day and night' could hardly have been more appropriate. Its association with the Javelin came to an end on 31 March 1963 with the usual disbandment, only to reform the following day, still at West Raynham, by re-titling the existing Target Facilities Flight there. They then flew a variety of Canberras and Meteors until in December 1975 it suffered the ignominy of becoming a Bloodhound surface-to-air missile squadron – still at West Raynham – and continued as such until final disbandment on 10 July 1991.

During these early years, the Javelin's accident rate had, almost inevitably, increased. Up to the end of 1959 a further 17 aircraft were lost in squadron service (see Appendix Three), with around six being due to engine-related issues and a further four suffering some form of loss of control. Of the squadrons discussed in this chapter only 41 and 89 suffered. The 41 Squadron accident occurred on 11 July 1958 when XA751 was abandoned in a spin while performing aerobatics at Horsham St. Faith. The USAF exchange pilot Capt Earl Taylor was killed, but his navigator Flt Lt Brian Bedford survived. According to an eye witness, during a loop the aircraft entered cloud and emerged in a flat spin. Both crew members ejected but the pilot's was outside the seat parameters. This was to have been Earl Taylor's final sortie before returning to the United States at the end of his tour.

The 89 Squadron crash came when FAW.2 XA779 M stalled and spun in on approach to Stradishall on 19 September 1958, killing Flt Lt Derek Kenney and his navigator Fg Off Gordon 'Randy' Lewis.

By the end of 1959 the Javelin force had grown to an impressive total of 12 squadrons at home and in Germany. Also now operating were 41 Squadron (actually 141 renumbered after less than a year), plus 3 (renumbered from 96) and XI Squadrons at Geilenkirchen, 25 at Waterbeach, 29 at Leuchars, 33 at Middleton St. George, 64 at Duxford and 72 at Leconfield. 3 Squadron had reformed after 18 months of inactivity (having last flown Hunters), while all the others had converted from Meteor night fighters. Although only two more squadrons would convert during the coming decade, events in a number of areas of the world were about to bring the Javelin back to the forefront of RAF fighter activity at a time when the focus was increasingly turning on the replacement of both the Javelin and the Hunter by the Lightning, which entered service first with 74 Squadron at Coltishall in June 1960.

CHAPTER THREE

FIGHTER COMMAND – THE FINAL YEARS

THE BOYS

Gp Capt Mel Evans
Pilot. Joined in 1959. Trained on Provost, Vampire and Hunter. 23 and 60 Squadrons Javelin. CFS and 3 FTS Jet Provost. 228 OCU and 17 Squadron Phantom. Flying Ops evaluator AAFCE. 4 FTS Hunter. 228 OCU and 23 Squadron Phantom. OC 6 Squadron Jaguar. Deputy director for Fighter Training at HQ Headquarters Tactical Air Command USAF.

Sgt Roy Evans
Nav/radar. Joined 1956. Trained at 2 ANS and 228 OCU. 153 Squadron Meteor. 25 and 11 Squadrons Javelin. Left RAF 1965 and became an air traffic control officer.

Sqn Ldr Jim Froud
Pilot. Joined in 1952. Trained in Southern Rhodesia on Chipmunk and Harvard, and in the UK on Meteor and Mosquito. 33 Squadron Hornet, later Vampire and Venom, CFS, 5 FTS Vampire, 29 and 64 Squadrons Javelin, 2 FTS Jet Provost, Phantom 14 Squadron, Jaguar 6 Squadron, 226 OCU, 54 Squadron. Retired 1991.

Wg Cdr Peter Masterman
Navigator. Trained as a pilot on Chipmunk, Harvard and Meteor. Changed to navigator. 59 Squadron Canberra '59. 228 OCU and 29 Squadron Javelin. Canberra B(I).8 Geilenkirchen. Retired after 33 years' service.

With further contributions from **Brian Bullock** (Chapter Two) and **Eric Marsh** (Chapter One).

FROM PEAK TO DECLINE

In the winter of 1959/60, the RAF's fighter strength in Germany was bolstered by the addition of another new Javelin unit. In January 1959, 5 Squadron had reformed at Laarbruch by renumbering the incumbent 68 Squadron which flew the Meteor NF.11. It began receiving Javelin FAW.5s in January 1960 and was fully operational on the type by the early summer, the last Meteors being withdrawn in June. This was another squadron with a long fighter heritage and it had spent most of the Second World War in the Far East flying Mohawks, Hurricanes, Thunderbolts and Tempests. After two years back in the UK flying a mixed bag of types on anti-aircraft co-oper-

XH393, a T.3 coded T3, of 5 Squadron Geilenkirchen in August 1965. (Adrian Balch collection)

ation duties, in 1949 it had reformed in Germany at Wunstorf to fly Vampires and later Venoms, being disbanded in 1957. The next significant change to Javelin strength came at the beginning of January 1961 when both 3 and 87 Squadrons were disbanded. No. 3 was immediately reformed at Geilenkirchen to fly the Canberra B(I).8 by the simple expedient of renumbering 59 Squadron there, while 87 Squadron disappeared completely and has not been reformed since.

Just one new squadron was destined to receive Javelins, 60 Squadron at Tengah, Singapore. This squadron had never been home-based since reforming in 1920 after the Great War, flying DH.10s from Risalpur in what is now Pakistan. The Second World War saw it flying Blenheims, Hurricanes and Thunderbolts in South East Asia Command, switching to Spitfires in Singapore at the start of 1947. Having re-equipped with Vampires in 1950 and Venoms in 1957, two years later it switched roles to night fighting with Meteor NF.14s. By 1961 the Meteor was seriously outclassed and in July the first Javelin FAW.9 arrived to begin replacing them. The squadron had the distinction of making the last operational flight by Meteors on 17 August when two aircraft carried out a sector reconnaissance.

The other significant change in the new decade was the arrival in strength of the significantly improved 'second generation' Javelins – the FAW.7, 8 and 9. The Mk.7s had started appearing in 1958 and went to 23, 25, 33 and 64 Squadrons. The reheat-equipped FAW.8 joined the fleet right at the end of 1959 when the Air Fighting Development Squadron (AFDS) at Coltishall received their first of four examples, and in November that year the first to reach an operational unit arrived at Wattisham for 41 Squadron. The only other unit to fly the Mk.8 was 85 Squadron at West Malling, later moving to West Raynham.

Lastly came the FAW.9, with the first two being delivered to 25 Squadron at Waterbeach on 4 December 1959. Thereafter it rapidly took over as the principal variant for the remainder of the Javelin's operational career, serving with 5, 11, 23, 29, 33, 60 and 64 Squadrons. The last of the first-generation Javelins, the Mk.6 left 11 Squadron in March 1962, and when 85 Squadron was disbanded in March 1963, the only Javelins remaining in service were Mk.9s. By then the replacement Lightning had joined four squadrons and the Javelin force had been reduced to eight.

23 SQUADRON

Mel Evans poses with 23 Squadron FAW.9 XH894 R. (Mel Evans)

Having successively flown Blenheims, Havocs, Mosquitoes, Vampire NF.10s and Venom NF.2s and 3s, 23 Squadron was well versed in the art of night fighting. In the Javelin era, its motto 'Always on the attack' might well have been adapted to 'Always on the move'! First receiving FAW.4s at Horsham St. Faith in March 1957 they moved to Coltishall two months later, back to Horsham St. Faith in September 1958, Coltishall again in July 1960 and then, just for a change, Leuchars in March 1963.

On 16 March 1961, 20-year-old Pilot Officer **Mel Evans** took off from Leeming on his first solo in the Javelin, after three hours dual instruction. Five and a half years later, on 19 October 1966, Flt Lt Mel Evans landed XH910 at RAAF (Royal Australian Air Force) Butterworth, his final flight in the Javelin which took his total hours on type past 1,200. The intervening years saw him develop his experience from a raw, young pilot learning the skills of a UK air defence pilot by day and night, and in all weathers in the rarefied cold air high above the North Sea, where the Javelin was in its designated arena preparing to meet the aggressors from the east, to a seasoned, skilled operator of the aircraft at very low levels just above the steamy jungles and waters of Malaya and North Borneo, where the aircraft coped with an environment that had not featured in its design specification. Along the way, the full capabilities and potential of the Javelin were explored and developed, pushing the extreme corners of the aircraft's performance envelope and pushing the limits in height, speed and manoeuvre to extract every bit of capability ready to meet the Indonesian threat.

> "I joined the air force in 1958 and started basic flying training on the Piston Provost before progressing, still as a teenager, to the Vampire to gain my wings. From there, I went to Chivenor where we did 30 hours of day-fighter training on the Hunter T.7 and F.4 to get us from the speed of the Vampire to the speed of the Javelin. We were introduced to basic fighter tactics and manoeuvres, with gunsight handling and tactical formations – bread and butter stuff for the fighter world. The Hunter was a delightful aircraft to fly, with beautiful controls and handling, but for me it was really another training vehicle on my way to a very different role. When you see the

Hunter and the Javelin side-by-side there's a huge difference between them.

"Before we could commence flying the Javelin there was one more box to be ticked. We had to have six hours night flying in the last six months. To acquire this we were sent to Valley in Anglesey to fly the Vampire T.11 once again. Opening up the throttle to start the first take-off was quite a shock after the Hunter; it felt as though the engine had failed, such was the power response. We soon adapted to the ways of the Vampire and, after a night dual trip and three solo general-handling trips, we were sent off solo at five-minute separation to do a one-hour cross-country flight, turning over Jurby Isle of Man and landing to refuel at Shawbury, before reversing the route back to Valley. It was blissfully quiet as we cruised along in the very dark skies. Suddenly, a microphone clicked on and a voice said, 'God I'm pissed off'. 'Station calling, say again your call sign.' 'I'm not that pissed off,' came the reply.

"I started my Javelin conversion with 228 OCU, Leeming, in February 1961. We had three weeks of intensive ground school before starting the flying phase. After three dual sorties in the T.3 dual-control version, I was sent on my first solo. Flying the Javelin solo was thereafter a rare event. The next 'solo' flight was in the FAW.5 with 'my' navigator. A happy feature of the Javelin was the large cushion of air it created beneath it just before touchdown. This made hard landings almost impossible. Not so popular, particularly with the 'old hands' converting to the Javelin, were the toe brakes and Maxaret anti-locking units. During the course at Leeming, we witnessed a number of accidents that were attributed to the brake units. Another unique feature of the Javelin was the power of its air brakes. At 430 knots, the maximum speed at which the air brakes extended fully, the retardation was 1 g, the equivalent of 100% braking in a car. For this reason it was essential to warn the navigator before using them, unless you wanted to have all his pencils. The provision of this powerful control, which was selectable anywhere between fully closed and fully extended, was to enable the speed to be rapidly reduced when closing on a target, particularly at night. There was virtually no trim change during selection which made it a useful control in formation.

"After a brief period becoming familiar with the handling characteristics and performance of the aircraft, there was a concentrated period of instrument flying to achieve the necessary standard to operate in the 'night all-weather' role. Fundamental to a successful air interception, was the need for the pilot to follow accurately the commands from the back-seater as he interpreted the indications from the radar. There was a standard set of commands that instructed the pilot to manoeuvre the aircraft precisely in turn rate, height adjustment and speed control. If the pilot's response did not match the navigator's expectations, the radar picture could then be misinterpreted, giving rise to incorrect subsequent action. Even in perfect visibility, it was vital that the pilot responded accurately and quickly to the navigator's commands. This technique was strongly emphasised from the very beginning and I determined that I would follow it religiously and only look out when the navigator handed control of the intercept to me by declaring that the target was 'dead ahead at 200 yards'. This worked well until the day that, as we were closing in behind the target but still in a 60 degree banked turn, I felt the hairs on the back of my neck go rigid. For some reason, I looked up to the windscreen. As I did, the wingtip of the target appeared in the top of the windscreen about 30 feet ahead and travelled down the vertical length of the screen. Suddenly, two very large jet-pipes went past followed by the other wing. I did not tell my navigator what had just happened. Instead, I told him that we seemed to be in a 'classic weave' behind the target and I was calling off the intercept. If the target aircrew had seen the incident, they never mentioned it. This was my only 'close shave' in a Javelin and it taught me to listen very carefully to the reported position of the target during the intercept – whether I was fighter or target.

"We successfully completed the Leeming course and were posted to 23 Squadron at Coltishall. The squadron was equipped with the Mk.9 version of the Javelin which had the more powerful engines with added reheat. This system, though denigrated by some, was a huge performance enhancement for the Javelin. The system relied on the basic fact that jet engines become more fuel-efficient with altitude, while the mechanically-driven fuel pump has a constant output at any particular rpm. This 'unused' fuel pressure was directed to a ring of nozzles in the jet-pipe aft of the engine, where it was ignited and controlled by a circle of petals that changed the size of the jet-pipe diameter to meet the increased thrust. At 20,000 feet the increase in thrust amounted to 12% but by 40,000 feet this became almost 20%, a significant increase in power that enabled the Marks 8 and 9 to reach and operate at 50,000 feet. Many people believe that the system did not provide additional thrust at low level. Indeed, if engaged on the runway, there was a very satisfying thump as the fuel ignited, followed by a reduction in the engine rpm to about 86%. I did a personal test of the system at 1,000 feet, where I applied full 'cold' power against full air brake and the speed settled at 300 knots. On engaging reheat, the speed increased to 303 knots, indicating an increase on total power – and another satisfying thump.

"23 Squadron's Mk.9s had been modified for in-flight refuelling, but before we could try our hand at 'jousting' we had to prove our competence as a night and all-weather intercept crew able to be trusted with the air defence of the UK. The specific goal was to demonstrate that we could successfully and consistently take a night intercept from initial radar contact to a stable position directly behind an unlit target, at any altitude, and achieve a visual identification of the unknown aircraft. Once the identification was achieved, we had to establish contact with the target and establish its further intentions, being ready, if necessary, to use internationally agreed signals to lead the target to a landing at a designated airfield. At the same time, we had to be prepared to take offensive action if necessary. Interestingly, our instructions listed our defensive priorities as missile attack, gun attack and, when out of weapons, ramming. To help the pilot acquire the target visually, the Javelin was fitted with a collimator mounted ahead of the gunsight. Once a radar lock was achieved and the target was directly in front of the fighter, a small dot was projected onto the collimator glass indicating the vertical and horizontal location of the target. This could be used to bring the pilot's eyes to the exact position of the target or, if necessary, provide an aiming point for the gunsight.

"There was one feature about the Javelin that I really appreciated and missed on all the aircraft that I flew subsequently; the cockpit lighting was excellent. All the main instruments were marked with luminous paint and the cockpit had two types of lighting. The red lighting provided clear sight of all the controls, switches and handles in the cockpit, particularly during start-up checks, without destroying night vision. At the end of the runway, the red lights could be dimmed right down or off, leaving the essential instruments clearly visible in the glow of the ultraviolet (UV) lights. When clear of the lights on the ground and settled into the inky blackness, the UV lights could be gradually dimmed until they were visible with night vision at a maximum. This feature was fundamental to achieving an early VID (visual identification) on a moonless night.

"Having achieved combat ready status, the joys of sitting on the ORP at five-minute readiness became one of the regular features of life during the Cold War. As I remember it, we sat out there for one or two hours and then handed over to the other crew for a similar period of rest in the warm, red-lighted crewroom. As a 'new' pilot, I was fascinated by the whole process. On occasions it would be very foggy, but we were still available to scramble as long as we could see three runway lights ahead. Sometimes it would be snowing and the giant snow blowers would be clearing the runway continuously, but always it would be cold. Eventually, the boffins came up with electrically-heated underwear. These undergarments had an electrical cable sewn into the fabric and a cable that plugged into an extension lead passed up to the cockpit. In the event of a scramble, the cable was unplugged and tossed to the ground crew. It was not possible to completely close the hood when using this facility. Talking of hoods, the Javelin may have been the last jet fighter built to be able to fly with the hood open, just as the older Hunter could. This feature proved useful out in the tropics to help cool the cockpit after take-off.

"We deployed to Cyprus for an air defence exercise [see Chapter Four]. All too soon we returned to Coltishall and to the routine of practice intercepts a hundred miles out over the North Sea at altitudes up to 50,000 feet. From time to time, the opportunity would arise for an interception against a Vulcan, which was easy to see, both visually and on radar and relatively easy to 'kill' with a Firestreak missile, but our training procedures required a 'guns kill' to complete the practice. The maximum permitted 'g' for a Vulcan was 2. At 50,000 feet the wing-loading of the Vulcan was such that it could achieve that g – and climb! With smart use of their tail-warning radar and a well-timed turn, the Vulcan crew could deny us a 'guns kill'.

"Another interesting exercise that we had to do from time to time involved climbing at night to 50,000 feet over one of the North Sea firing ranges to exercise the guns. We were not firing at a target, just checking the function of the guns. If the aircraft was rolled inverted just before firing, the navigator was able to 'watch' the rounds trajectory on the radar screen. It was when we were returning from one of these exercises, that I noticed a very bright light high above the canopy moving in a similar direction but slightly faster. We were still at 50,000 feet and this was 1962. I asked our controller if there were any other aircraft in our vicinity. He replied that there was none and asked why. I described the scene and he asked if we could follow the light. After confirming our fuel situation with Harry Wyld in the back, I agreed to follow for a limited period while we were heading in the general direction of home. Eventually, the light was moving too far ahead and away from our required route. (Once on the ground I completed the relevant form and heard no more of the incident!) At this point, we were able to employ another feature of the Javelin to ensure that we would have sufficient fuel on return to base. From 50,000 feet both throttles were closed to idle and the angle of descent adjusted to give a speed of 215 knots. This was the 'best glide' speed. Once the glide was established, one of the engines would be shut down completely. During this relaxing descent, the Javelin would cover 147 nautical miles in 27 minutes and use just 84 gallons of fuel – not bad for a 20-ton beast.

"I never had an opportunity to intercept a 'Bear', but Harry and I were selected to go as part of the squadron participation on the guided weapons course at Valley on the Isle of Anglesey. As the junior pilot, I was not selected to be one of the 'prime firers' but I was a reserve ready to step in if the primary went unserviceable – which did not happen. However, we did have a ringside seat for each firing. Traditionally, the target was an unmanned vehicle, a Jindivik, not too dissimilar to a Second World War flying bomb, but using a small jet engine. These targets were relatively expensive so a mechanism had been fitted that allowed the target to deploy a small package of flares from a winch. When the fighter was in position, the flares were ignited and the missile fired at the flares. Each of our missiles passed close enough to the flares to achieve a 'kill' – on its way up the wire to impact the Jindivik and destroy it.

"September 1962 was a memorable month. The squadron's Mk.9 aircraft were being sent away for modifications to the structure and fuel systems to enable the carriage of the Hunter-style 230-gallon external fuel tanks. One tank was carried on each of the four pylons, providing an extra four tons of fuel to improve fuel reserves on long deployment flights. As the Mk.9s went away they were replaced with a few Mk.7 airframes to keep us flying. Eventually, there were insufficient Mk.7s and we were allocated a few old Mk.5s. On the 20th of the month the Coltishall-based AFDS asked if they could borrow my services to fly one of their Mk.8 Javelins as a target for their Lightning, operating at low level over the sea. During the month, I also completed my instrument rating renewal in the T.3 and thus flew five marks of Javelin in that month."

The sorties from Coltishall gave something of a taste of Fighter Command's future for Mel. He flew an AFDS Mk.8 XH976, without a navigator, to act as a target for a Lightning T.4 to practise PIs. Two such sorties were flown on the 20th, the first for PIs at the very low altitude for a Javelin of 500 feet, and the second at 1,000 feet. **Mel Evans** contines:

"Playing target is not a very memorable event. What was memorable was exploring the Mk.8's autopilot. We were under radar control for the set-up and the target height was pre-briefed. The big attraction for me was the opportunity to add the Mk.8 to my logbook. I'm afraid it was sometimes nice to fly solo!

"I had been on 23 Squadron for some time and was becoming confident in manoeuvring the Javelin close to the operating limits, when two events occurred in quick succession that had a profound effect on my confidence and capability flying the Javelin. At the end of an annual assessment flight with an examiner from the Fighter Command Instrument Rating Squadron (FCIRS), I had completed an instrument approach to Leuchars. I was asked to overshoot and climb to 10,000 feet overhead the base. As I levelled out, the examiner asked me to roll inverted and pull through. He obviously sensed my hesitation and assured that it would be fine. 'Just roll inverted, put out the air brakes and pull the nose smoothly back to level flight.' As the aircraft returned to level flight, I was amazed to discover that we were at 5,000 feet. On the ground, he explained that the manoeuvre was a useful way of positioning for a tactical formation rejoin to the circuit in good weather. I never had cause to use it but it taught me a lot about the capability of the Javelin. Shortly afterwards, I was scheduled to fly staff continuation training with one of the squadron's most experienced pilots. The briefing had set out the requirement to cover various aspects of aircraft handling specific to the Javelin. Once airborne, I did some hard turns and rolls at his request, then he took control and said he was going to show me that the Javelin was no different from other fighters of the period and could loop with the best of them, if you knew what you were doing. At this point I was seeing the page in the Pilot's Notes that said, 'Aerobatics in the looping plane are prohibited'. He then performed a perfect loop with no drama whatsoever. 'Your turn. Just remember to keep a steady pressure to achieve 4 g, 3 g at the vertical and 2 g over the top. Use the trimmer to follow the changing speed.' We practised several more and I became perfectly comfortable doing the aerobatics. On the ground, he explained that the perceived difficulty was down to the complex flying control system that tried to maintain any trimmed speed by introducing a control change to correct any deviation. If the speed reduced below the trimmed speed, the control system would 'lower the nose' to regain the target speed. When inverted at the top of the loop, the speed would be considerably reduced causing the control system to 'lower the nose', thus ensuring that the speed would continue to reduce. Using the trimmer during the speed changes, watching the g meter and the horizon produced perfect loops. This was not a vital skill for an interceptor pilot, but in the very different scenario in Malaysia it could have been vital to be able to use the aircraft in the vertical plane in direct combat.

"As a graduate of the RAF's aviation medicine high altitude and pressure breathing course in September 1961, I was well versed in the effects and problems of high flight. The Javelin was designed for moderately high altitudes – we regularly operated up to 50,000 feet and the aircraft was appropriately equipped to operate the pressure breathing jacket designed to work with the g suit to provide a basic pressure suit in conjunction with the Mk.21A pressure regulator oxygen system. At 48,000 feet the cockpit altitude was about 26,000 feet and therefore the P2 oxygen mask was necessary at all times. Compare this with a modern airliner or fighter, where the cockpit altitude is rarely higher than 8,000 feet. At the time the Javelin was designed, there was obviously concern about the effect on the crew if there was an explosive decompression through the sudden loss of pressurisation at very high altitude. During the course we were subjected to a decompression from 25,000 feet to 53,000 feet and that was dramatic enough, with the chamber atmosphere turning to fog in an instant and oxygen under pressure being forced into the lungs. Under these conditions it was necessary to force the air out of the lungs, and then stop the pressurised air from bursting your lungs as you relaxed slightly to allow air into them. It was interesting to see how large the neck swelled under these pressures. Another feature of operations at these cockpit altitudes was the possibility of suffering from the 'bends'. In normal operations lasting an hour or ninety minutes, it was rare to encounter the 'bends'. If it did occur, an immediate descent to a low altitude would remove the pain immediately. When we began the longer flights using flight refuelling the possibility for the 'bends' was greatly increased. Position yourself in the middle of the Indian Ocean, as happened to me on a flight from Gan to Singapore, and the option to descend and leave your fuel supply tanker, was not so easy. Suffering the joint pain for a couple of hours was often the best option.

"A formation of Hunters of the Royal Danish Air Force arrived at Leuchars for a cultural exchange, and to buy whisky. One aircraft managed to burst a tyre during the landing. The visit was only over one night, so there was an urgent need for a replacement tyre/wheel. Leuchars had none and the nearest available was at Royal Naval Air Station Lossiemouth to the north of us. Road transport would take too long so my boss, always ready to help, dispatched me to Lossiemouth in a Mk.9 with the unfortunate Danish pilot in the navigator's seat. We arrived at Lossiemouth and refuelled while the wheel was procured and stowed; I presumed that the only bay large enough for it was the engine access area. We were strapped in ready to go when the crew chief came on the intercom to say that the wheel would not go far enough up into the engine compartment to allow the panel to be closed. It seemed the only possible option was to try and position it on the rear seater's lap. Did we want to try that? I discussed the implications with my Danish passenger and he was desperate enough to give it a try. I sat quietly in my cockpit while the wheel, which now looked enormous, was passed up to the rear cockpit. Amazingly, it fitted in and we were able to close the canopy. I flew the return trip very gently and made a very careful approach and landing. I did not wish to consider the likely outcome had it become necessary to abandon the aircraft. I suspect it was a very relieved Hunter pilot who climbed from that Mk.9 cockpit. I still cannot imagine how the wheel fitted into the rear cockpit."

Eric Marsh found himself posted to 23 Squadron in June 1964, only a couple of months before the first Lightnings arrived to replace the Javelin '9Rs they had at that time.

"When I finished on 60 Squadron in Singapore, I came back to the UK. I joined 23 Squadron at Leuchars, but not for long, because it converted to Lightnings. Although the Javelin was generally reliable, you had to be very careful with the cartridge starter. You had a couple of cartridges to start the engines, with a single cartridge being fired into one of them.

"I was on 23 Squadron when it happened; an officer from air ministry, wanting to get his hours in so he could claim flying pay, used to come up

23 Squadron aircrew with FAW.9 XH707 T during missile practice camp at Valley 1963. (via Mel Evans)

so that he could fly in an aeroplane. This fellow wasn't au fait with Javelins so he sat in one with me, and I briefed him and so forth and on start-up we had a double cartridge fired down one cylinder…bang! It blew the starter completely and an engine fire developed. (This was usually caused by a sticking flap-valve that directed both cartridge exhausts into the same engine instead of one to each engine.) I told him I thought we'd better get out; he was senior to me but I told him to get out on the right-hand side because it was the left-hand side that was billowing flames. I got out quickly, but when I got to the wingtip and looked round he was still there, with his helmet on struggling with his umbilical oxygen chord which stretched all the way back into the cockpit. He hadn't unfastened it, so I had to push him back so that I could release the oxygen chord.

"We flew a formation of four aircraft over the new Forth Road Bridge when it was opened; I was No.3 in the formation. We did one flypast on 24 August 1964 and a second one on 21 September, which was my last flight on 23 Squadron. I stayed at Leuchars but went to the Fighter Command Ferry Squadron; we were going to ferry Javelins out to Singapore. We started out from Leuchars, flew down to Cyprus with in-flight refuelling, but then had to return to the UK. The whole project was abandoned because Rangoon, one of our planned ferrying stops, was also handling Russian aircraft and they thought it was a conflict of interests. We came back along the south coast to Lee-on-the-Solent for them to be loaded onto boats – destination Singapore. Lee had rather short runways and traffic lights on the road at the end, and one of the aircraft came in with some brushwood in his undercarriage.

23 Squadron flypast for the opening of the Forth Road Bridge 24 August 1964. (Eric Marsh)

"My total Javelin flying time was 1,286 hours and my last flight in one was on 22 March 1966 in T.3 XH966. Then I went off to Manby on a Jet Provost jet refresher course followed by CFS to train as an instructor on Chipmunks, then to Nottingham UAS. After that I left the air force for civil aviation with BOAC."

Eric's work on the Fighter Command Ferry Squadron saw him ranging far and wide, including a number of trips out to Akrotiri, 'Deci' (Decimomannu) in Sardinia, El Adem in Libya, RAF Germany and frequent hops between Leuchars and Coltishall, supporting the remaining Javelin squadrons.

Thus 23 Squadron began changing over to the Lightning F.3 in August 1964 and continued to fly them from Leuchars until moving down to Coningsby in October 1975 to re-equip with the Phantom. The squadron relocated to Wattisham in 1976 and Port Stanley in the Falkland Islands in 1983, and then to the new Mount Pleasant airfield in 1986. From 1988 to 1994 it flew Tornado F.3s at Leeming before disbanding. Two years later it surfaced again at Waddington as part of the Sentry AEW (airborne early warning) Wing, finally disbanding in 2009.

25 SQUADRON

Yet another long-time night-fighter unit, having flown more less the same types as 23 (less the Venom NFs), 25 Squadron (motto 'Striking I defend') was one of the fairly small number of units to fly the FAW.7 when its first examples arrived at Waterbeach in December 1958. A year later FAW.9s joined them and all the '7s had gone by January 1961. In October that year the squadron moved to Leuchars, which is where nav/rad **Brian Bullock** joined them.

XH882 L, a 25 Squadron FAW.9 with a pair of Firestreaks, coming into land. (via Mick Speake)

"I arrived at Leuchars mid-October 1961 on a Sunday evening. After booking in at the mess I went to the bar to meet some of the 25 Squadron guys. Imagine my reaction when nobody knew anything about 25 Squadron! It was certainly not based at Leuchars. Arriving at SHQ the next morning I discovered that 25 Squadron was actually at Waterbeach, but was moving to Leuchars in about three weeks' time. So, having contacted the CO, a nav Wg Cdr James Walton, I was given the task of sorting out the office set-up in the designated hangar. Initially I flew with a variety of pilots, eventually teaming up with Flt Lt Mike Gawtree. He was quite a rarity, possibly unique, he had been a nav/rad on a squadron before becoming a pilot.

"At the end of May 1962 the squadron was detached to Gütersloh. The Russians were again threatening to close the Berlin air corridors and we were warned we might have to escort a military transport aircraft into Berlin. However, the threat subsided and in the meantime we were kicked out of Gütersloh because of a VIP visit and seven days later, after being at Brüggen we returned to Leuchars at the beginning of August. In mid-October, following several practices, we made a rather unusual flypast over Leith docks and down the middle of Princes Street in Edinburgh, all for the benefit of King Olaf of Norway.

"On 5 November 1962, 25 Squadron was disbanded and became a Bloodhound unit. About half a dozen of us walked across the tarmac to an adjacent hangar to join 29 Squadron."

Roy Evans, having begun his first tour as a nav/rad on 153 Squadron with Meteor NF.12s and 14s at the end of 1958, found himself switched to Javelins on 25 Squadron at Waterbeach. He stayed with the unit when it moved to Leuchars.

"I was a nav/rad on the Mks.7 and 9, starting in 1958 at RAF Waterbeach, moving with 25 Squadron to RAF Leuchars in 1961, then on to RAF Geilenkirchen in December 1962 to join 11 Squadron. Re-equipping this squadron with the bulk of 25 Squadron aircraft and most of its aircrew, finally leaving in September '65 with a total of 1,362 hours on Mks.7 and 9. In addition I helped three different pilots to destroy three little Jindivik drones with Firestreak air-to-air missiles. The nav/rad had charge of the attacks, irrespective of rank. This was especially valid when the pilot/captain of the aircraft was a senior figure, for example when the station commander or wing commander flying was involved. I first met Jack Broughton [see Chapter Four] on 25 Squadron, then crossed over with him to RAF Germany (RAFG) in 1962, where apart from being an 11 Squadron colleague he was also our station rugby captain; I was the hooker and he was in the second row.

"Various squadrons were equipped with different marks of Javelin, each with sometimes different features. Flt Lt Keith McRobb joined 25 Squadron from 72 Squadron at Church Fenton equipped with Mk.4 and 5 aircraft. I flew with Keith to do a familiarisation trip and a double-engine air-test. The latter was done up to 45,000 feet east of Waterbeach, then Keith said he'd never pulled through a Mk.9 and did I mind. Of course not, so there we were in Mk.9 XH884 C carrying two Firestreak missiles. When Keith rolled us onto our back, he then pulled through in a dive, shouting 'Whoa!' as we went supersonic, the Mk.9 with reheat nozzles and missiles weighing about five tons heavier than a Mk.4. 'Never mind', said my intrepid pilot, 'luckily, we're over the sea.' 'No matey', said I, 'we're over Great Yarmouth!' Luckily, nobody ever discovered who dropped a sonic bang on that coastal resort, and it was a valuable lesson for Keith.

"There was fierce inter-squadron rivalry in the night-fighter world, and it was so in May 1961 between 25 (ourselves) and 64 Squadron based at Duxford. Exercise Matador was held over the North Sea involving the night-fighter force defending against V-force and Canberras attacking inbound to East Anglia. As was normal, crews met in Cambridge the week before the exercise, swapping bragging-rights. The line-chiefy of 64 asked how many aircraft we had serviceable and we truthfully said 16 out of 16. 'No way' said the line-chiefy, he had 12 and thought that was good! Early morning on Monday 13th, after bagging two V-bombers and two Canberras, 25 Squadron aircraft received the message: 'Waterbeach Exercise BLACK [terminated], divert to Duxford.' 64's chiefy had not only his aircraft on his ORP but also 16 of 25's lined up in front of them! Chiefy's face was a picture, and two days later, after returning to Waterbeach on the Tuesday, 64 Squadron were again the hosts to us on a further diversion – lovely!

"The Waterbeach station commander was ex-Battle of Britain but he was built like a bomber, being about 120 kgs. In fact he had to check the port and starboard cockpit consoles before he sat in the aircraft, as it was impossible to visually check them when he was in situ! One day in 1959 he asked the 25 Squadron CO if he could fly later on that morning. The news of his impending arrival at the squadron sent most of the nav/rads not on essential duties into a 'flap', and they quickly found reasons to go on other errands, anywhere other than 25 Squadron, before the arrival of our heavyweight station commander. This day was no exception, and when the staff car, complete with groupie's pennant, arrived, whilst pilots were plentiful, nav/rads were definitely not. After checking the aircrewroom, coffee bar etc., the groupie entered the nav briefing room, also apparently devoid of nav/rads. But our intrepid heavyweight had played this game before. Opening a large map-cupboard, one unfortunate flight officer was discovered hiding, so groupie said, 'Hello Bas (Whorwood), fancy finding you here. Get your kit on, we're going flying!'

"On 22 August 1961 a 'Lane-Ex' was planned over the North Sea. Radials from Waterbeach were drawn up starting 50 miles from base, extending to 150-200 miles out, with lanes approx. three degrees wide, which meant fighters were allocated a unique lane, from 20-30 nautical miles wide. As all available aircraft had already been allocated, and my pilot was sick with a head cold (a definite showstopper for high altitude fighter work), I was resigned to a spectator's role. However, after lunch the engineering chaps worked a small miracle, and they managed to make a fourteenth aircraft serviceable, and in the uncanny way senior pilots have of discovering facts, the wing commander flying quickly materialised and I was in the frame to fly with him.

"We briefed, then as the bulk of the squadron aircraft had already been scrambled, we had carte blanche to enter the Lane system wherever there was 'trade' (bomber forces), and kill whatever we could! This was luxury, so off we set, yours truly checking all targets on a south-westerly track with my IFF (identification friend or foe) equipment, which showed if radar echoes were friendly fighters or not. After approximately 20 minutes, I discovered a target, with another couple in attendance, and after a quick assessment I told the wingco we had a target at our 11 o'clock position, range 18 miles, so it was quite fast and high, and it looked as if we were in business. I told the pilot we would throw a hard left turn (45 degrees of bank) at range 12 miles, losing altitude as necessary to maintain a minimum speed of Mach 0.93, as the target was already a few degrees above us, but a snap-up when we had the target at 12 o'clock 20 degrees above. This should let us get acquisition with our Firestreak missiles at about 1-1.5 miles range. The 12 miles point came, 'Port hard' said I, and off we went; should be a good kill, most probably a V-bomber. As we were about to pass through heading 270, our aircraft reversed turn! 'What the Blue Blazes are you doing?' I asked, completely forgetting who the pilot was, not that it made a lot of difference, I was in command and the driver was most definitely in the wrong, irrespective of rank. As we steadied on a south-westerly heading, there was our target in our dead-ahead position, but now nine miles away. I was livid, told the pilot our pidgeons (steer and range to base) and then refused to say anything else to him until we landed back at base.

"As we pulled up on the pad, I left my cockpit, jumped off the port wingtip and shot off into our line-office, where my sick pilot Bob Kelly was the ops officer. I was just telling him about the cock-up, when in came our CO Jim Walton, who heard me exploding. He told me to leave the pilot to him and cool off over a coffee. When the wingco flying appeared, complaining that the sergeant had refused to speak to him after pidgeons, he was told in no uncertain terms that if he wished to continue flying in 25 Squadron aircraft in future he must obey his navigator's orders, or else find another Javelin squadron! I did eventually get an apology from him at the same time as he gave me my elevated rating of 'above average' on my next assessment, which was only fair considering!"

From 1973 25 Squadron had Bloodhounds at North Coates on the Lincolnshire coast, moving to Brüggen in 1971 and Wyton in 1983, where it remained until 1989 when it took on Tornado F.3s at Leeming, disbanding in April 2008.

29 SQUADRON

Of all the Javelin squadrons, 29 (a former Blenheim, Beaufighter, Mosquito, Meteor unit) had the distinction of flying them the longest, starting at Acklington in November 1957 and ending at Wattisham in May 1967 when it re-equipped with Lightnings. Having left a Canberra squadron, **Peter Masterman** liked the look of the Javelin and joined 29 at the end of 1959.

"After flying Chipmunks, Harvards and Meteors as a trainee pilot, defective eyesight resulted in me being sent to Canada to train as a navigator; that was not easy. I think I was the only one who wore glasses and we were learning astro-navigation. Could I see the stars? No. They then found me one of only two sextants that they had and could I then see the stars? Well, sometimes! The sextant normally issued to trainee navigators was the Mk.9B – B for bubble. They managed to get me a Mk.9BM – BM for bubble magnifying. Without it I think I would have failed the course, which would have been a

29 Squadron FAW.6 XA817 E starting-up at Leuchars June 1960. (Peter Masterman)

pity because after Canada I never saw or used a sextant again! It took more than two years of intense navigation training for me to be able to calculate roughly where I was on the surface of the planet. Now I can go to Halfords, buy a Sat nav for £100, and discover exactly where I am – really annoying!

"I spent ten years in Germany including – after my Javelin tour – a full tour on Canberras, which was my favourite aeroplane; the Javelin wasn't! In early 1959, my three-year tour with 59 Squadron flying, first the Canberra B.2 at Gütersloh, and then the Canberra B(I.)8 at Geilenkirchen in Germany was coming to a close and I was wondering where I would be posted next. I was told to report to air ministry to discuss my next posting – something which had never happened before or since! To enjoy my flying, it was necessary for me to see where I was going and to enjoy the sky, the sun, the moon and the stars: the last thing I wanted was to be 'buried' in the back of a V-bomber together with another navigator and an air electronics officer. Despite its long gestation, which was marred by a number of fatal accidents, the Javelin appealed to me. I had seen it fly at a Farnborough Air Show and I had had a look over a couple of Javelins which were always in bits in a hangar at Geilenkirchen. The Javelin was nicknamed 'The Dragmaster' and 'Supersonic Flat-Iron' together with other less than complimentary names! I wanted to fly it. The thing I liked about it (and the Meteor because I often flew in one), was that I could see out. One quite good thing about the Javelin, was the term 'kick the tyres, light the fires'; with the Canberra, you often had to do hours of flight planning.

"When interviewed at the air ministry, the interviewing officer seemed surprised that I wanted to fly the Javelin. I recall that he told me to go away and think about it over lunch. After I confirmed my wish, he said he would arrange a posting to Leeming, the Javelin OCU. However, he added that I would have to wait six months because the Canberra T.11, a Canberra bomber with a Javelin radome, was being introduced at Leeming for navigator training. In the meantime, I was posted to Northolt to help in the production of aeronautical information documents.

"On arrival at Leeming with four other navigator trainees, I was somewhat dismayed to hear of the high failure rate of navigators. This was because of the hand and eye co-ordination and manual dexterity required to operate the 'joystick' which controlled the radar scanner in pitch and azimuth. Constant adjustment was necessary in order to keep an evading target aircraft in radar sight. Further, the 'joystick' had a knurled ring at its base operated by one's index finger to strobe the target in range. There was also a button at the top of the 'joystick' which one pressed to lock-on to the target. Operating this was hard enough for a normal person, but it was especially difficult for me as I am left-handed. Although, oddly enough, I bat and bowl at cricket right-handed!

"After completing ground school I progressed to the Canberra flying phase and was soon in difficulty operating the AI 17 scanner. I was not encouraged when two of my four navigator colleagues got the 'chop' and I feared that I would be the third. However, I struggled on until, Eureka! – I suddenly got the hang of it and thereafter there was no stopping me! I progressed to the Javelin stage where initially pilots and navigators were trained independently before crewing-up. I got on well with Chris Cowper who shared my interest in cricket and music, so we agreed to crew-up. I was keen to fly with Chris on our first solo together, but I was feeling unwell and had a sore throat. All went well until our descent from high level when I had difficulty and pain in clearing my ears. Chris and I were due to fly again that afternoon, but I felt that it would be unwise for me to fly so I took to my bed in the officers' mess. At about 5 p.m. my bedroom door was flung open by Chris who was in a state of high excitement and he shouted 'Get up Masterman, we are going to the pub!' I protested, saying that I was ill, however, carried away by his excitement I got up, got dressed and jumped into his car. When we got to the guardroom, the RAF police would not let us out and told us to wait there for a bus which would take us and others to the North Yorkshire Moors to put out a fire caused by a Javelin crash. I had not heard Chris swear before but I think he said, 'F**k that, I was the pilot!' We were then let out and went to my favourite pub in Copt Hewick, a small village near Ripon, where we drank far more than was wise. I lost touch with Chris but by coincidence we met some years later – I was staying at the RAF Club in Piccadilly. I came down in the lift to the ground floor and as the lift door opened there was a loud exclamation 'Bloody Masterman! You chickened out hours before I bailed out!' and there was Chris waiting to go up in the lift. We went to the bar and carried on drinking where we had left off a few years earlier!"

Chris Cowper's accident occurred on 29 September 1959 in FAW.5 XA662/N of 228 OCU. The starboard engine caught fire at 30,000 feet after turbine failure and the second engine was shut down after a fire warning. The aircraft crashed at Leyburn, Yorkshire. **Peter Masterman** again:

"Bob Nietz, a USAF staff navigator on an exchange tour had taken my place to fly with Chris, who suffered a serious back injury and never flew in the RAF again. These were the days when, after ejecting, crews were taken not to the nearest hospital but to the nearest bar! Chris told me that whilst descending with their parachutes, he and Bob were so close that they were able to shout to each other! Chris later flew with BOAC.

"The Javelin had a very bad reputation and killed a lot of people, and I was very lucky to be ill when my pilot bailed out. Ejecting from a Javelin could cause a serious back injury and I don't think many people bailed out of one without incurring one. I remember those accidents, but when you're young you don't worry. I enjoyed flying the Javelin, but you wouldn't get me in one today! That centre-line closure where the blades came off – muggins here was sitting between the engines. The blades came off and often went into the other engine, but did I worry? Not really; I had a couple of incidents where we did have centre-line closure, but we closed it down and were able to get back.

"I then crewed-up with a Sqn Ldr Shaw and flew with him on his first Javelin solo. However, I barely got to know him because he suffered from asthma and departed. I then crewed-up with Sqn Ldr Corbishley, a New Zealander. I also flew with him on his first solo. But he seemed to have difficulty in seeing his hand in front of his face and he too departed. I was becoming a permanent fixture at Leeming and beginning to get a reputation! At around this time my flying logbook records that I twice flew supersonically in the Javelin. This was known as a 'boom ride' and entailed climbing up to 40,000 feet or so over the North Sea, doing a half-roll and pulling through. Overall, I thoroughly enjoyed my time at Leeming. During the summer I regularly played cricket, not only for Leeming but also for the pub in Copt Hewick where the landlord was a retired Fleet Air Arm lieutenant commander who captained the pub cricket team. When not flying Javelins, I often flew in Meteor NF.14s which were used as targets for the Javelin. Moreover, whilst at Leeming I met my future wife! Monica was a nursing sister and midwife at Harrogate General Hospital.

"Eventually, I crewed-up with John McLeod and we completed the OCU course and were posted to 29 Squadron at Leuchars near St. Andrews in Scotland, which is where my father was stationed in the early 1930s. I was pleased that after my early difficulties with AI 17, my end of course assessment was 'above average'. However, Sod's Law dictated that, after mastering AI 17, I was posted to 29 Squadron whose aircraft were equipped with AI 21 which was totally different!

"I see from my flying logbook that our first flights from Leuchars were GEE approaches and let-downs. Air-

29 Squadron FAW.9 XH958 J in the frost at Leuchars. (Ken Brereton)

crew today would have no understanding of the navigational problems in my day. The Javelin was fitted with GEE Mk.3, a development of the radio hyperbolic navigation system fitted to Lancasters and Halifaxes during the Second World War. It told the navigator when and where he had been, from which he had to calculate the aircraft's present position. Advection-fog was a regular occurrence at Leuchars, and the airfield could quite suddenly be 'clamped' in fog. Turnhouse, now Edinburgh airport, was used as a 'bolthole'. A GEE lattice line coincidentally was located in line with the main runway at Turnhouse: this made GEE let-downs relatively easy. However, it was the cause of our first fatal accident when the navigator selected the wrong lattice line and the aircraft crashed into a hill and both crew members were killed. I believe that this accident gave rise to the RAF Dependants' Fund where servicemen pay a nominal amount into the fund each month so that the station commander can sign a cheque to give short-term financial help to wives or other dependants. I suppose the apogee of my modest career was, I was station commander at West Raynham which had a fantastic history with the AWFCS. I never believed I would be station commander there but sadly I had cause to use the Dependants' Fund on three occasions. We were also urged to make our wills and take out life insurance.

"With Leuchars on the coast, the navigator could depress the AI scanner to pick out the coastline which was a great help in bad weather when approaching from the sea. Also, I think there was a lighthouse on the extended centre-line which was a further help. At Christmas, a crew would row out to the lighthouse and give the lighthouse keeper a crate of beer! I recall that at low tide, a Canberra bomber's fin and rudder stuck out of the sea – a fair warning not to undershoot on landing!

"I witnessed a mid-air collision in early 1960. We had scrambled for a 'stream' take-off during a major exercise. Whilst climbing through 30,000 feet over the east coast, I saw the fin, rudder and elevator of a Javelin spinning down to earth like a sycamore leaf. The two aircraft ahead of us had collided. As a result we had one crew swimming in the North Sea and one crew on the ground near Scarborough. Mercifully all survived, but not without injury."

The collision occurred on 21 May 1960 at 42,000 feet between XA823 P and XA835 Z. P was abandoned and dived into the sea north-east of Scarborough, Yorkshire; Flt Lt J S Wilson and Fg Off E Wood were both OK. Z was abandoned on reaching the coast four miles north-west of West Hartlepool, County Durham. Again, Flt Lt D J Wyborn and Flt Lt J S Clark were OK. **Peter Masterman** continues:

"In order to eject the crew over the high elevator of the Javelin, the ejection seats were fitted with two explosive cartridges which often caused back

XH723 R leading XH792 O, XH963 E, XH774 B FAW.9s and T.3 XH396 Z of 29 Squadron, Cyprus 1964. (Adrian Balch collection)

injuries. Much later, I was serving at CTTO (Central Trials and Tactics Organisation), at High Wycombe. In my office was Roger Lloyd who, like me, was a former Javelin navigator. We were discussing Javelin accidents, and I told him of an accident I remembered at Akrotiri, Cyprus when a Javelin collided over the airfield whilst intercepting a Canberra. The Canberra's pilot and two navigators were killed together with the Javelin pilot. Miraculously, the Javelin navigator ejected just before impact. Roger went white and said that he was the Javelin's navigator. Incidentally, also in my office was Tony Alcock, a descendant of John Alcock of Alcock and Brown who in 1919 completed the first non-stop crossing of the transatlantic in a Vickers Vimy aircraft. I believe that when Tony Alcock returned to flying the Phantom, they found a navigator called Brown and they repeated the transatlantic crossing!"

Roger Lloyd's accident took place on 26 October 1961 in XH906 Q of 25 Squadron. It collided with 32 Squadron Canberra B.2 WD995 north of Akrotiri. The pilot of the Javelin was Flt Lt John Morris. **Peter** again:

"Most of our practice interceptions were called 'mutuals', where a pair of Javelins would take turns at intercepting each other having been positioned head-on or at 90 degrees by fighter controllers at Boulmer. The navigator would detect the 'target' at about 18 miles and at around 11 miles the navigator would instruct the pilot to turn through 210 degrees. For much of the turn, the target would be out of scan, but would re-appear towards completion of the turn. The aim was to roll out 800 yards behind the target and lock-on, whereupon the range meter would function and we would close to 200 yards before claiming a 'kill'. The navigator would call 'Judy' (don't ask me why!) when lock was achieved. Whilst closing, the target would often try to evade and the navigator would give instructions to follow, for example, 'turn right, right hard, right as hard as you can, reverse left, left hard' etc. When training at Leeming, these instructions were recorded and played back for analysis by staff in front of the crew: this could cause both hilarity and embarrassment. Often at night, interceptions were carried out with the target aircraft's navigation lights out. Occasionally, if the target was not detected in the final stage of interception, there would be an anguished cry of 'lights on!' or 'height difference!' Sometimes the target would be uncomfortably close.

"When a crew was declared 'operational' they were eligible for the QRA roster. Two aircraft per squadron would be placed at cockpit-readiness on the ORP. This entailed sitting strapped in the cockpit all night ready to fly out over the North Sea to chase away Russian aircraft (usually Tupolev Bears), intruding into UK airspace to gather 'elint' (electronic intelligence). This was especially prevalent during Cold War naval exercises. We would sometimes wave to their rear gunner, and he would wave back. We were not authorised to shoot them down, but if they did not turn back we were authorised to fire a burst of four 30mm cannon across their nose to encourage them to turn about. It never came to that though. In winter, we would sit in the cockpit for one and a half hours, by which time we were almost frozen solid. We would then be relieved by another crew and retire to the crewroom and get warm over a coke stove before climbing into the cockpit again. To pass the time we would read by torchlight, although I had a small radio-cassette player and would listen to either Miles Davis or Gustav Mahler, or something in-between. We would usually wear immersion suits in case we had to eject over the North Sea. These were extremely uncomfortable because one was completely sealed in what was a rubberised suit. It was vital to go to the lavatory before climbing into the cockpit. We also wore anti-g suits, a form of laced-up corset around one's abdomen, thighs and legs. In high 6 g manoeuvres the corset would inflate preventing blood pooling in the lower parts of the body. When daylight came, thankfully, we would be relieved by the day fighters of 43 Squadron who flew Hawker Hunters. When relieved, we would usually take off and carry out practice interceptions – after being awake all night!

"Leuchars was thought to be too far north to face the Warsaw Pact threat. As a result, we often were detached to either Leconfield in Yorkshire or Wattisham in Suffolk for QRA. With other regular detachments to Norway and Sylt in Germany, my wife and I rarely saw each other in the early months of our marriage.

"It was believed that the first casualties during any war would be the control and reporting centres, such as Boulmer in Northumberland, which controlled our fighter force. A technique was therefore developed of 'loiter lanes'. These were lanes laid out in the form of a fan around the North Sea and were designated alphabetically. In exercises (and in war) we would be despatched to the entrance of our designated loiter lane to loiter, flying a racetrack pattern, When targets were within range, and on receipt of a code word, we would fly up our lane using our AI radar to detect target aircraft. Our squadron commander would arrange visits to Boulmer so that we were able to meet our fighter controllers. I played cricket against Boulmer – we won. We also competed in a drinking competition – we lost!

"Towards the end of a detachment in Norway I suffered a serious back injury. The Javelin was a large aircraft with the cockpit a long way from the ground. At our home base we had special ladders for climbing in and out of the cockpit. When away, we had to climb in and out by walking on the wing via the trailing edge which was relatively close to the ground. Whilst on an exercise chasing V-bombers at altitude we made a rapid descent into the airfield. Getting out of the cockpit with my nav bag in one hand and my bone dome under my arm, I stepped on to the wing which was covered in ice. I slipped and fell, slithered down the wing and landed on the concrete – ouch!

"At first, I seemed to be uninjured and was able to fly back to Leuchars. However, the pain in my back became severe, and after time in station sick quarters, I was admitted to the RAF Hospital at Nocton Hall near Lincoln. I was placed in 'traction' which was similar to the medieval torture known as the rack. A dance known as 'the twist' was popular at the time – I think the singer Chubby Checker was responsible. If I could have got out of bed, I swear I would have strangled the next person who said, 'Been doing the twist have you?' After a thoroughly miserable month in bed, I was no better. So it was decided to immobilise my back by placing it in a plaster cast which thankfully relieved the pain. I remained in plaster for more than three months but was able to walk and returned to Leuchars. We had a good time up there, it was a very happy station actually and we were very sorry to leave there, but with my back injury there was no way I could fly for the time being. 29 Squadron was no longer there, having been detached to Zambia as a result of Rhodesia's Unilateral Declaration of Independence.

"Clearly, my flying days were over for the time being, and I started what was to be a long association with Bloodhound and Rapier surface-to-air guided missiles. When I got my flying category back, I said to the station commander: 'Sir, it's about time I went back flying.' He said, 'Where do you want to go to?' I told him I wanted to go back to my old squadron in Germany. I went to lunch, came back, and he said, 'I've got you a posting back to your old squadron'. But it took a year of further training to get back to where I was before. I did eventually get back to flying my favourite aeroplane, the Canberra B(I).8 at Geilenkirchen. But that, as they say, is another story. After some 33 years in the RAF, I retired on a Friday at High Wycombe, Bucks. The following Monday I started work as the university precinct services manager at Newcastle University where I worked until my retirement 12 years later."

To complete the story, 29 Squadron's Lightning phase came to an end in December 1974 when it switched to Phantoms at Coningsby, changing again to Tornado F.3s in April 1987, disbanding in October 1998. It reformed in September 2003 as the Typhoon OCU at BAE's airfield at Warton, Lancashire, before moving back to Coningsby in June 2005, from where it continues to operate.

TRAPPERS

With many active Javelin squadrons, it fell to the lot of the Fighter Command Instrument Rating Squadron (FCIRS) to travel around the various units and check their standards – the so-called 'trappers'. Having completed tours on such diverse types as the Hornet, Vampire and Venom before joining the Javelin world, **Jim Froud** found himself in the trapping role.

"I was on 29 Squadron in Cyprus when I got a call to come back to England, and I joined the instrument rating squadron at Middleton St. George. The reason I joined was that the OCU had closed down, and they were planning to form another squadron. They needed two instructors, so myself and Flt Lt 'Inky' Inkleton-Webber joined the FCIRS to help convert people back onto the Javelin; I arrived there in about May or June 1962. I'd only been there for a time when they changed the plans, no longer did they want to train another squadron. We had the first students come in, but of course we didn't do much with them apart from training one or two to go onto other squadrons. I stayed with the FCIRS and amazingly enough, we had six instructors, one adjutant, one sergeant, four Javelin T.3s and no ground crew – all our maintenance was done by centralised servicing.

"I went out trapping two different squadrons, 25 Squadron at Leuchars and 64 Squadron at Waterbeach, taking two of our own aircraft with us. When I was trapping 25 Squadron, I was doing the final circuit with one chap and coming in to land, when a four-ship formation turned up. We decided we would go round again to let them land. We went round again and the next time we came in we couldn't get one of the legs down; we finished up with the port undercarriage and the nose wheel, but nothing else. We tried getting it down by putting negative g on and what have you, but we couldn't, so we had to land on two wheels. As I was completely au fait with the Javelin T.3 from the rear cockpit, I thought if anyone's going to kill me it'll be me! I got the chap in the front cockpit to operate the flaps when I wanted them and bring the hood back as we were landing. So, I did the landing from the rear cockpit and I let it swing right at the end, because I would probably do more damage by keeping it straight; we finished up virtually still on the runway. The boss came rushing out to Mike Gawtree in the front cockpit, and said to him, 'Well done, absolutely superb Mike' and Mike said, 'Well I didn't do it, he did it'. He came to me and said, 'You landed it from the rear cockpit?' I nodded. He said, 'You stupid b*****d!' I thought, well thank you very much, there's no justice in this world.

"Then in April 1963, the QFI on 29 Squadron was grounded, so they came hunting around for me again, and back I went to Cyprus. All the Javelins varied; I flew a T.3 first, then the 5, the 6, the 9 and the 9R; all of them had slightly different handling characteristics. The T.3 didn't carry so much fuel and it only had two guns in it. The Javelin was an effective fighter but it was never a happy aeroplane, I have to say that, with so many things going wrong with it. If people asked you what you were flying and you said 'Javelin', they never said, 'You lucky blighter!' I enjoyed my time on it, I flew it for seven years and got just under 1,000 hours on them. It wouldn't be my favourite aeroplane; the Hornet and the Jaguar fill that role."

After continuing his Javelin tours in Singapore, Jim went on to have a long career as an instructor and on the Phantom and Jaguar fleets before finally retiring in 1991.

FAW.8 XJ130 R and another from 41 Squadron Wattisham in a practice interception against an Olympic Airways Comet 4B. (41 Squadron Association)

CHAPTER FOUR

THE JAVELIN ABROAD – RAF GERMANY AND BEYOND

THE BOYS

SAC Ken Beere
Airframe fitter. Joined in 1965. 71 MU Bicester. 29 Squadron Akrotiri and Zambia '65-'67. 56 Squadron Lightning. Left the RAF in 1970 and worked in technical training at British Airways.

Cpl Bryan 'Taff' Elliott
Air radar. Joined in 1958. Trained at Cosford and Yatesbury. 29 Squadron Javelin. 60 MU Dishforth. 23 Squadron Javelin Leuchars. Coltishall. 29 Squadron Javelin Akrotiri. 56 Squadron Lightning. Wattisham. Left the RAF in 1971.

Sgt Malcom Elliott
Engine fitter. Joined in 1954. Halton apprentice. Changi. 33 Squadron Middleton St. George '60-'63. 228 Squadron Whirlwind Acklington. 37 and 38 Squadrons Shackleton Khormaksar. Marham. Left the RAF in 1968.

Gp Capt Kel 'Johnny' Palmer
Pilot. 228 OCU 1952. 96 Squadron Meteor. Instructor 228 OCU. US exchange flying F-4, F-101, F-106. 23 Squadron '61-'63. MoD. Air staff Cyprus. Director College of Air Warfare. MoD. SHAPE. Retired 1983.

With further contributions from **Jack Broughton** and **Brian Bullock** (Chapter Two), **Mel Evans, Roy Evans** and **Peter Masterman** (Chapter Three).

RAF GERMANY

Javelins were first stationed in Germany in July 1957 when 87 Squadron at Brüggen received its first FAW.1s, (which had previously flown with 46 Squadron at Odiham), to begin replacing the Meteor NF.11s it had flown since 1952. Just over a year later Mk.2s also arrived, but these only stayed for a couple of years. In late 1959 Mk.5s also joined the squadron, which was flying a mixture of 1s and 5s when it disbanded in January 1961. The squadron's wartime service had encompassed Hurricanes flying in France during the dark days of May 1940 and after returning to the UK, eventually going out to the Mediterranean theatre, re-equipping with Spitfires and disbanding in Austria at the end of 1946.

Top: FAW.9 XH753 R of 5 Squadron Laarbruch. (Richard Andrews collection)
Left: 5 Squadron Laarbruch FAW.9 formation in 1965, XH773 D nearest the camera. (Adrian Balch collection)

Next to re-equip was 96 Squadron. During the war it had flown Hurricanes, Defiants, Beaufighters and Mosquitoes before curiously switching to the Dakota and Halifax in the Middle and Far East, disbanding in 1946. It too had reformed in 1952 to fly the Meteor NF.11, latterly at Geilenkirchen where it took on Javelin FAW.4s in September 1958. Less than a year later in January 1959, it was renumbered 3 Squadron and continued with the same aircraft until also disbanding in January 1961. 3 Squadron was formed in May 1912, its motto, 'The third shall be first', a reference to its claim to have been the first squadron to fly heavier than air machines. It too had an illustrious war as a fighter operator, flying Hurricanes, Typhoons and Tempests and from 1948, Vampires, Sabres and Hunters until it became one of the victims of the post-Sandys cuts in June 1957.

This flurry of activity was followed by the establishment of two further Germany-based Javelin units, 5 and XI (11) Squadrons, which were the only ones stationed in the country to fly the ultimate Mk.9. First formed in 1915, 11 Squadron spent the 20 years from 1923 as a light-bomber unit, switching to Hurricanes in India, followed by Spitfires, Mosquitoes, Vampires and Venoms, disbanding at Wunstorf in November 1957. In January 1959 it reformed at Geilenkirchen with Meteor NF.11s and that autumn Javelin 4s started to replace them. FAW.5s came in 1961, 9s in 1962 (in which year the earlier marks all left), and the unit continued to operate until disbanding on 11 January 1966 – the last Javelin squadron in Germany.

5 Squadron had started life even earlier, in 1913. By the time of the Second World War it had long been established in India, where it remained for the duration, successfully equipped with the Wapiti, Hart, Mohawk, Hurricane and Thunderbolt. Post-war saw it use the Tempest, then return to the UK and fly a mixed bag of types from Pembrey and Llandow until disbanding in August 1951. When its Javelin FAW.5s arrived in January 1960, it had been flying Meteor NF.11s at Laarbruch for a year. These were replaced by FAW.9s and the squadron moved to Geilenkirchen at the end of 1962 for its last three years of Javelin operations.

The early years of the 1960s marked a particularly chilly era in the Cold War. The heightened tension following the Cuban missile crisis, the building of the Berlin Wall and much sabre-rattling by the Eastern Bloc, led to an increased presence of RAF fighter units in Germany. It is curious then that by that time two established Javelin units had gone, leaving 5 and 11 Squadrons to continue supplying the night all-weather air defence, supported by UK-based units on detachment.

11 SQUADRON GEILENKIRCHEN

Among the aircrew stationed on the Javelin force was **Jack Broughton**, who had completed his first tour on type in the UK with 89/85 Squadron.

> "Germany was a totally different kettle of fish for us in 2 ATAF (Allied Tactical Air Force). I didn't know anything that was going on in the UK – I didn't know very much of what was going on in the rest of the world! On 11 Squadron at Geilenkirchen we had three flights, A, B and C Flights. C Flight was always commanded by a squadron leader engineer. As a tactical air force unit all the engineering work was carried out on the squadron. The squadrons had their own engineers, and A and B Flights were commanded by squadron leaders and the squadron CO was a wing commander. There was a rad/nav leader who was a squadron leader navigator and then there were about 16 crews.
>
> "We had about 12 or 14 Javelin Mk.9s. It was a night/all-weather squadron so, during the week, one flight would be on days and the other on nights. The idea was that everyone would go in on Monday morning. The crews that were going to be night flying that week would do a night-flying test, and then went off at lunchtime. They then came in for whatever the night-flying commitment was. In the winter, you might start flying at 1600 hours and in the summer, at 2200 hours; you would swap over at the end of the week. In addition to this there was a QRA commitment; that was mounted by two aeroplanes waiting at the end of the runway, with crews

Javelin aerobatic team members, 11 Squadron Geilenkirchen 1963, John Galley second left, Peter Goodwin third left. (Roy Evans XI Squadron Association)

either in or out of the cockpit, depending on the readiness state. For example, I was in the cockpit when President Kennedy was killed in October '63. On the intercom, the telecom briefing was that John F Kennedy had been shot, and we were automatically brought up to two minutes' readiness. We spent the next 24 hours waiting to start the engines in case the Russians took advantage of his assassination. You had two minutes to get airborne and people at the end of a 24-hour shift were generally scrambled during the last hour or so, just to get you airborne and to feel that you'd achieved something, whether there was anything to achieve or not. We had one flight on nights, one on days, and then the additional commitment to QRAs. There were two squadrons on the station, 5 and 11, with equal numbers of crews on each. I'd been around for a while so I knew quite a lot of 5 Squadron crews as well.

"I was never scrambled for real, but was involved during the Hughie Green episode when he tried to fly into Berlin without permission, and was fired upon by the Soviet air force. I was living in quarters in Cologne, 50 miles away from base and the squadron was called out on this particular day, sometime in the afternoon. It took an hour to get to the airfield and by the time I got there I was nominated to take command of four aeroplanes and fly to Gütersloh near the East/West German border, which we did that afternoon. Four crews were based at Gütersloh for four days and each day we had a couple of sorties in the morning, two in the afternoon and two at night. We were going backwards and forwards, up and down the border, until it was all resolved and then we went back to base."

On 4 April 1963, television presenter Hughie Green (a wartime transatlantic ferry pilot) was flying himself from Stuttgart into Berlin in his Cessna 310 G-AROK to record a show, allegedly without getting the correct prior permissions. On entering one of the three, 20-mile-wide approved air corridors over East Germany, he was buzzed by a number of Russian fighters, one of which lowered its undercarriage and rocked its wings to indicate to Green that he should follow it and land. Having ignored this, MiG 21s sent cannon fire close to his aircraft, more than once, to reinforce the message. Still continuing on his legitimate way, a Yak 25 then came on the scene and attempted to divert him from his course using jet blast, causing one of Green's engines to stop. He signalled to the pilot who took it to mean that he would follow, but having restarted the engine he went flat out for the last 27 miles and landed at Gatow airport.

Germany-based Javelin squadrons were required to maintain two aircraft at immediate readiness on Battle Flight/QRA 24 hours every day of the year. Up to a further four aircraft were required to be at 30 minutes' readiness and all had fully loaded cannons and live Firestreak missiles. **Jack Broughton** continues:

"When we took over from the older Javelins at the beginning of '63, they closed down the armament ranges at Sylt. The RAF Germany squadrons then held their annual APCs at Leeuwarden, a Royal Netherlands Air Force base. We went to Leeuwarden, up in the north of Holland twice: 1963 and '64. That was good fun, an interesting time. We used to have a Meteor tug which the navigators had to see to. The aircraft had a long cable and the navs wound it backwards and forwards behind the aeroplane before take-off. At the end of it was the banner and a metal pole with a weight on the end so that it flew upright. The idea was that you flew in a pattern, you got into a 'perch' position, you turned in, then reversed and fired at the banner while you were still 15 degrees angle-off from the tug so that you didn't shoot it down. The bullets were all coloured, so with four guys on the flag you had yellow, blue, green and red [see also page 43]. It was quite a religious ceremony when it came back and they laid it out. The squadron leader came out and counted the holes and everybody looked on very sagely. We also went to Malta on an Exercise Maltex, and once to Valley to fire Firestreak missiles on the Fighter Command missile practice camp.

"Important changes of tactics were occurring whilst I was in RAF Germany, and by '63 there were already mutterings at high level about concentrating our air defence. Initially the Vulcans flew at high level, then switched to low level; we then realised that the fighter force was going to have to do the same. We operated quite a lot at low level over northern Germany, which was challenging because there were Nike and Hawk anti-aircraft missile batteries forward, and we were operating behind them in clutches. We were practising in a number of low-flying areas, which was quite a challenge.

"The Javelin was an excellent bomber-destroyer; comfortable and safe. The pilots were mainly chosen because they were experienced and good at instrument flying. Mostly the Javelin was employed as a bomber-destroyer because it wasn't an ideal combat fighter, but you would get the odd pilot who enjoyed air-to-air combat. It was much better as a bomber-destroyer with the weapons and the radar required. The interception profiles were all devised to get you in behind the target at half to three quarters of a mile, so you could close in and identify the target at night.

"You'd get a bunch of pilots who were gung-ho, and another group who were a bit deadbeat and that tended to inhibit nav/rads who flew with them. We also had another set of pilots who preferred to do a good approach to an airfield, a good let-down with the navigator checking the GEE. We had GEE-3, which was very good because you could home on to the airfield and become quite efficient at it.

"We did lots of PIs, 'mutuals' they were called – mutual practice interceptions with another Javelin. We also flew them with other types, particularly on exercises in Germany, where flying was more rigidly controlled; it was almost exclusively under the control of the sector operations centres. When you went off on a sortie almost inevitably you went off as a pair, then you'd split off in the climb at 30,000 feet, then you did whatever sort of intercept you wanted. In the UK you had more flexibility because you were that much further away from the Russian border. At AWFCS we set up electronic countermeasure raids where the B-66s and B-45s from Sculthorpe came in from the North Sea. You'd get maybe 36 aeroplanes all jamming the radars – magnificent you know! I don't think you could replicate that now; there aren't enough aircraft in the air force!

"During my RAF career I flew 3,200 hours; 1,850 were on Javelins and I loved every minute – it was the aeroplane that formed my career. One of the things for navigators in this night-fighter radar business was that if you were very good at it you were the exception and you could then devote part your life to doing other things, organising the rugby team or whatever. But if you weren't, you had to struggle even to become just acceptable. We were checked every so often by TACEVALs (tactical evaluation) and exercises like that but to me, it was like putting on a comfortable old shoe; I just loved it. I flew with about half a dozen pilots altogether. The one that I did the AWFCS course with, Peter Poppe, unfortunately died in Singapore when he flew into the bay. Another of my friends flew the Javelin and disliked it, it just wasn't his scene and that applied to other people as well. If you were a bit extravert, gung-ho,

FAW.4 XA756 C of 11 Squadron Geilenkirchen on its acceptance air test, 19 January 1960. (Brian Bullock)

> you could have a marvellous time and enjoy your flying. For others it was a struggle."

The accident in Singapore happened on 8 November 1965 when 64 Squadron FAW.9 XH959 U hit the sea while on a night ASR (air-sea rescue) search for another Javelin which had crashed earlier in the day (see also page 171). It was thought that the pilot, Flt Lt Peter Poppe may have lost the horizon; his navigator Flt Lt Bruce Unsted survived.

Brian Bullock also moved from the UK to Germany, again joining 11 Squadron.

> "For me, it was quite a relief to be posted to 256 Squadron at Geilenkirchen in mid-September. Back to Meteor NF.11s, but rumour had it that this squadron would convert to Javelins about three months hence. I was to be part of a nucleus of Javelin-qualified nav/rads. Actually it was to be almost a year before our Javelins arrived – small world, they were Mk.4s from my previous squadron 41, and a welcome return to that familiar armchair. In the meantime, 256 became 11 Squadron and our sister squadron at Geilers became 3 Squadron, also equipped with Javelins.
>
> "With the Meteors we had an interesting variation with our PIs and cine, firing our guns at ground targets in the Nordhorn range and initially, this was continued with the Javelins. Unfortunately, it soon became obvious that the construction of this aircraft was not suitable for the extra stresses imposed on the airframe, and this activity ceased quite quickly. We did continue with air-to-air gun firing at towed targets, which was carried out at Sylt. The island was famous for nude bathing, but my two visits, one Meteor and one Javelin were during the winter months, when our activities were restricted to flying and drinking – no strolls on the beaches!

"In RAF Germany the QRA Battle Flight duties were mounted from home airfields, where the aircraft operated from the ORPs at the runway ends, usually at two minutes' readiness in cockpits. There were more scrambles than in the UK, usually to intercept aircraft flying west out of the ADIZ (Air Defence Identification Zone). These were mainly probes by Russian or East German military aircraft. I was scrambled three or four times but never got radar contact before the hostiles did a 180 and returned to base. However, usually they were American military aircraft that were intercepted on their way back after inadvertently penetrating the ADIZ.

"We were doing some Jav-to-Jav air combat when under positive g my seat ran up the rails until my bone dome was hard against the hood. I advised the pilot and prepared myself for ejection. The pilot made a very smooth approach and landing, and we were instructed to park on the ORP. We were soon surrounded by a clutch of ambulances, fire engines and a Land Rover full of armourers. Apart from the armourers, everyone was cleared from the area and we sat very still as they removed the hood from the outside at arm's length. They were obviously very apprehensive, expecting us to go up at any time. Eventually we were both cleared to climb out, and we scrambled clear onto the wings and to the rear.

"Another incident at Geilenkirchen was during the squadron's conversion from Meteors to Javelins, and as I have said before, as the most experienced nav I flew with many of the pilots on their first solos in the T.3. I was with a senior officer on one man's solo when we heard a terrible grinding noise and the port engine fire-warning light came on. We quickly went through the shutdown procedures and the warning light went out. However, before I realised what was happening at the front, this idiot was starting the relight procedure. I shouted for him to close the engine down, but almost immediately heard a huge bang and there was a ball off flame at the rear. Again I prepared for ejection after giving the pilot a steer for base. Fortunately, we were quite close. We were requested to do a low flyby over the tower and were informed the fire was out but a large section of the port jet-pipe was hanging outside, and a section of the rear fuselage was missing. After a quick circuit and landing we were parked on the ORP with the usual emergency vehicles in attendance, most of the occupants with wide-open mouths! On inspection, we found about nine feet of the rear fuselage around the port engine jet-pipe had completely melted away. I threw caution to the wind and gave my press-on pilot a piece of my mind!

"I was actually at Geilers when a pair of 41 Squadron Javelins came in and did a rather fast run and break. No.2 pulled back and operated his ailerons at the same time and the two wings flapped and became detached. What was left of the aircraft continued and ended up in the married quarters area. Luckily, although bits and pieces of the aircraft landed all over the place, no one on the ground was injured. I think the crew tried to eject but both got the 'chop'. I was at the swimming pool at the time when I heard these things; everyone got up because of the horrible noise. Everything happened so quickly; it's difficult to remember one's impressions. I saw the wings clap but the debris fluttered vertically down, while the engines and fuselage went forward at reasonably high speed. The wings floated down like bits of fabric and I thought they might hit the Tiger Moth we had on the station flying club, which was due to fly that morning."

On 29 August 1961 FAW.8 XH971 A of 41 Squadron broke up due to pulling excessive g during a run-in and break to land at Geilenkirchen. Pilot Flt Lt John Hatch and his navigator Flt Lt John Nothall were both killed. **Brian Bullock** again:

"At one stage I lost my regular pilot for a couple of months. In that time I was chosen, from a cast of thousands, to be the station adjutant. The CO was Gp Capt later Air Marshal (AM) Desmond Hughes, an ex-Battle of Britain pilot who had retained his love of flying. I flew with him in the Javelin a few times and my initial trepidation rapidly disappeared, he was a very smart and competent operator – and a very nice chap to boot. A pleasant interlude in April 1960 saw the squadron detached to RCAF Soellingen in southern Germany for ten days. We flew PIs on most days, Javelins versus CF-100s and cross-fertilisation where the Jav nav/rads flew with the Canadian pilots in the CF-100s, and our pilots flew the Javelins with Canadian nav/rads. I managed only one flight, but was impressed with the pick-up range of the radar equipment in the CF-100. Their standard PIs were head-on set-ups which made use of their extra range, and our pilots found the CF-100 very pleasant to fly.

"Coming to the end of my second Javelin tour (I'd been on four squadrons at that time, with number changes), I decided on a change of role and volunteered for the Vulcan force as a nav/rad. I was posted to 1 Bombing School at Lindholme, but on the day before leaving Geilenkirchen I was called to see someone in station headquarters, who told me it had all been changed. Apparently, there was a sudden shortage of experienced Javelin nav/rads and I was required to fill a post on 25 Squadron at Leuchars. I was not impressed."

Nav/rad **Roy Evans** joined 11 Squadron after a tour on 25 Squadron at Leuchars, and recalled an unfortunate ejection and lucky escape for one member of the squadron.

"One of our pilots, Norman Glass, was flying a PI with Fg Off Alan Evans, when his 'playmate' went u/s, so they went in search of some 'trade', which they found in the shape of four F-84Fs of the Belgian air force. After some serious dogfighting the Javelin got right in behind the leading F-84F, hit its slipstream, and went into a spin. The stall warners cut in, severing intercom contact between the two crew members. Passing 20,000 feet, Norman was trying to tell Alan that the Javelin was coming out of this serious spin. Unfortunately, Alan couldn't hear this good news and as the aircraft passed 18,000 feet, Alan followed orders and ejected. He landed in a field near Cologne, was helped onto a tractor by the farmer, and by the time a German air force helicopter found him, both the farmer and Alan were rather drunk from the farmer's bottle of schnapps! Norman did indeed get the Javelin out of the spin, landed back at base minus the rear canopy, with the long 'broomstick' from the nav's ejection seat sticking up. One of the very few times that a spinning Javelin had been successfully recovered – well done.

"As a result of the Hughie Green episode [see page 95], the Allies had a contingency plan called Exercise Quicksand, (involving aircraft from RAF, USAF and the French air force), in order to provide protection for aircraft using the Berlin air corridors. On 10 March 1964 my pilot Flt Sgt Bob Kelly and I were part of a four-ship force of 11 Squadron Mk.9s to fly to Celle near the East German border to await Quicksand. We were billeted with the Irish Guards on St. Patrick's Day! Upon entering their barracks in flying kit I sought out the duty officer to place my authentication codes under lock and key until I needed them. The Irish lieutenant, rather hungover, was not impressed with this small English RAF navigator – in flying kit – in his barracks demanding secure help, but grudgingly did as I requested. That evening, Bob and I joined the other three commissioned crews from our squadron in a bar/cafe in the square in Celle for a few beers, and a couple of hours later we decided to return to barracks and asked for our bill. The waiter indicated a small, old German sitting near us and said this gentleman had paid for our drinks. Apparently the locals were so afraid that the Soviets would invade West Germany, that any sign of Allied forces – such as eight RAF fighter aircrew chaps – was so welcome that he treated us for the evening. We thanked him profusely and retired to bed.

"Eventually on 13 March we got airborne, joined up with four USAF F-100 Super Sabres and four French air force Vautours and orbited just west of the central corridor into Berlin, awaiting any calls for assistance. With our four shiny Firestreak missiles each, and whatever weaponry the Yanks and French had on their aircraft, we felt ready for anything, but in retrospect I think the Soviets had the edge! Anyway, after 30 minutes the controlling GCI ground radar told us all to return to our respective bases, but we had let the Soviets know we were still awake and ready.

"Every year on most RAF stations occurred an event which most people considered a waste of time and effort, and this was the AOC's inspection. The only good thing about this was the fact that the station got a good old clean, which was mostly needed once a year. Geilenkirchen had its AOC visit as usual in 1964, and almost the last event of the day was his inspection of 11 Squadron, the 'West End kids' of the station. The AOC and his entourage had arrived on the station in the morning of the visit by road from HQ at Rheindahlen, some 30 kms distant, and after inspecting 11 Squadron, its aircraft and personnel, he was entertained in the squadron's aircrewroom to coffee and biscuits before being flown back to Wildenrath in the squadron's T.3. It was a rather expensive taxi to get VIPs to their further destinations, and one of the squadron's senior pilots was then the designated taxi-driver; in this case it was Norman Glass. Having given the AOC a short briefing on the safety aspects of the T.3, and how to evacuate it in a hurry, Norman and the AOC left the aircrewroom, went to the line-hut to sign out, get a ground crew team to assist with the start-up and then see the aircraft on its way. Then all the squadron personnel heaved a sigh of relief that the VIP gent was on his way, and we could all relax and return to normal.

"The AOC was installed in the front cockpit, with his hat, complete with its gold braid 'scrambled-egg' placed upon a console in front of its owner, and start-up ensued. All went well until the cockpit canopies were motored shut, and as the front one went forward, the famous hat was caught up somehow. It was thrown forward, downwards and then out and into the port-engine intake. One of the start-up crew was a tall engine fitter, and the other crew member signalled that something was amiss to Norman and to shut down the engines. As the engines began to wind down, 'Lofty' as the tall fitter was known, grabbed onto the front of the engine intake and disappeared head first into it to grab the hat before it was shredded! Wg Cdr Bill Marriot was the 11 Squadron boss at that time, and when he heard the engines shutting down, he rushed out onto the pan, looked at the T.3, and saw just a pair of large boots sticking out of the intake. His heart almost stopped as he envisaged one of his ground crew being killed! Fortunately, airman and hat were unharmed, and after a bit of a clean-up, the hat was restored to its owner and they all went happily on their way as planned, and Bill Marriot's palpitations disappeared.

"In the summer of 1965, Geilenkirchen was closed to re-surface the runway, so all three resident squadrons had to move for a week, and 11 Squadron went to Gütersloh, in the middle of West Germany, 104 miles from Geilenkirchen. As we were then away from our families and homes, it was decided to fly over the weekend, so we did this on the Saturday. The weather was fine and the locals decided that a squadron of Javelins needed inspecting, so the area under the approach lights for Runway 27 had a horde of civilians parked in it as they enjoyed a picnic between the lights. Not realising how much danger they were in, the citizens of Gütersloh waited for the airshow to continue. The efforts of the military police plus the civilian police did nothing to move the voyeurs, and it looked as if the eight aircraft we had flying from our new base would have to divert to another airfield. However, help was at hand as the intrepid Norman Glass was one of the pilots airborne, just returning from a pairs sortie. Norman was appraised of the situation and requested to make a simulated power failure approach to overshoot the runway, and this permission was given.

"Completing a very high circuit, Norman flew his aircraft very quietly around the final turn of his circuit, and floated down the last few hundreds of feet, with half airbrakes out until he was over the approach lights, where he popped the airbrakes in as he applied almost full power, and as the power came on, so the jet-wash sent umbrellas, coats, rugs, people, tumbling out from among the approach lights. Where the assorted police had failed, Norman succeeded and whilst the mayhem was occurring, all eight aircraft managed to land back at Gütersloh before the crowds returned. Such was the power of an occupying air force in those days. One would not get away with it in these days; a court martial would be in order more than likely!"

The ultimate replacement for the Javelin in RAF Germany's air defence role was to be the Lightning F.2s of 19 and 92 Squadrons, which moved out from Leconfield in 1965. Throughout the Javelin's period of service, the squadrons based in Germany suffered a total of eight write-off accidents (see Appendix Three). 87 Squadron lost three, both 3 and 5 lost two (including one due to centre-line closure), while 11 Squadron lost just a single aircraft in a start-up fire.

After their Javelin days were over, the squadrons had mixed fortunes, with both 87 and 96 disappearing for good. Of those destined to have a future role to play, 3 Squadron continued on in 1961 by the simple expedient of renumbering 59 (Canberra) Squadron, then switched to the Harrier at Wildenrath in 1972. In 2006 it became the first operational Typhoon squadron at Coningsby.

When 5 Squadron gave up its FAW.9s in October 1965, it moved to Binbrook and two months later started operations with the Lightning F.6, which it flew until 1988 when it moved to Coningsby and the Tornado F.3, disbanding in 2003. A year later it reappeared at Waddington to fly Sentinel R.1 airborne stand-off radar (ASTOR) aircraft. Finally 11 Squadron, which after a short period of disbandment, (during which time the number was allocated to 228 OCU at Leuchars as a 'shadow squadron') reformed there in April 1967 to fly the Lightning, doing so until 1988 when it too changed to the Tornado F.3. These were given up in 2005, but two years later 11 Squadron returned to fly the Typhoon at Coningsby.

SQUADRON DETACHMENTS

29 Squadron

Home-based fighter squadrons had detachments to Germany and other European countries on a regular basis. **Peter Masterman** had experience of that while serving with 29 Squadron.

> "Each year we would be detached for six weeks or more to Sylt for air-to-air firing (away from my wife yet again). Sylt was an island in the North Sea to the west of Schleswig Holstein in northern Germany. The island is linked to the mainland by a railway line on a narrow causeway. It was weird to be in a railway carriage with the sea on both sides. We took the train to visit the notorious Reeperbahn in Hamburg. The Reeperbahn is the centre of Hamburg's nightlife and is known as 'die sundigste meile' (the most sinful mile). We did not sin though – honest!
>
> "When we went to Sylt it was so funny. My pilot was a very devout Roman Catholic and there were times when he wouldn't drink at all, then come Saturday, when we were not flying, he would get stoned out of his mind. Air-to-air firing involved aiming at a target flag towed by a Meteor. Our scores were much lower than those achieved by the Hunter and Sabre day fighters. I believe that this was due to the Javelin having wing guns whereas the Hunters and Sabres had guns mounted in the fuselage. Our guns were 'harmonised' (focused) for a specific range – about 800 yards I think. As a result, if we fired out of this range, many of our rounds would miss what was a relatively small target. Mind you, it would take only a small number of hits by our Aden cannon to destroy an aircraft. On one occasion we fired all four cannon at night: the noise was deafening and we lit up the sky.
>
> "When using the air brakes, the pilot was supposed to warn the navigator before he shoved them out, because if the navigator was looking into the AI he'd get his nose shoved into the screen! I once took off with a young pilot who I shall never forgive; we got to about 500 feet and he did a twinkle roll, but didn't tell me he was going to. I was much senior to him and I said: 'If you ever do that again without telling me, I'm going straight to the station commander!' He got the message.
>
> "Later in my tour we received FAW.9 Javelins equipped with re-heat and Firestreak air-to-air missiles. One of the problems with the Javelin was that the speed rapidly bled off when the aircraft was put into a hard turn – it wasn't named the 'Dragmaster' for nothing. Re-heat enabled us to maintain our speed in steep turns. It also produced a sheet of flame behind the aircraft, and occasionally we received telephone calls from members of the public saying that they had seen an aircraft on fire. We would demonstrate

the Firestreak infra-red missile to visitors on the ground by getting someone with a cigarette to walk about 50 yards in front of the missile. The missile scanner would follow the cigarette.

"On two occasions my squadron was detached to Norway, once to the Norwegian airfield at Gardermoen, now Oslo International Airport, and once to Ørland in northern Norway. Whilst there, I hitched a lift in a Sea Otter floatplane and we landed on the water in Stavanger fjord. After a weekend in Stavanger, the floatplane was supposed to pick me up but the weather was so bad I had to return by boat – yuk!

"We used to chase the Norwegian Sabres up and down the fjords. However, we would not fly in poor visibility, and who could blame us with all those mountains? As a result, the Norwegian aircrew called us 'the penguin squadron' – we had wings but couldn't or wouldn't fly. I remember that we were dismayed at the price of alcohol in Norway. However, the Norwegian aircrew introduced us to their 'moonshine' (home brew) – a headache in every glass!

"When returning to an airfield, it was common practice to approach at low level and high speed. When overhead the airfield we would turn into the circuit pulling a high 6 g force ('bank and yank') and deploy the airbrakes at the same time. This produced a very impressive loud 'ripping' noise. However, whilst in Norway we heard that a Javelin, when performing this manoeuvre, had disintegrated over Geilenkirchen killing both pilot and navigator [see Brian Bullock's account on page 98]. We were surprised because the Javelin was thought to be such a rugged aircraft – put crudely, 'built like a brick sh*t house'. Thereafter, we returned to the airfield more sedately!"

A 33 Squadron FAW.7 behind the wire at Middleton St. George. (Steve Bond collection)

33 Squadron

Malcolm Elliott was an engine fitter who spent three years on 33 Squadron at Middleton St. George, which included a lengthy detachment to Geilenkirchen in early 1962.

> "I arrived at Middleton St. George in about June 1960 as a junior technician (J/T) just arrived from a tour at Changi and was posted to 33 Squadron. At that time the CO was Wg Cdr David 'Tiger' Hughes DFC AFC, a South African, well respected. Hughes was succeeded by Wg Cdr Caryl Gordon who had taught the Duke of Edinburgh to fly.
>
> "In QRA scrambles the ground crew were required to plug in the cable to allow arming of the missiles etc. and refit the belly panel which accessed the starters. Just after Wg Cdr Gordon had qualified, he was on a QRA when the alert sounded. He started both engines, signalled for the crew to fit the panel, and moved off before they had the chance to reconnect the arming cable. He got airborne but couldn't raise the gear because the cable was hanging out between the gear door and the wing, so he had to return with all the ground crew standing outside the hangar, most embarrassing.
>
> "In the early 1960s the Russians started a blockade for aircraft flying into Berlin; there were three corridors from West Germany to Berlin. At this time, each Javelin squadron did a detachment to Germany in turn. When it was 33's turn the blockade had become quite serious [see page 93]. So off went 33 Squadron to Geilenkirchen on the German side of the border with Holland. One of the aircraft had a triple hydraulic failure while at Wildenrath; on landing it undershot, taking off the undercarriage and ending up in the trees. The pilot ejected from the aircraft, which was just as well because the radar in the nose was forced back into his position. Christian, his flight sergeant navigator, was still trapped in his seat. It took some hours to extract him from this position, and apparently the ejection seat seat had started to break from the impact and the firing pin was perilously close to the cartridge which, had it fired, would obviously have killed him. He returned to flying duties at a later date."

The aircraft involved was FAW.9 XH794 X and the crash occurred on 9 March 1962. The pilot was Sqn Ldr S Burrows. **Malcolm Elliott** again:

> "As the situation over the corridors got worse, six aircraft were detached to Gütersloh in the event that a shooting war started. At three o'clock one morning the station alarm sounded and all the Javelin chaps dashed to the aircraft, got strapped in ready to go, only to be told that it was a station practice and not meant for them!

"In October 1961 33 Squadron went on detachment to Cyprus. On the way, one aircraft suffered a centre-line closure on one engine and diverted to Pisa. I flew out with several others to Pisa via Idris and Malta to change the engine. We returned by train through Paris, quite a time for a short detachment.

"There was an American pilot Capt Jackson 'Jack' Bailey who bought an MG A to take home when he was tour-ex; he had an American back-seater too which was quite unusual. We also had a master navigator called Bert Farey. Bert was about six feet tall and weighed around 16 stones. He was lost when the aircraft they were flying entered a spin; both ejected and their 'chutes deployed. Bert was seen to enter cloud but did not come out at the bottom. Unfortunately, as far as I know his body was never found despite extensive searches."

On 18 May 1962 Master Pilot J Crowther was flying FAW.9 XH755 Y when control was lost, resulting in a spin. The crew abandoned the aircraft which crashed seven miles east of Tynemouth in Northumberland. The pilot survived but, as Malcolm says, navigator John 'Bert' Farey lost his life.

LONG-RANGE DEPLOYMENTS – 23 SQUADRON

The Achilles' heel of many fighters is a short duration due to the restricted internal fuel capacity. In that regard the Javelin was no different, but in the early 1960s, the art of air-to-air refuelling, had first been trialled with an operational squadron in 1951, using 245 Squadron's probe-equipped Meteor F.8s at Horsham St. Faith and three Avro Lincoln tankers flown by Flight Refuelling Ltd. From 1960, some of the existing fleet of Valiant bombers began being used as tankers, finally enabling routine long-range deployments of fighter aircraft for the first time.

Kel Palmer returned to the UK from an exchange tour in the United States where he had flown many of their jet fighters. He was posted to fly Javelins with 23 Squadron, who were destined to be the trailblazers for long-range tanker-supported deployments.

"On my return from a tour in San Diego flying the F-4, my new post was to 23 Squadron at Coltishall and I was bursting to start my conversion to the Javelin Mk.9. If it is possible to select one out of all my tours, 23 Squadron stands out. About ten days after getting off the good ship *Queen Mary*, we did a Javelin conversion on the squadron using a T.3. It was an interesting time and the comparison that I found, having come off F-101s, F-106s and F-4s, and on to Javelins was really, in terms of performance, going backwards a lot.

"As a combination of job satisfaction, location, and the capacity to enjoy life, the 23 Squadron tour first at Coltishall and then at Leuchars, is the one that provided most professional satisfaction. I was 32 years old, a newly promoted squadron leader, flying a new and exciting aircraft on a famous squadron, and based in a lovely part of the UK. What made that tour special was the indefinable ingredient that, if not already present, cannot be concocted. It's the difference between being merely a good team and the one that wins all the trophies. It is the mix of personalities, the chemistry, the interchanges and the characters of those that make up the team. On 23 it wasn't just the skills, style and experience of the aircrew, it was encapsulated too in the engineering and administrative support to the squadron.

Top: Valiant tanker and 23 Squadron FAW.9s at Gan en route to Singapore in January 1963. (Steve Bond collection)
Bottom: 23 Squadron FAW.9 XH894 R refuelling at Gan en route to Singapore in January 1963. (Steve Bond collection)

"When I was in the States, 38 Group really got off the ground. As a tactical group they decided that, instead of having lots of squadrons overseas, you would deploy from the UK. This meant you had to have tanking, etc. and I'd done a fair amount of that in the States. We did 16 hours from the USS *Coral Sea* into Vietnam, for instance, but they had a lot more tankers and it was a rather busy system. The tanker side of things wasn't new to me but what *was* different for the RAF was that you had a fighter designed to fly for one-and-a-half to two hours (with tanks on) but you then had to do a very long trip to Aden, picking up tankers on the way. We'd never done that before but you had to be strapped in a Javelin for 11, 12, 13 hours and you had to take some sandwiches or something. The point was would the aeroplane be able to keep up with you? At first I remember we had a daft guy called John Irving who was our squadron leader engineer and the biggest nut case ever. A brilliant man but an absolute nut case and the first thing he pointed out was that on a trip that long we would run out of engine oil so we had to do a check, roaming around the UK for 15 hours, to make sure we didn't do that.

"We were the first squadron to do the refuelling trail out to Singapore. We did the shakedown trials to Aden, and the first big detachment was to Singapore. We took off from Leuchars and picked up the tankers somewhere around Paris, then carried on, depending on the winds, either to Malta or all the way to Cyprus. If we were going all the way to Cyprus, we had tankers coming up from Akrotiri to meet us somewhere between Crete and Cyprus. Once we got to Tengah we were there for a period of time, and then did the reverse route back home.

"This then meant regular detachments; so instead of performing just the classic air defence role, the squadron was in-flight refuelled over long distances to bases in Malta, Cyprus, Libya, the Persian Gulf, Aden and Singapore. Instead of flying PIs or gunnery/missile sorties of some 80 minutes duration, we were flying non-stop legs of 12 to 14 hours with the help of tankers that sometimes accompanied us, or rendezvoused with us to top up our fuel. Falling on my feet again, I joined 23 as this new role was being introduced and had the job of leading the planning, training and eventual execution for a role that no one in the RAF had done before at squadron level.

"Not all the challenges were of major operational significance or technical complexity, but most were important. For instance, the tankers transferred fuel but nothing else. What about engine oil and oxygen in an aircraft designed to fly for two hours maximum? There was no room to fit anything else, except under the wings, and those pylons carried fuel or missiles. There were no toilets in a Javelin, nowhere to cook food or store water, nowhere to stretch your legs, and no bunk or comfortable chair in which to grab some sleep or take off your bone dome for a rest.

"In-flight refuelling was relatively easy during the daytime in calm conditions, but could we do it at night, or amongst the tops of towering cu-nims over the Indian Ocean with the nearest diversion being a dinghy if you couldn't get the probe into the tanker's basket? A solution had to be found to all the problems, and we had perhaps the most fun (in retrospect) in solving that of having a pee at thirty-odd thousand feet over the Empty Quarter, or wherever we were at a given moment of need. One of our trial kits consisted of a tube joined to a condom, the lower end of the tube running into a plastic bottle strapped to the inside or outside of one's calf. The first problem with the 'penikit' was that it was a fairly fragile affair that often leaked or was knocked as you climbed in or out of the cockpit. The second, and decidedly the most annoying, was that having been strapped tightly to a seat for hours, one lost all sense of feeling in the family-jewels area and ended up cheerfully peeing oneself, until a warm sensation crept around one's ankles. The expression 'fill your boots' suddenly took on a different meaning. Generally, after a 12-hour trip to Aden, the ground crew didn't want to get anywhere near us. Despite all that, it was a very happy squadron.

"In the end, we abandoned any 'stopcock' type solution and some bright spark designed an absorbent nappy. You simply had a hot flush followed by a long cold soak. When, in 102 degrees, you opened the hood after 12 to 14 hours, the ground crew quickly dispersed and watched as you poured yourself out of the cockpit and waddled away awkwardly to the nearest shower. I'd rather not answer the next and obvious question, but suffice to say that a combination of pills and diet prevented most disasters, except when one's last meal was taken in a part of the world renowned for Delhi belly or Montezuma's revenge. In the early days (1963), 12 Javelins set out for Singapore, and on the leg from Bahrain we were diverted to avoid some disturbance in Iran, and arrived en masse at 35,000 feet 50 miles from Karachi with very little fuel. Knowing Karachi then to be a difficult air traffic set up, I found a space in the ceaseless natter to advise them that we were approaching an urgent situation so, 'please, pretty please, could our formation have priority over the chaotic civil traffic?' For some reason, at that time Pakistan controllers were anti-Brits (something to do with their relations with the Indians) so instead of using my cultured Mancunian accent, I became very oriental, high-pitched and 'goodness gracious me'. I did that all the way down and when I called for final landing the wag in the tower said, 'Red Eagle one, clear to land – and when you land you'd better be black!'

"We over-nighted at Karachi and set off at dawn with the tankers for the staging island of Gan in the Maldives. One by one, starting soon after take-off, the crews of the fighting 23rd called in apologetically, 'Red Leader, from Red whatever, making emergency diversion to such and such an airfield'. They were spread out along the western coast of Pakistan, India and Ceylon so that when I arrived at Gan I had only one other 'chick' (Dave Mitchell's) left out of 12. Because of dicey food in Karachi, we learned like thousands of Brits before and since, that when visiting certain outposts of the Empire, it was wise to take your own water and sealed sandwiches. Gan then was an isolated tropical island with waving palms, blue seas, sharks, incredible marine life – and NO girls! We were happy to have planned thoroughly, because on a full detachment using the odd staging base never used before, we took 12 out on time and brought them back on time, missing one of the UK's worst winters on record. It was a great detachment all round.

"Some guys were simply not happy being strapped to an ejection seat for all that time. I can remember some who said they'd rather go and fly the tankers themselves, but basically it was a case of getting used to that different sort of flying, most of which was rather boring. The other thing which was different then was that a lot of the places we flew through were *their* bases and we were either going to refuel ourselves or, when we got there, we were going to rely on some of their dusky gentlemen to stuff fuel in our aircraft.

"I think we normally worked on the basis of three Javelins to two tankers, and generally we were spaced about 15 minutes between sections of three. As I have said, we used to go into Karachi when we got to the Far East and then down to Gan. It's quite different now of course: it's a sexy holiday place. It was a nice place to go, then, and we often used to be taken out shark fishing, if we got stuck there. Probably the most difficult ride was down to Singapore. You were often crossing tropical fronts, with cu-nims up to about 50,000 feet and if flight refuelling coincided with that, it made life quite exciting. Normally we'd refuel at between 30,000 and 36,000 feet. The limiting factor there was the Valiant, rather than the Javelin, but actually, the Valiants were good.

"One other 38 Group detachment deserves special mention, if only because of the contrast between the pain and the pleasure. The pain was the first ten days of a detachment to El Adem, a staging post-cum-gunnery practice camp some 15 miles south of Tobruk in Libya. The climate and the terrain were awful, and just to make matters worse we were under canvas suffering all the deprivation that came with flying at night, and trying to sleep in the day when the day fighter squadrons of Hunters were doing their exercise flying. When we flew by day on air-to-ground gunnery sorties, it was hell to climb into an aircraft that had baked in the Sahara sun for hours. By the time you were strapped in, you were soaking with sweat, eagerly waiting until you could switch on the cold air to clear the mist and cool down. Then, when you landed and opened the canopy, first you got hot again and simultaneously collected a mouthful and a hair-full of blowing sand. When not flying, it was our nightly custom to leap aboard the squadron Land Rover and drive into Tobruk which is, or was then, a dump. A bunch of old dilapidated buildings, but nevertheless heaven compared to an oil-lit tent out in the bundu.

"On one such occasion the Land Rover carried six of us, with the boss and me in the front and four others in the back. The boss decided halfway home that he needed a kip, so he pulled over, put up his feet and fell asleep – as did we all. I was rudely awakened by him shouting 'Come on Palmer, let's go for a beer in Tobruk!' There were groans of dismay from the back when they realised his intentions, and I wholly agreed. But the groans turned to ribald mirth as he revved up the engine, but all that happened was that we rocked back and forth. We leapt from the vehicle thinking we had a flat tyre or were stuck in the sand. We certainly didn't have a flat, in fact we had no wheels at all. The Land Rover was jacked up on four piles of stones! Even allowing that we were all smashed out of our brains, it was still a remarkable feat, in pitch dark, to jack it up with six men aboard, nick the wheels and leave it propped up on stones. The following morning, about three hours later, we were out on air-to-ground range. As we lined up on the cone targets in loose formation, the Arabs were actually scurrying around below us to pick up our discarded shell cases. Had they known what time we'd slumped into our camp beds, and what state we'd been in, I doubt if they'd have been so confident that we'd hit the targets rather than them.

"Ten days were more than enough in Libya, and I'll swear that 23 Squadron were so keen to get away that most of us got airborne before starting our engines. We were bound for the lovely island of Malta for a ten-day air defence exercise. Mid-June in the Med, no sand, living in the splendour of a superb officers' mess, and the fleshpots and restaurants of Valletta to look forward to. El Adem was soon but a dim memory. As aircrew go, I was a good boy in Malta.

"As to day-to-day ops in the UK, until the 38 Group role came along it was a typical fighter squadron. Because we were a night/all-weather unit, we would probably do a day sortie and then maybe fly twice at night, until about four in the morning, depending on the time of year. It was nearly all PI stuff, the standard fighter role, bearing in mind that when I came back from the States there were new squadrons being formed almost every other month. The Meteors were going out, the Hunters were already in, the different marks of Javelin were coming in, the Canberra squadrons were building up and there was the Swift as well. It was a great time, and I was trying to work out where I might be posted after Coltishall; in fact, I went to Staff College. I think there were about 35 bases I could have gone to, all over the world, including Singapore, Cyprus, Malta and about five bases in Germany. It was an exciting time.

"As for the Javelin, I was probably a superior sod when I came back from flying the F-4 because it was a Mach 2.2 aeroplane, and its weapons system was so much better than the Javelin ever became. Having said that, the Javelin was a nice aeroplane, it was good to fly. We were doing a very big operational role, without having anything like the performance of the F-4, but it was a very friendly aeroplane. One of its good points was when we went to do trials and so on, rather than the big squadron operations. I remember sitting on the pan at Bahrain just as the sun went down and we refuelled the aeroplane with a bunch of Arabs, using a hand pump. There were several Arab bases in those days; what is now Dubai was just a couple of runways with holes in them and you got your fuel at the end of the runway from a bowser. It was an interesting time and you could do it with a two-man crew in those days; that was an acceptable way of operating.

"The Javelin was good as far as reliability went. To put it in perspective, there was nothing particularly difficult about it, and the radar system was positively bucolic compared to what I'd been used to in the States. It was reliable, we very seldom lost an aeroplane en route because of unserviceability. When I was at Leuchars we did have one or two incidents on the squadron with guys going in on the approach. We also had a mid-air collision in India on one occasion, however I suffered nothing personally.

"My tour on 23 and living in Scotland ended as we converted from Javelins to the RAF's 'hot pursuit ship', the Lightning. My finale was to head a small team of crews to ferry Javelins between the UK, Germany, Cyprus and Singapore so that the right mark of Javelin (the FAW.9R with a flight-refuelling capability) would be based where needed. We would then fly back their old aeroplanes in 500 to 600-mile stages. I chose the code name Operation Heavenly because it promised to provide some interesting flying to staging posts in countries that the RAF did not normally visit. In the event Heavenly never happened because the only IFR tanker then in service, the Valiant, was grounded overnight and forever due to main spar fatigue, and the exchange of aircraft was delayed for months. When it bit the dust, my allotted three years in a 'command post' was up and I received a posting that made me cringe – administrative plans at HQ Fighter Command. After 14 years on flying tours they put me behind a desk."[6]

Mel Evans also experienced deployments using in-flight refuelling while on the same squadron. His first such trip took him to Cyprus, a few months later undertaking the long trail to Singapore.

"Once we had achieved combat-ready status, we were able to learn the skills of in-flight refuelling. The squadron had a commitment to deploy anywhere

FAW.9 XH846 C 23 Squadron taking off from Coltishall flown by Mel Evans. (via Mel Evans)

in the world to meet national requirements. We were packed and ready for the building of the Berlin Wall, and the Cuban missile crisis. It was not very long before my nav and I were following a Valiant tanker from Coltishall to Cyprus, a flight of four hours 20 minutes. It was while we were in Cyprus, participating in an air defence exercise, that I had an incident which was the only time I 'bent' a Javelin. After a frustrating morning sitting on 'alert' in the cockpit, watching targets 'attack' the airfield, we were finally scrambled to intercept an 'incoming raid'. After take-off, I pointed the aircraft in the direction given by ground radar, climbed to 5,000 feet and allowed the speed to build. My nav picked up a target and directed my eyes in its direction. When I saw it, we were closing rapidly at right angles to the Hunter's track. If I turned too soon we would be ahead of the target and if I turned too late we would never see it again. At what I judged to be the right point, I pulled the Javelin into a very hard turn and rolled out immediately behind the Hunter and in a perfect firing position. I called the 'kill' over the radio and the Hunter broke off its attack, turning north towards its own base. I was feeling pleased with myself and, as the controller had no other targets for us, I decided to escort the Hunter from our area. At the Troodos Mountains I turned about and set course for base, enjoying the beautiful snow-covered scenes below. As I was gazing around, I noticed a strange marking on the top surface of the wing. I turned to look at the other wing and saw more clearly that the aircraft skin was rippled. I immediately looked at the g meter and saw that it read almost 6 g. Until the ventral fuel tanks were empty, the Javelin's maximum g was 3, thereafter the maximum was 5. Back on the ground standing in front of the aircraft, the wings looked slightly 'gull-winged'. The boss was not pleased! After viewing photographs of the wings, Gloster Aircraft declared it fit to be flown home for a wing change – one of the more experienced pilots was selected to do it. I was surprised that the job had not been given to me as the person responsible."

As previously outlined, Mel also raised some of the issues for aircrew arising from these lengthy transit flights.

"In January 1963, after a concentrated period of flight-refuelling practice using the new external tanks, the squadron deployed to Singapore to 'prove' the reinforcement capability. As the junior pilot, I was specially selected to be in the last section but, as a bonus, I would be the 'running spare' for each section departing ahead. This required that my nav and I were 'ready to go' and started engines with each section, ready to step in if anyone was

6. Kel Palmer, *A Roving Commission* (iUniverse, 2007) with later additions.

unserviceable. This occurred after each of our overnight stops in Cyprus, Bahrain, Karachi and Gan in the middle of the Indian Ocean. Along the way, I progressed steadily forward and arrived in Singapore with the leading section. One year later, we repeated this deployment but on that occasion it was 'for real' as we joined the ranks of 60 Squadron to defend the Malaysian territories of the Malay Peninsula, Singapore and North Borneo. Before that happened, 23 Squadron had moved to Leuchars in Scotland to put us in the way of the Russian 'Bears'.

"There were some 'interesting' complications to long flights at these high cockpit altitudes, starting with inputs; that is eating and drinking. Making sandwiches that were one inch square enabled the release of the mask to pop in a square and immediately secure the mask.

"Drinking was more tricky. After the first person punctured the issued can of fruit juice and turned his cockpit yellow, other options were explored. A flexible vessel with a valve to control the rate of release was essential. I expect that most took the same route as me and chose to forgo in-flight drinking. This also helped with the final problem – output. Initially, the boffins at Farnborough were tasked to produce a suitable item of equipment to resolve the problem. Their solution was a large, condom-like fitment, connected by plastic tubing to a bag stowed in the lower pocket of the flying suit. Two serious problems emerged when the device went to trials. To fit the device and achieve a proper seal, it was necessary to have a firm erection. Maintaining this for up to five hours may have been difficult. The plastic tube connecting to the bag could become kinked and/or trapped by the leg-restraint garters, resulting in a warm feeling. Most of us chose the simple but effective option of a standard hot water bottle. This solved the problem of changing pressure but did require that, unless you were unusually blessed, the parachute and ejection seat straps had to be undone for a short period [see also page 108].

"There was another feature encountered during the long transit flights. Flight refuelling between Valiant and Javelin normally took place at or above 40,000 feet, with both types in their best operating conditions. Over Europe this normally kept us clear of cloud, but on one occasion over the Indian Ocean we encountered high cloud at our operating altitude. At times, the cloud became quite thick and we had to move into close formation with the tanker, with one aircraft on each wingtip and one underneath the Valiant's tail. At times, the cloud was so thick that I could not see the full length of the wing. This situation continued for one and a half hours, during which we passed through one of our refuelling brackets. This required some very careful shuffling of aircraft very close to the mothership to take turns in the refuelling position.

"The confidence given by having attended the missile camp was in the back of our minds as we departed the island of Gan on the final leg of our journey to reinforce 60 Squadron. As this leg would take us just north of the Indonesian island of Java, we had fitted live Firestreak missiles on two of our pylons – just in case. This was not universally popular with the Valiant crews who did not relish four hours with us following them carrying live missiles. We reached the squadron base without further event and began the process of theatre familiarisation, ready to take up defensive patrols from RAAF Butterworth in the north, Singapore in the south and from Kuching and Labuan in Borneo."

CYPRUS AND ZAMBIA – 29 SQUADRON

Having spent a short time with 25 Squadron at Leeming, **Brian Bullock's** tour of the Javelin world continued with a move to 29 Squadron at Leuchars, just before they left to take over the air defence of Cyprus.

"In late 1962 at Leuchars, the 29 Squadron CO announced at a dining-in night that the squadron was posted to Nicosia in Cyprus with effect from February 1963. That was a very, very hard winter, and after some days of heavy snow, followed by frantic snow-clearing (we cleared about two feet of snow off the runway) we departed a frozen Leuchars on 26 February for the sunny Med, calling at Wattisham, Orange, Decimomannu, Luqa and El Adem. En route we mislaid our CO and one of the flight commanders due to aircraft unserviceabilities. As a result my pilot Ian Robertson and myself led just two Javelins, out of the original 12, into a very warm Nicosia on 28 February. Thus two scruffy flight lieutenants were greeted by a welcoming party that included senior air staff from Headquarters Middle East Air Force (MEAF). Luckily, after all the handshakes and explanations some cold beers were dispensed and needless to say, our CO was not best pleased.

"At Nicosia we replaced 43 Squadron Hunters who proceeded east to Aden, and we took over the QRA commitment. Very quickly the scrambles started. In the first week I found myself shadowing an Olympic Airways Comet that had strayed off track at 30,000 feet. At the end of the month we closed on, but did not intercept, a target that finally disappeared back into Turkish airspace.

"Life on the squadron settled in to a mixture of high and low level PIs and a lot of air-to-air gun firing on banners. The Greek Cypriots, aided and abetted by mainland Greece, were pushing for autonomy, and on the Turkish side there was a sabre-rattling reaction. Incursions into Cypriot airspace increased, with most aircraft turning back to Greece or Turkey well short of the island. On the ground there was open warfare between Greek and Turkish Cypriots, and at about 1000 hours on Christmas Day 1963 all personnel were recalled to the squadron. Our Javelins were to be flown the short distance to Akrotiri. We departed in dribs and drabs, and I recall a

15-minute flight in darkness, arriving at Akrotiri at about 1800 hours just in time for a night-flying supper in lieu of a Christmas dinner!

"Our first scramble was on Boxing Day morning, when we identified a US Navy A-3D Skywarrior at 36,000 feet. The next ident a few days later was a friendly Shackleton at 500 feet; no evasion, but quite a challenge at a little above stalling speed. Patrols were now being flown frequently in various sectors of Cypriot airspace at altitudes between 3,000 and 43,000 feet. The squadron returned to Nicosia on 6 January, much to the relief of our families, many of whom were living off base and very vulnerable. Gun battles were often heard from our house, which was a bit disconcerting.

"In between patrols our scrambles very often came to nothing, but we did identify a B-66, a couple of F-84Fs and a Turkish F-100 that nearly penetrated the Akrotiri zone and caused us to prepare for our first live air-to-air firing on another aircraft. It was early April when the squadron made a permanent move back to Akrotiri. At this time we were practising unusual PIs at around 10,000 feet, obviously in preparation for even more incursions. We had plenty of air-to-air gunnery. On one sortie, my pilot achieved a very creditable 29% hits on the flag. We were also flying sorties to home on to the SARBE aircrew locator beacons in case any of our pilots got shot down. We would have to home onto them and give them air cover, but these practices were not very successful.

"In a masterpiece of Foreign Office diplomacy, the squadron made a goodwill visit to Athens-Elefsis airport at the end of June 1964 to visit the Greek air force. The atmosphere was very cordial, typical aircrew to aircrew and, at this level, our Greek friends strongly condemned their government for encouraging the Greek Cypriots' actions. It was just a jolly, two days on an island in the Greek air force holiday camp. Very enjoyable, but questionable whether it was a good thing to do at that time.

"In August, a three-day local AIDEX, Exercise Cyprex 5, gave us plenty of tracks, mainly Canberras, between 700 and 52,000 feet. We struggled to close on one of the high level photo-reconnaissance (PR) versions, which must have been well above 52,000 feet. Some low level 1,000-feet Lightnings were also intercepted. The day after the exercise finished we were scrambled and eventually identified an Israeli Noratlas, flying at 1,000 feet at 120 knots. Thank goodness for the Javelin's huge airbrakes as we were in great danger of overshooting, which we did twice. It was somewhere down near the south of the island, and after enquiries we were advised that it was doing a nav training flight.

"A few days later we escorted a PR Canberra taking photos for the United Nations in the area around Morphou in the north-west of the island. We were detailed to be fully-armed ready to fire if any unidentified aircraft approached. On another occasion we were detailed to search for a Turkish navy R-class patrol boat reported to be in the Kyrenia area, but no joy. Our bread and butter sorties continued, the accent being on PIs between 500 and 1,500 feet, and air gunnery.

"There were just a few chances to get back to some basic navigation. The Javelins required periodic major inspections, for which they had to be flown back to the UK, usually to Shawbury. I arrived there one Friday afternoon and the civilian tradesmen had removed the hood before the engines had stopped turning! They obviously wanted to get away early. I was the nav officer on 29 Squadron and devised an idiot's guide for the flights from Akrotiri to the UK and back; this was regularly updated by NOTAMs (notice to airmen) etc. I had to volunteer for a number of these flights, even getting some use from the very poor radio compass fit in the Javelin – oh for GEE coverage!

"I'd been on the squadron for a while, angling for a slot on A (Fighter) Squadron at Boscombe Down, and finally I got it. I was lucky and left 29 Squadron in June '65, just before their unfortunate detachment to Zambia."

On 11 November 1965, Rhodesian Prime Minister Ian Smith (a former Spitfire pilot with 237 [Rhodesia] Squadron), unilaterally declared the country to be independent from the United Kingdom; the first British colony to break free in such a way since the United States in 1776. The British Labour government under Prime Minister Harold Wilson elected to respond by imposing sanctions. These included a Royal Navy blockade of the oil supplies Rhodesia received via the Mozambique oil ports at Beira and Lourenco Marques. One unfortunate side effect of this blockade was the fact that Zambia received its oil supplies from Rhodesia, who turned off the tap. In December 1965 RAF Britannias commenced flying oil into Zambia, and were quickly followed by aircraft from other civil and military operators. To guard against any possible Rhodesian threat to the oil lift, 29 Squadron was ordered down to Zambia to provide an air defence capability. They arrived on 3 December 1965, with Ndola as the headquarters and principal operating base, with a detachment at the capital, Lusaka.

FAW.9 XH891 R 29 Squadron Ndola airport, Zambia, 1966. (Ken Beere)

FAW.9 XH894 again, now E of 29 Squadron Ndola, Zambia 1966. (Ken Beere)

Only recently out of trade training, **Ken Beere** was among the ground crew flown down to support the Javelin operations.

"I joined in 1965 at the age of 17 as a direct entrant, just before my 18th birthday. I went to Bicester, 71 MU and applied for an overseas posting at the end of the year. I was posted to 29 Squadron and arrived at Akrotiri in December '65. While I was there we had a base alert and I had to do a night guard on a Canberra's A-bomb. It was odd sitting on an A-bomb's trolley, smoking a fag at 2 a.m., armed with a pick-axe handle!

"We went down to Zambia on 9 January 1966. I did the Zambia tour and eventually went back to Cyprus. The routing for us was via Muharraq (Bahrain), or El Adem – Nairobi – Ndola in a Hastings or a Britannia. The whole squadron went down apart from the two T-birds (T.3s). We stayed down there for about a month at a time, before rotating back to Akrotiri for a couple of months. There were four Javelins at Lusaka (which became RAF Lusaka, BFPO 645) and the rest were at Ndola; there was talk at one time that Ndola would be made into a one-year overseas tour. The flying was quite restricted because of the fuel shortage. They were bringing in 45-gallon drums of fuel in Britannias and Royal Canadian Air Force Hercules."

Other aircraft used during the oil lift included Britannias of British Caledonian and Lloyd International, BOAC VC 10s, plus Air Ferry Carvairs and DC-4s. **Ken Beere** continues:

"The living quarters at Ndola were a bit rough. All the squadron personnel were in one huge shed, known as the Zambia Hall of Industry; it leaked when it rained and was very humid when it was hot. It was divided up into seven squares by hardboard sheeting; all the beds had their head to the wall and feet towards the centre. We had no lockers, one table in the middle of the room and there were clothes hanging from everywhere. We had a local gentleman named Isaac, who did all our washing and ironing for five shillings a week and swept the place out in the mornings.

"I was on first-line servicing, i.e. replenishment and a general check-over, but this also included a number of mainwheel changes and a hydraulic reservoir change (a six-hour job). I also had to do progressive servicing and modifications if necessary. At first I was the only airframe chap on the line, so I had to do all this by myself and sign for it, so I was kept pretty busy! At one point I finally had a day off after eight straight days working. This was during a time when we were changing wing pylons from the wet pylons to carry drop tanks, to the ones that were wired up for the Firestreaks. We also had to remove the inboard pylons if an aircraft needed an undercarriage retraction test, in order to allow clearance for the jacks. They sent two chaps up from Lusaka to Ndola to help me. They were both LACs but weren't Javelin 'trained' at all and had never worked on them before.

"Talking of Firestreaks, they were kept in a small hangar. Although the RAF Regiment was there to protect us, we had to do guard duty sitting in a chair outside the hut all night, armed with a .303 rifle and five bullets, to stop anyone from taking our missiles.

"We had a great spate of airframe snags. My friend and I changed four brake units in two weeks. Then we had an aircraft of which the undercarriage wouldn't lower, so the pilot 'porpoised' the aircraft and they finally came down. When he finally landed we did a retraction test and found that the uplock was misaligned. I had a hood seal change and a hydraulic pressure switch change, all in one day. I later went onto both first and second-line servicing, and we still only had seven airframe chaps.

"In June '66 the airfield at Ndola was closed because the runway was cracking up, not for the first time, and there was no flying for about two weeks. I spent one session at Lusaka, which is where I had a start-up fire, a fairly common thing on Javs. The drop-down panel with Dzus fasteners covered a big bay with all the hydraulics, avionics and stuff like that. After start-up, you had to duck underneath, stick your head up in this hole and check that nothing was on fire, with an extinguisher standing by obviously. So they start one – you have a look, OK; start two – have a look, OK, and then you had to put the panel up, which meant you were enshrouded in AVPIN fumes. So it was a big breath, get under there and whack the panel on as quickly as you could – eyes streaming.

"On this particular day at Lusaka, they started number one, started number two and as number two started, a great sheet of flame came out of the hole. Panic stations, 'Cut! Cut! Get out!' to the crew, grab the fire extinguisher, stick it in the hole, fire it off and we all legged it into the distance. The Zambian fire brigade came rocketing up and took over. What happened to the aeroplane I can't remember.

"There was one FAW.9, XH764 coded C for Charlie, which did a wheels-up landing in May, and was sent to 103 MU at Akrotiri to have a mainplane change. The Javelin's brakes were not weak, but they had a propensity to overheat, and the wheels were made of magnesium alloy. The main undercarriage legs were prone to cracking or something, although I never had any experience of that. This aircraft had to be ready to fly down to Ndola by 30 December. On the 28th we worked all day getting it ready – check all the wire lockings, put all the panels back on, connect all the supplies, check the whole aircraft – and then it went up for a test flight. I was in the starting party and we got it away safely. When it came back, the pilot said it was a lovely aircraft to fly. Again, we did the necessary and he went back up again for the long test flight. Two hours later it came down and went to the compass swing pan, prior to going down to Zambia. It hadn't been there more than five minutes when the starboard undercarriage leg and wheel caught fire. The nav and pilot got out and the fire brigade arrived to put the fire out but the airframe was Cat 3/unfit to fly as the mainplane and fuselage were badly warped and burnt. Charlie was once again in the MU for quite a long period as they had to reskin the burnt areas.

"I've no idea what caused the fire, maybe a hydraulic leak. In pre-inflight refuelling days, the Javelins had been fitted with four long-range fuel tanks. The inboard tank was quite close to the undercarriage and was full of fuel vapour, so we all kept a great distance from it."

This aircraft was fated. Having been repaired again in 1966, a year later it suffered a heavy landing at Manston, Kent while en route to 27 MU Shawbury and remained at Manston as a gate guard. **Ken Beere** again:

"As Zambia was a copper-mining country, copper dust used to get all over everything. We used to get lots of it piling up on the wings, so they decided that we needed somebody to come and brush it all off. We had a couple of local labourer lads and I was charged with taking one of them out to an aircraft to show him what to do. I got up onto the wing, but he wouldn't walk out onto it. He didn't speak English, so I think he was just a bit frightened that it was going to snap off or something. So I had to walk out to the wingtip and bounce up and down a bit to prove that it was quite safe. I then gave him a brush and showed him what I wanted him to do, being very careful not to knock off the vortex generators that were sticking up all over the place. It was part of my pre-flight routine to walk out and check the vortex generators, the lights and the wingtips and do a little bounce on the tip. One day, when I was bouncing on the wingtip, I noticed that the fin was flapping about; I thought 'Crikey, that's not right!' I went back into the line office and reported it, but I have no idea what happened to it after that.

"We didn't have any training back then [before joining the squadron]; as far as I was concerned it was on the job training when I got there. I stayed

FAW.9 XH789 G of 64 Squadron after overshooting Akrotiri with hydraulic failure, 30 July 1959. (via Steve Sanders)

on 29 until the middle of '67 when the squadron went back to the UK and re-equipped with Lightnings. They were replaced in Cyprus by 56 Squadron Lightnings, which we continued to do the maintenance on. Again, no introduction, no training, no general familiarisation courses; 'there's a Lightning, get on with it' sort of thing.

"I only did five years in the air force. I enjoyed my work, I liked working on the aeroplanes, but what went with it I didn't. Although I had been offered another five years, the trouble was I was a bit of a party animal, so I decided to leave and came out as a senior aircraftman (SAC). I then did 20-odd years at British Airways, training etc., manuals, procedures and so on."

Having completed a fitter's course, and a posting to the 'Special Installation Squadron' on 60 MU at Dishforth, air radar man **Bryan Elliott** also served with 29 Squadron at Akrotiri, later being detached to Zambia.

"When I was on 29 Squadron in Cyprus in 1966, one morning I was walking from the tech area towards the ops buildings, we had a 'Battle Four' up and I was watching them coming into land. Suddenly the second aircraft reared up (he'd got caught in the leader's slipstream). I heard the characteristic roar as the power went on, but by that time he was almost vertical. The thing that was uppermost in my mind as I looked at the underside of the almost vertical aircraft as it wallowed in the sky was, how far it would come towards me, and although it must have been some 400 yards from me, I took off towards the line in somewhat of a hurry. The nose started to come down, but he didn't have the height (he was only some 2-300 yards from the threshold) and both crew ejected. The nav ejected when the Javelin was just off vertical, I saw the seat go out but he was shielded from the airflow so his 'chute didn't deploy, and he was still in his seat when he hit the ground. The pilot ejected when the Javelin had reached the horizontal, and in my mind's eye I remember him going out and seeing the 'chute, but he appeared to carry on up into the shrouds. He then fell clear and the 'chute fully deployed just as he hit the ground. The Javelin then fell in the bomb dump (great place to site a bomb dump, on the approach to the runway!) and finished up with its nose in the entrance to a bunker that had a load of live Firestreak missiles inside. Both the crew lived, the pilot broke both his legs but apparently got up and ran to where the navigator landed! I ran across to the line, and they told me to get the pilot (a master pilot) of the third Javelin out as soon as he taxied in, and get him into an adjacent one that was ready for flight. I went up the ladder to the cockpit and as I came in view he looked at me and said, 'Christ, that was one hell of an undershoot!' I think it was the nav's second or third ejection, and they said he couldn't cope with another one, so when he was fit they posted him to a Canberra squadron where they had to go out the side door. Not good at low level!"

Fg Off J W Pierce was flying XH848 L on 14 December 1966, with Flt Lt Paul Burns as his navigator. On approach to land at Akrotiri their aircraft was caught in the wake vortex from the preceding Javelin, causing loss of control, pitch up and a stall. **Bryan Elliott** continues:

"We were programmed to do live firing of the Firestreaks on the range near Aberporth, which meant coming over to Valley for a few weeks. One of the navs related a story to us about their firing on the range. Apparently in the final stages of an interception the Javelin was at some height, climbing inverted, and the stall warning had been going for some time. The nav said that he spent most of that time holding onto the ejection seat upper handle. I believe the pilot went on to fly with the Red Arrows. Then on two occasions a missile was fired (from the same aircraft) which totally ignored the flare, flew up the wire and blew the Jindivik out of the sky!

"I was doing a scanner change on the line at Akrotiri. On final checks we used to see if we could pick up an echo of any passing ship and track it. I was engaged in changing a scanner one night and had got to the end of the installation (or so I thought). I fired up the radar, and during the completion checks picked up an echo from a ship at some considerable distance. I tracked it for a few minutes and went to carry out the final task which was a pressure check on the wave guide. This check proved there was a major leak which annoyed me as this seemed to be an excellent radar, I went up into the nose-wheel bay to check the wave guide assembly and was horrified to see I hadn't connected it up! The flexible section was hanging down, only overlapping the corresponding wave guide by a small amount. I connected both up and the pressure check was successful. By all rights, the original configuration should not have worked but I'd got a signal at a fair range and tracked it. Perhaps I'd discovered a new theory on microwave propagation – we'll never know.

"I was very lucky to get detached from Cyprus to Zambia when the Rhodesia crisis came about. The ground crew were supposed to turn around every eight weeks or so but I was single, playing rugby for the local town (Ndola) and enjoying life, so I volunteered to stay permanently which suited the married guys in Cyprus, who could stay at home. We did have one incident when the undercarriage collapsed on one of the Javelins when landing, and I spent a few days stripping out all the radar gear from it; the aircraft ended up in a children's playground in Ndola and looked a sad sight."

This was XH890 M which came to grief as described on 2 June 1966. It was struck off charge as Cat.5 the next day and abandoned on site when the RAF detachment left for home. The remains of the aircraft were still in the children's playground well into the mid-1970s. **Bryan Elliott** again:

"We did hear of questions being asked in the Zambian parliament about what the Javelins were doing, as nobody ever saw one flying (not surprising due to the height they were at). However, one of the aircrew took it into his head to show them and apparently went down Cairo Avenue (the main street in Lusaka) at fifth floor level. This is hearsay and I've no way of proving it. On another occasion, someone stood up in the Zambian parliament and asked why couldn't the visiting aircraft be used to aid the Zambian economy? Furthermore, he highlighted crop spraying as a possibility! COMBRITZAM [Commander British Forces in Zambia] in Lusaka then brought out a spoof modification leaflet regarding drilling holes in the rear of the ventral tanks and fitting spray nozzles!"

CHAPTER FIVE

RIGGERS, SOOTIES, LECKIES, PLUMBERS AND FAIRIES – THE GROUND CREW

THE BOYS

Cpl John Augoustis

Air radar. Joined in 1959 as a boy entrant. Trained Cosford. 72 Squadron Javelin Leconfield. 92 Squadron Hunter Leconfield. Coningsby, Vulcan. St. Athan, Beverley, Victor and Vulcan. Sealand. Left the RAF in 1970 and remained at Sealand as a telecommunication technical officer.

Sgt Ken Brereton

Air electrician. Joined in 1959 as a boy entrant. Trained St. Athan. 29 Squadron Leuchars '60-'63. Watton ASF Canberra, Varsity, Hastings. 209 Squadron Labuan single and Twin Pioneer 1965. 201 Squadron Kinloss Shackleton 1966. Nimrod handling flight. 202 Squadron Leuchars 1972. Left the RAF in 1973.

Chf Tech Dave Curnock

Engine fitter. Joined in 1955 as a Halton apprentice. Shackleton ASF Gibraltar. 229 OCU Hunter and Meteor. 60 Squadron Javelin Tengah and Kuching '64-'65. 24 Squadron Hastings and Hercules. 48 Squadron Hercules, Lyneham and Akrotiri. Left the RAF in 1977 and worked as a technical author.

J/T Cliff Edwards

Airframe fitter. Valiant and Anson, Marham. Visiting Aircraft Flight Luqa '65-'68. RAF College Jet Provost, Varsity. 205 Squadron Seletar Shackleton. Left the RAF in 1973. Became a senior manager in Shell Aviation and a safety management expert in his own company.

Wg Cdr Piers Gardiner

Air traffic control officer. Joined in 1965. First tour Strubby. Tengah. Area radar at Eastern Radar, Watton. LATCC (Mil) West Drayton. HQ MATO. Watton. HQ NATS. HQ 11 Gp. MoD. SATCO Waddington and Stanley. Retired 1994.

Cpl Doug Mansfield

Air radar, later retrained as a navigation instruments technician. Joined in 1959. Trained at Yatesbury. 72 Squadron Javelin Leconfield. 19, 23 and 74 Squadrons Lightning. 390 MU Singapore. Left the RAF in 1994.

Flt Lt Alan Mudge
Armourer. Joined in 1957. Halton apprentice. IRF and 228 OCU (11 Reserve Squadron) Leuchars, 64 Squadron Tengah. 3 Squadron Harrier. Left the RAF in 1980 then spent seven years in the Volunteer Reserves.

Sqn Ldr Bill Ragg
Air radar. 33 Squadron Javelin Middleton St. George. Hunter. Lightning. Commissioned as air loadmaster. 30 Squadron Hercules, Lyneham. Retired in 1997.

Sgt Mick Speake
Photographer. Joined in 1962. Trained Wellesbourne Mountford, later air camera fitter (ACF). 29 Squadron Javelin Nicosia '63. Akrotiri. 1 AIDU Northolt. 3 MFPU Laarbruch. ACF St. Mawgan Shackleton, Nimrod. 8 and 208 Squadrons Hunter. 210 Squadron Shackleton. MARDET Singapore. 3 Squadron Harrier. 23 Squadron Phantom. Technical instructor School of Photography Cosford. Left the RAF in 1983. Technical author, later PR manager in South Africa.

With further contribution from **Bryan Elliott** (Chapter Four)

THE GROUND CREW

While aircrew have the high profile job of flying the aeroplane, they are the first to acknowledge that they cannot do so without the support of large numbers of back-up personnel. Foremost amongst these are the aircraft engineers, often working in extremes of weather on the flight line, or on second-line servicing in the hangars and workshops.

In typical RAF fashion, individual trades have acquired sobriquets by which they are far better known amongst their peers. Some of these are quite obvious, others less so. Airframe mechanics and fitters are 'riggers', a title that goes back to the earliest days of aviation when assembling aeroplanes was referred to as rigging, involving such tasks as flight controls assembly and adjustment, and tensioning the inter-wing flying wires on biplanes. Especially since

64 Squadron, Cpl Sam Sumner marshalling and SAC Al Mudge ready to do the tyre check. (Alan Mudge)

the advent of the jet, the engine men have been known as 'sooties', simply a reflection of the soot-covered hot end of the engine and its exhaust. 'Lecky' is straightforward – an electrician.

Somewhat more obscure are 'plumber' and 'fairy'. Armourers became 'plumbers' during the Second World War when their responsibility for hydraulically operated gun turrets on the heavy bombers meant they had a lot of pipework to contend with. Finally, the radar/radio man, known as a 'fairy', supposedly a reference to fairy lights and originally applied to electricians before radar became a separate trade in its own right. All the engineers particularly remember the Javelin's predilection for start-up fires, and the generally poor accessibility to systems and equipment. Overall however, they do tend to express – if somewhat reluctantly – a fondness for it, together with pride in a job well done.

AIRFRAMES – THE 'RIGGER'

Ken Beere gave an insight into the details of a rigger's work on Javelins with 29 Squadron in Zambia in Chapter Four. Fellow rigger **Cliff Edwards** had been involved in scrapping the Valiant fleet at Marham after it suffered terminal fatigue issues. Although this was where he first encountered Javelins, it was not until he was posted away to Luqa, Malta that he got his hands on them.

> "In 1964 I was working as an airframe fitter at Marham on the Valiant. Early in the year they were scrapped due to wing spar cracking and I, with many others, was deployed on parting out the Valiants, and then cutting out the hotspots (areas that had a radioactive signature above a defined limit) on the wings, fuselage, and tail. As part of my trade training I had

FAW.9 XH846 J of 60 Squadron surrounded by ground equipment at Tengah. (60 Squadron)

learnt to do repairs to fabric-covered aircraft. Marham's station flight had a 'station hack' Anson with sections of fabric wing skins that needed repair. I volunteered to do this as it was a better option than chopping out bits of aircraft skin on the Valiants.

"It was during my short stay on the station flight that I first encountered the Javelin, when two of them diverted into Marham for a night stop. My role related to this visit was limited to 'gofer and gawper' whilst the aircraft were turned around, refuelled and readied for the morning departure by the station flight ground crew.

"In early 1965 I was posted to Luqa in Malta and joined the visiting aircraft flight as the B shift aircraft fitter. During my three years in Luqa I was fortunate, in some part, to work on a large number of different types of aircraft which included those from the RAF, Royal Navy, USAF, US Marines, and the Italian air force. During 1965 we saw a few visits by Javelins which, with others such as Canberras, were often en route to the firing ranges close to El Adem in Libya.

"My one significant memory related to the Javelin was when I was working in conjunction with my colleague, who was the engine fitter, and we shared the workload depending on need and opportunity. My mate was a small guy, and I was tall and in those days somewhat athletic with interests in sport, such as throwing the hammer and rugby. I say that in way of explaining that one of the minor tasks we undertook on visiting Javelins was to re-arm the engine cartridge starter system on the Sapphire Mk.SA7 and SA7R engines. The breech blocks for the two starters were accessed through a panel in the belly, aft of the cockpit area and forward of the engines. The breech blocks were located at the back of this bay, a reach of about two-and-a-half feet. My mate the engine fitter, whose job it was to change these cartridges, found them difficult to reach and heavy to lift. The cartridge was quite large, about four inches in diameter and ten inches long and weighed, together with the breech cap and insertion tool, around 15 to 20 pounds. Therefore, on some occasions I would fit the cartridges to be helpful, albeit that it was not my job. Our sergeant would come along and check they were correctly, installed and tightened and would sign off the job. I had very little in the way of exposure to the Javelin, but I did enjoy these aircraft when we had something to do on them."

ENGINES – THE 'SOOTY'

Dave Curnock had been enjoying his tour at Chivenor – 'Heaven in Devon' – where he looked after the target-tug Meteors on 229 OCU, when in 1964 he was posted to 60 Squadron's detachment at Kuching in Borneo. He spent the next two years working on Javelins until being posted back to the UK to look after Hastings transports.

"The 60 Squadron motto, *Per ardua ad aethera tendo* – 'I strive through difficulties to the sky' – could not have been a more appropriate description of life on the squadron's Kuching detachment. I was posted to Kuching as a corporal engine fitter on a 12-month unaccompanied tour in early June 1964. I had absolutely no experience whatsoever of working on the Javelin, in common with the majority of the other ground crew members who had, like me, been posted in to relieve the personnel on temporary detachment from the squadron's base at Tengah, Singapore. In response to the threat caused by the Indonesian Confrontation, this detachment had been sent to Kuching primarily to provide air defence cover: other roles included the provision of escorts to Hastings and Valetta transport aircraft during supply-dropping missions to forward area troops, and carrying out low level patrols over the jungle and parts of the sea area close to the Indonesian border. Later in 1964, we were reinforced by 64 Squadron, some of whose aircraft, FAW.9Rs, rotated through the Kuching detachment. We sometimes had FAW.9s, armed with four Firestreak missiles; although these were admirable in the air defence role they lacked the range of the FAW.9R, with its two Firestreaks and two 230-gallon under-wing fuel tanks, for escort and patrol duties.

"It was soon realised by the powers that be that we, the newcomers, urgently needed familiarisation with the Javelin, so we were swiftly sent to Tengah to gain some practical experience on type. Here, we were set to work in the squadron's rectifications hangar where we performed a variety of tasks. Most of the 'experience' gained proved to be of little use in our subsequent endeavours: tasks such as the replacement of engine control systems, auxiliary gearbox changes etc., were unlikely to be performed on an operational first-line unit. On the last day of our training, it was realised

Operational turnround on 60 Squadron FAW.9 XH751 N at Tengah. (60 Squadron)

1. FAW.1 XA563 on a pre-delivery test flight. (MoD via Tony Buttler)

2. FAW.4 XA635 and FAW.1 XA552 formate over Gloucestershire in 1956. (Adrian Balch collection)

3. 41 Squadron's first FAW.4 XA637, delivered in February 1957. (via Sandi Taylor)

4

5

6

7

4. FAW.5 XA667 O of 228 OCU's 137 Squadron near Leeming in April 1961. (Adrian Balch collection)
5. 23 Squadron line-up at Coltishall, with FAW.9 XH894 R in the foreground. (Mel Evans)
6. Capt Earl Taylor USAF and Flt Lt Brian Bedford 41 Squadron. Earl Taylor lost his life in a crash at Horsham St. Faith on 11 July 1958. (Steve Taylor)
7. 23 Squadron FAW.9 XH894 R during a quick turnround competition. Navigator Flt Lt Harry Wyld sprinting across the wing. (Mel Evans)

3. 23 Squadron FAW.9 XH890 M in 1961 prior to conversion to FAW.9R standard. (Adrian Balch collection)

9. FAW.9 XH753 Z from 11 Squadron Geilenkirchen at Abingdon's Battle of Britain display 14 September 1963. (Steve Bond)

0. Ground crew awaiting the action. Taff Lewis, Robbie Robertson, Pete Whatmore and Mick Tarrant, 228 OCU Leuchars, November 1965. (Alan Mudge)

1

2

14

15

11. A very smart FAW.9 XH957 S from 5 Squadron Geilenkirchen, at Cameri in 1965. (Adrian Balch collection)
12. FAW.9 formation from 29 Squadron Leuchars, XH792 A leading. Circa 1961 or '62. (Peter Masterman)
13. 29 Squadron FAW.9 XH962 P and 25 Squadron XH882 L in 1961 or '62. (Rex Wickens)
14. FAW.9 XH792 A 29 Squadron Leuchars, circa 1961 or '62. (Peter Masterman)
15. A 29 Squadron pair over Malta during a deployment from Nicosia in 1963. FAW.9 XH962 P nearest the camera. (Steve Bond collection)
16. XH712 K heads a line of 29 Squadron FAW.9s at Akrotiri in January 1966. (Adrian Balch collection)

16

17. XH889 H and XH712 K start the line of 29 Squadron FAW.9s detached to Nairobi in December 1965. (Adrian Balch collection)

18. Ndola airport, Zambia, in 1966 with 29 Squadron on detachment from Akrotiri. (Ken Beere)

19. Undercarriage retraction tests on a 29 Squadron FAW.9 at Ndola, Zambia, 1966. (Ken Beere)

20

21

20. Sqn Ldr George Beaton's personal FAW.9 XH898 GHB, 228 OCU Leuchars 17 September 1966. (Adrian Balch collection)

21. 228 OCU FAW.9s break to land, Leuchars 17 September 1966. (Adrian Balch collection)

22. T.3 XH397 B of 228 OCU at Leuchars July 1966. (Adrian Balch collection)

22

23

24

25

23. FAW.9 XH763 C of 64 Squadron at Tengah March 1966. (Martin Fenner collection)
24. Wg Cdr P D Wright, OC 64 Squadron in his personal FAW.9 XH834 PDW over Singapore June 1966. (Adrian Balch collection)
25. T.3 XH435 D on start-up, 228 OCU Leuchars November 1965. (Alan Mudge)

26

27

28

29

26. T.3 XH445 Z of 64 Squadron basks in the sun at Tengah in 1966. (John Mounce collection)
27. 64 Squadron's disbandment flypast at Tengah 10 June 1967. (Sqn Ldr Tony Douglas-Beveridge)
28. 64 Squadron's disbandment formation 10 June 1967. (Sqn Ldr Tony Douglas-Beveridge)
29. 60 Squadron FAW.9 blasting off from Tengah at dusk. (60 Squadron)

30

31

32

33

34

35

36

30. 60 Squadron's packed flight line at Tengah. (Mike Bryant)

31. 60 Squadron diamond nine formation, with a single T.3 bringing up the rear. (60 Squadron)

32. A 60 Squadron pair on finals at Tengah. (C J Donovan via Peter Day)

33. 250 feet – who's kidding who? 60 Squadron air-to-ground firing at Song-Song October 1967. (60 Squadron)

34. "And then I shot the bloody flag off", says Joe Warne to sympathetic ground crew after an air-firing sortie. (60 Squadron)

35. Close-up of the business end of 60 Squadron boss's FAW.9 XH839 MHM. (60 Squadron)

36. Borneo Jet Force line at Kuching: thick mud, rattle of wheels on PSP, smell of AVPIN and tractor fumes, flap and creak of the windsock. (60 Squadron)

7

8

39-40

41

2

43

37. FAW.9 XH725 P of 60 Squadron passing Horsburgh lighthouse in the Singapore Straits, crewed by Flt Lt Jacques David and Flt Lt Tony Forster. (60 Squadron)

38. FAW.9 XH841 D of 60 Squadron turning over the Johore Straits for the run-in and break. (60 Squadron)

39. Firestreak loading demonstration for the cameras. (60 Squadron)

40. Operation Gas Iron II, Hong Kong July 1967. Gerry Barnard, Dave Sumner, Dinger Dell, Andy Anderson, Keith Fitchew, Geoff Clark, Ian Campbell, Gus Geeve plus one. (60 Squadron)

41. Kai Tak roller landing by 60 Squadron, taken from ATC. (Mike Miller via Peter Day)

42. Kai Tak with 60 Squadron FAW.9s XH759 A and XH961 H on finals. (Keith Fitchew via Peter Day)

43. Nine-ship from 60 Squadron turning in for a run on Tengah. (60 Squadron)

THE BOYS TODAY

Bill Hustwayte

Brian Bullock

Doug Mansfield

Dave Curnock

Alan Mudge

Eric Marsh

George Lee

Jack Broughton

John Augoustis

Mel Evans

Mick Speake

Peter Day

Peter Wallington

Peter Masterman

Mike Gill

44

45

46

47

44. Mel Evans keeping his 60 Squadron FAW.9R XH877 W low as he escorts a 52 Squadron Valetta into Kuching in 1964. (via Mel Evans)

45. A&AEE Boscombe Down's FAW.2 XA778 at Moreton Valance in February 1961. (Adrian Balch collection)

46. Stream landing at Tengah by 60 Squadron. (C J Donovan via Peter Day)

47. The last Javelin to fly. FAW.9 XH897 of A&AEE A Fighter Test Squadron, Boscombe Down in 1971, now preserved at Duxford.

by the technical hierarchy that none of us engine men had ever ground-run a Javelin, so a visit to the blast pan ensued.

"Once back at Kuching, we relieved the incumbent detachment members who rapidly disappeared back to Singapore, leaving us to take stock of the situation. The 'we' to which I refer, comprised four engine fitters, four airframe fitters and two each of the electrical, instrument, wireless/radar, and armament trades. Due to the requirement for 24-hour coverage seven days a week, the available manpower was split into two shifts, each comprising two engine fitters, two airframe fitters and one each of the remaining trades, with changeover at midday. We were now expected to keep one Javelin 'on state' (nowadays called QRA) at five minutes' readiness, the second at 15 minutes, and the third to be used as a back-up for the other two (when this was possible!) The readiness requirement eased to 15 minutes at night. Our office/crewroom and spares store were housed in tents adjacent to the ORP at one end of the runway. Some months later, we moved into more palatial surroundings, namely two local-style basha huts that were located around 200 yards from the ORP, hardly an optimal distance for a rapid response. The aircrew hut was air conditioned; ours was not.

"The original ORP was constructed from pierced steel planking (PSP), as was the access road to our small tented complex; because of the damage this material caused to high-pressure aircraft tyres, no turns were to be made while on the PSP. On returning from a sortie, the aircraft taxied to a point on the runway alongside the PSP, from where we pushed it with a tractor backwards, in a straight line, to a position from where it could taxi forward directly onto the runway on the next sortie. Later a new, much larger, concrete ORP was built that provided greater flexibility regarding aircraft parking positions and could, on occasion, accommodate three Javelins in the unlikely event that all three should become serviceable. Once a week we had to push the aircraft to the rear of the ORP; this was, I believe, connected with airfield operational and/or insurance requirements to do with the visit of the weekly, Malaysian Airways-stickered, BOAC Comet airliner from Singapore.

"Our squadron Land Rover, quite a well-used example, had previously been used by somebody quite important, as witnessed by the bracket on the front bumper that had formerly held a senior officer's 'star' plate. To this bracket was now affixed a plate carrying the 'insignia' of the Borneo Jet Force (BJF), an unofficial designation shared at that time by us on 60 Squadron and 20 Squadron with their Hunter FGA.9s which were intended for operations against ground targets. The acting station warrant officer (a flight sergeant) was unimpressed with this, and did his best to apprehend the driver whenever our Land Rover appeared on the domestic site – but never succeeded. Varying the route taken during shift changeovers was a challenge he could not overcome! The insignia of the BJF was definitely unofficial but it was usually represented as being the markhor's head (mountain goat!) as depicted in the official 60 Squadron badge, with the words Borneo Jet Force beneath. Between the goat's horns were the digits '60'.

"To an engine fitter, as for most trades, the Javelin posed many challenges. We claimed that the auxiliary gearbox was the first item to appear on the production line, around which the aircraft was assembled. I still bear the physical scars resulting from working in the area known as 'the bramble patch' at the front of the gearbox, where the hydraulic pumps and associated pipework, with their many safety lock-wired couplings, were situated. Access to the engines was quite tight; topping up the oil after a sortie was achieved via a belly panel between the two ventral tanks. On removing this panel, the first wave of heat gave some indication of what awaited you when the engine access doors were opened: a blast of searing heat almost took your breath away as you then juggled with the two jugs full of oil (hopefully, one per engine) and the oil filler cap which was also quite warm! Usually, at the same time, you became aware of a pair of legs attached to an instrument man appearing somewhere below the panel. His job was to take the readings from the fatigue meter situated in the roof of the central servicing bay: we engine men often took pity on the chap and read out the numbers for him while he wrote them on his pad.

"One of the first things to be learned by a new arrival when on starter crew duty was the movements required to participate in the 'starter crew tap dance'. This was performed on those not infrequent occasions when, without prior warning, a starter motor would spit its turbine blades down the exhaust pipe onto the ground, from where they bounced all over the place. This event was soon followed by us engine chaps spending several hours in the incredibly hot and humid forward servicing hatch (the home of the bramble patch) and down the intake duct as we replaced the starter motor.

"The starter system on the Javelin was notoriously unreliable. On one occasion, a starter problem led to the loss of an aircraft, an FAW.9R XH874 H from 64 Squadron that was written off following irreparable structural damage that occurred on 4 August, 1964. I had been rostered for night standby crew that evening and was in the shower block, at the domestic site on the far side of the airfield, when I heard running footsteps on the pathway outside and someone shouting '...there's a Jav on fire'. I grabbed my towel and ran outside in time to see the smoke rising from the distant ORP. My colleague on shift had been about to carry out an engine run to assist airframe men who had been working on the hydraulic system. On pressing the starter button there was (he told me later) an almighty explosion from below, followed by the starter crew man waving frantically as he ran towards the aircraft with the fire-bottle trolley. After selecting the electrical power and fuel cocks to 'off', he swiftly vacated the cockpit. The civilian airport fire service arrived and proceeded to hose the area with water, not a particularly good idea, before the RAF firemen arrived with their foam tender.

"The subsequent investigation determined there had been a crack in a starter fuel (AVPIN) pipe; during the start cycle the leaking fuel was pressurised by the starter initiation cartridge system and had leaked between the aircraft skin and the starboard ventral tank. This fuel was then ignited by hot gas from the starter exhaust, triggering an explosion. The force of the blast had blown off the starboard ventral tank, which then split open as it hit the ground. Being full of fuel, this caught fire under the aircraft, burning much of the adjacent aircraft structure, in particular the fuselage frames supporting the engine rails. The Javelin then became a 'Christmas Tree' and was cannibalised for spares after being struck off charge on 27 August. Removing the starboard engine proved particularly tricky as the inbuilt engine rails were badly distorted following the fire.

"The shortage of spares, special tools and equipment were the key protagonists in an engine change saga that developed after an engine incident on a ground run in which I, thankfully, was not involved! The engine needed to be run at high power: due to local airfield constraints we were forbidden to run at high power settings on the ORP, so the aircraft was crewed by its normal complement of aircrew and taxied to the opposite end of the runway for the procedure. The shortage of equipment included the lack of engine intake guards; whether these would have protected the engine against the ingestion of a metallic foreign body is a matter for conjecture. Actually the resulting damage to the engine was terminal. We had no engine change kit or spare trolley/stand for our detachment, although there *was* a spare port engine available; this in itself was fortunate, being that the Sapphire engines on a Javelin were 'handed' – port or starboard – and we needed a port! The scaling of tools and equipment was such that there was only one 'off-base' engine change kit, to be shared between Kuching, Butterworth and Labuan detached flights of 60 Squadron. Needless to say, it was elsewhere when we needed it, at Labuan in this instance. An urgent signal ensured the kit arrived at Kuching by air, next morning.

"Later that day, after we had changed the engine, but before we had done the post-engine change ground run, a signal arrived stating an urgent requirement for the kit and trolley/stand at Labuan: these were duly sent to station stores for immediate air dispatch. During the engine runs a fuel leak was discovered from the fuel control unit; its location required engine removal for access to the leaking seal. By now, the engine change kit was airborne en route Labuan! Signal duly sent, etc. Three days for an engine change was well beyond the norm and having one of our only three Javelins 'off state' could have left us poorly equipped to meet an aerial threat from the Indons.

"As things turned out, our Javelins never fired a shot or missile in anger. This was fortunate for all concerned, especially those of us on 60 Squadron. For whatever reason, and although we took pride in completing a 'quick turnround' during conventional servicing after a sortie, we had never practised an operational re-arming, either of guns or missiles. The next time we did so would be the first."

WEAPONS – THE 'PLUMBER'

The business end of the Javelin was of course, its armament, 30mm cannons on all marks, and Firestreak air-to-air missiles on the later marks. **Alan Mudge** had tours at Leuchars and Tengah and found that the weapons side of Javelin engineering support was not without its challenges.

"I was posted to RAF Leuchars in July 1964 to serve on station flight, handling everything from Chipmunks to Britannias, and taking care of first-line servicing for the four Javelin T.3s of the Instrument Rating Flight (IRF). SNCO i/c was Flt Sgt 'Kit' Carson, a genial Scot, who sported a most wonderful handlebar moustache, and was a good boss who looked after his troops. I soon realised that I was really enjoying flight-line work and this first contact with the Gloster Javelin. Having already served a full tour at RAF Tengah, I was keen to get back there as soon as possible, so when volunteers were sought to join 64 Squadron, operating the Javelin 9R at Tengah as 'reforce' personnel during the confrontation with Indonesia, my name was soon on the list. In December 1964 I turbo-propped out to the Far East, serving on the squadron until April 1965 then returned to Leuchars once more.

"During my time away, 228 OCU had been reformed at Leuchars, absorbing the four IRF T.3s. The object was to convert pilots and navigators, direct from flying training, plus a few re-treads from the recently disbanded Valiant squadrons, to the Javelin. They were then posted to the Far East onto either 60 or 64 Squadron. With my Far East experience on the Javelin, I was

Changing the port outer 30mm Aden cannon on a 64 Squadron Mk.9 at Tengah in 1967. Cpls Terry O'Neil and Tony Ash on top, JT Pete Waltuch under the wing. (Alan Mudge)

posted onto the strength of the OCU. All OCUs carry reserve squadron status so we were 11 (Reserve) Squadron, carrying their black double eagle on the tail. I remained on the OCU until July 1966, then once again returned to 64 Squadron at Tengah, staying with them until June 1967 when the squadron disbanded, completing my final few weeks, until my tour expired, on 60 Squadron. Going back to my early days on this aircraft, one pilot on the IRF whose name I remember, was Flt Lt Inkleman-Webber, known as 'Inky' or 'Inclement Weather' but addressed as 'Sir'!

"Boss of the OCU was Sqn Ldr George H Beaton, who claimed the only bare metal finish Javelin as his own, by having his initials 'GHB' painted on the tailplane. Two staff pilots who also come to mind are Flt Lt Geoff Roberts and, a Rhodesian, Flt Lt Peit du Plessis. While I was at Tengah, Geoff Roberts came out from Leuchars to do the instrument rating checks on some of the pilots, so I made sure that I was on his seeing-in crew as we'd had a pretty good pilot/linie relationship at Leuchars. When he noticed who the aircraft marshaller was, a very large grin appeared on his face and we had quite a natter before he headed off to sign in.

"We led quite exciting lives on the flight line, engine bay fires were common enough during start-up to have the full engine bay panel off, instead of the small battle flight panel. Following start-up, one linie would get his head and shoulders into the bay, between two roaring Sapphires, and look for any signs of a fire. If the aircrew saw the second linie heading towards the underside of the aircraft with the fire extinguisher, they developed wings of their own. In the Far East our only body covering was a pair of working shorts, but I don't recall anyone getting burned while carrying out this task. If the aircraft wouldn't start, one linie would stick his head into the engine bay, and welly the cracker boxes with the butt end of his GS (general service) screwdriver to free the contacts. We always ensured the pilot had both hands on the cockpit coaming before doing this, the second linie watching him like a hawk.

"On the OCU, whilst a novice pilot was getting the hang of turning the aircraft on brakes and engines, life could become exciting for the marshaller. One large aircraft bearing down on him, with the nose wheel having a mind of its own, could be quite disconcerting, and if said novice pilot was too hard on the brakes the aircraft would bounce up and down on its nose wheel. Linies often heard an unhappy staff pilot going into fluent Anglo-Saxon mode as he pointed out to the novice the error of his ways.

"Novice and staff pilot prepare for a trip. They're walking around the aircraft doing their pre-flight checks whilst the two linies on starter crew are lurking about waiting. The two aircrew approach the main undercarriage. One linie to his mate, 'That main-wheel tyre is looking a bit worn'. His mate replies, 'Should be OK as long as it doesn't make a heavy landing'. Novice pilot looks somewhat concerned, staff pilot grins and mouths, 'You pair of buggers'.

"On the line I did the armament turnrounds which were relatively straightforward; a few times I was working in the hangar. The Javelin was certainly an armourers' aircraft. Two ejection seats, a pair of bosom (belly) tanks, four 30mm cannon, two or four Firestreak air-to-air guided missiles, and the cartridge-operated missile emergency ejector units, kept us all gainfully employed. When we carried out air-firing practice at Leuchars, ammunition tanks were loaded to full capacity, 180 rounds per gun. There were no targets, the novice pilots simply pointed the aircraft at the North Sea and let rip. This was to give them some idea of the feel of the aircraft when four cannon were blasting away. The armament boss on the OCU was Chf Tech Ted Plusa, formerly of the Polish air force, until Herr Hitler forced him and many other Poles to leave their homeland. He treated every air-firing exercise like a real war, his favourite words during re-arms were 'faster, faster'.

"At Leuchars, a newly-serviced aircraft was started up outside the hangar for its air test. It promptly blew large parts of its starter system back into the hangar, obviously having a bad hair day and not wanting to fly, whilst the ground crews scattered in all directions! In future, following that incident, newly-serviced aircraft were towed to the flight line.

"Fg Off Pete McKellar, who later survived an ejection from a Javelin in Singapore, already had one claim to fame. While going through the OCU, his aircraft's undercarriage, following a number of attempts, would not come down. SOP before attempting a belly landing was to get rid of the bosom tanks. However, it all went pear shaped for him. Instead of pulling the handle to mechanically release the bosom tanks, he pressed the button on top. Result, the ejector units blasted both missiles off their pylons. One disappeared forever into St. Andrews Bay, the other came down on one of the hallowed golf courses. The undercarriage came down, probably shocked by the double blast, and McKellar landed, parking just off the end of the main runway. Off we hurtled with tractor and towbar for a bit of a giggle. However, as we chuntered along at a steady pace down the peri-track,

Exercise Angle Iron June 1966. Re-arming the 30mm cannons on 60 Squadron. (60 Squadron)

Geoff Roberts passed us in his car at a high rate of knots. Arriving at the aircraft he stuffed both aircrew into it and hurtled off again, bummer!

"When we did air firing, particularly at Leuchars, you could always tell when they'd been fired, because the muck that came back over the wing was filthy. All the fumes, dirt and carbon were just blasted straight back over the wing. Our staff pilots were also diverted, from time to time, on exercises where we carried live missiles to do a live shoot from Valley over Cardigan Bay, to keep their hand in. When we had station exercises, as a reserve squadron we were armed up live, just as the co-located Lightnings were.

"The 30mm Aden gun (Armament Development Enfield, where the cannon was manufactured) was developed from the German Mauser MG213C20, a 20mm-calibre five-cylinder revolver cannon. We just increased the size of the gun and the round to 30mm calibre. Workshop servicing of this gun was very precise, especially during assembly. There were many mechanical parts, some of which had specific gauging points; get these wrong and it would fire one round and then foul up. Stoppages during firing did occur for a number of technical reasons. One simple one was that the rounds were not aligned correctly in their links so, using a rubber hammer, we would tap any misaligned rounds into their correct position during the flaking (the correct positioning of the ammunition belt into the ammunition bay to ensure a smooth feed into the gun when firing) of the ammunition into the tanks. A stoppage meant a gun change, which on a good day would take about 20 minutes of hard graft. If there were enough armourers, a stoppage team was organised, thus allowing for maximum manpower on re-arms. The return springs in the gun were so powerful that initial cocking was carried out using 2,300psi air pressure. The cocking lever was operated three times, rotating the cylinder to bring the first round in line with the firing pin.

"Although as I said, you could change a gun in about 20 minutes or so, if you were changing all four, it kept you busy for a while. To fit one, you had a little triangle that sat on top of the Aden gun bay to attach a winch, and then the cable was lowered down, the gun was attached, winched up, slid into position and tightened down. The one thing you had to remember was to put the barrel in first, as it attached to the gun. To take the gun out, you unlocked the barrel and pulled it forward. Then before you fit the gun in, you slid the new barrel into the housing, put the gun in and then connected the barrel. If you forgot to put the barrel in it could be very embarrassing!

"The Firestreak air-to-air missile was a passive infra-red homing fire-and-forget missile, with a field of 20 degrees attack either side of the target. Fired from behind, it homed onto the emissions from the engine(s) of the target aircraft. The warhead, housed in the fore part of the missile, was segmented and shaped like a small barrel. It looked something like a very large hand grenade, and operated in a similar manner, upon detonation exploding into hundreds of steel segments, making the enemy pilot's life rather difficult as his aircraft's turbine blades and other vital parts were re-arranged.

"We had three types of missile. There was a total dummy one, which was mostly made out of wood. Then we had an acquisition round, which had everything bar the explosives and rocket motor in it, but all the gizmos worked to give the pilot training. Finally, we had the live round. The fitting/removal of the Firestreak guided missile was relatively straight forward. The pylons had a winch attachment point to hoist the missile up, although sometimes totally unofficially, it could be lifted up by two armourers while the third closed the hook into the suspension lug. This was not to be recommended if the engineering officer was prowling the flight line. 'Feet didn't touch the ground' comes to mind. When the acquisition or live round was switched on, liquid ammonia was used to keep the working components cool. There was around 15 minutes worth of ammonia per missile, enough for the pilot to acquire, lock on and fire the missile. The ammonia was stored in a metal container known as a bottle, fitted into a fairing and attached to the top of the missile behind the suspension lug; it was held in place by a worm screw. Upon switching on, a valve opened and ammonia flowed into the missile; when switched off the valve would close, or should have done!

"A leaking ammonia bottle could clear the flight line, especially on a windy day. To remove it an armourer clad in full breathing apparatus and

"What's this?", says Flt Lt Jim Adams to JT Kendall and Cpl Foakes, pointing to a Firestreak's nose, 60 Squadron 1962. (60 Squadron)

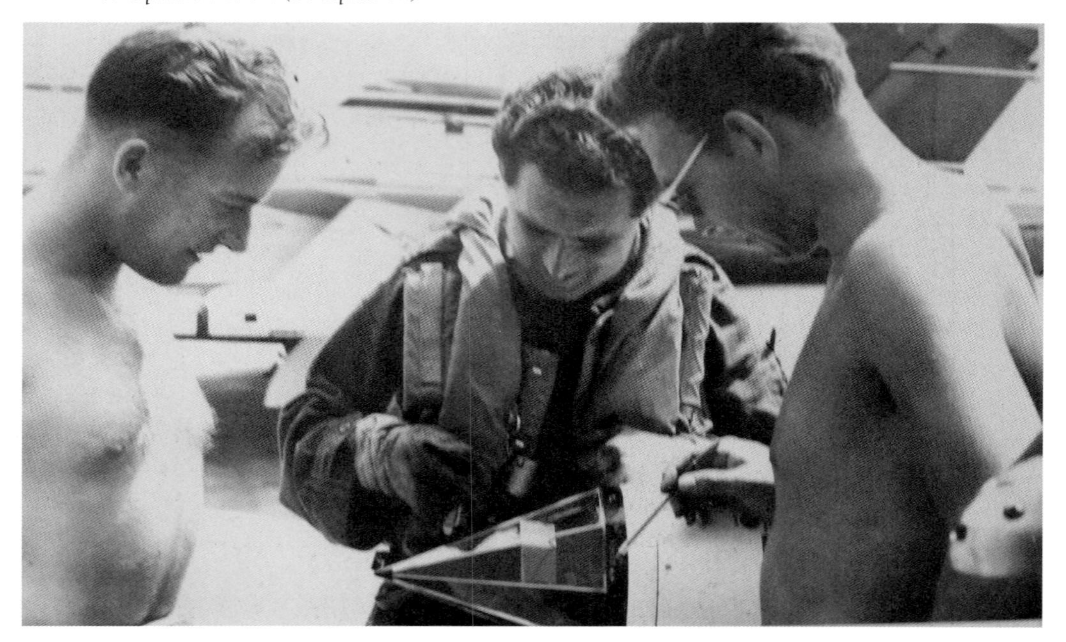

almost shoulder-length protective gloves, trotted out to the aircraft and, using his trusty GS screwdriver, removed the bottle from the missile. He then carried said bottle, holding the leaking valve end away from his body, to the grass area at the back of the pan where at intervals large drums of water were situated. The bottle was placed (sometimes thrown in from a distance) into the drum to safely expend the ammonia into the water. Remember that in the Far East he'd only be wearing working shorts. Sometimes, especially in a hot climate, the face mask of the breathing apparatus would steam up making the job even more difficult. A leaking bottle was easy to spot as, when the aircraft taxied in, a white cloud of vapourising ammonia could be seen around the missile. A good whiff of ammonia definitely cleared the tubes and brought a tear to the eye.

"In the Far East heat and humidity affected the missiles. The glass nose was manufactured in triangular segments, and these were glued together forming a pointed glass head, then a protective red, plastic 'noddy' cap was fitted over the head whilst on the ground; however, that did not stop the bonding glue from coming unstuck. One of the missile checks on 'before flight', 'turnround' and 'after flight' inspections was to check the length of any bonding that had come apart; this showed up as a white streak between the segments. If it reached a certain length the missile had to be changed because eventually the segments would separate. Sometimes, chiefies wearing right-angled berets appeared from the air-conditioned comfort of the missile site to see that we treated their pride and joy in the correct manner. A whiter shade of pale, they sweated buckets in their tailored KD (khaki drill) uniforms as they watched us armourer linies, in oily working shorts, carrying out turnround servicing on the missiles. The noise and activity on the flight line soon sent them scurrying back to where their life was more civilised.

"On the line in Singapore we just had a pair of shorts, our normal shoes and our Far East socks rolled down. The only thing we had on top of that was a pair of ear defenders, needed when you were stuck up between two roaring engines in the engine bay with a torch, looking for potential fires. The same dress was used during night flying as, being on the equator, the nights were also very warm and humid. We had no protective fireproof clothing, and no high-vis jackets. During the monsoon season it was warm rain so no worries. My biggest nightmare was one of the torch wands failing during night marshalling. The spot for the nose wheel was clearly marked, with not a lot of space between adjacent aircraft's wingtips. Our pilots taxied quite fast and could turn the Jav on a sixpence using brakes and engines when they saw the marshaller's wands. Orange sodium lights on the pan didn't help as they cast weird shadows onto the concrete. I loved flight-line work – a few years later when promotion put me into the hangar on second-line servicing, for a while I was not happy.

"During the confrontation with Indonesia both 60 and 64 Squadron carried out Battle Flight duties. A pair of aircraft were kept at readiness with another pair on standby, as we had a fair number of scrambles during this period. The Battle Flight aircraft cannon were loaded with high explosive ammunition, and were cocked into the gun. The first five rounds were ball ammunition (solid steel heads). In the tropical heat parked out on the ORP high-explosive rounds had the potential to 'cook off" (involuntarily explode) in the gun with disastrous consequences. Each round contained about eight ounces of high explosive, one round exploding could cause sympathetic explosion of other rounds in the belt of ammunition. This could result in the wings falling off. Oh dear.

"I had a ground crew air experience flight while on 64 Squadron, sitting on my own handiwork so, no worries mate. I can still clearly remember hurtling down the runway with the second aircraft a few feet away on my left. It was a wonderful hour flying in a four-ship formation around the skies of Singapore and South Malaya. However, I would never become a pilot. Many years later, a Harrier pilot mate, an A1 QFI, decided he'd teach me the rudiments of flying – not in a Harrier I hasten to add – but in a Cessna 172. It was found that I had no perception of the horizon, vitally important for both military and civilian pilots.

"Nos. 60 and 64 were the two largest fighter/night-fighter squadrons operating in both FEAF and the RAF. Operations in the Far East were the swan song for the Gloster Javelin. Both squadrons were disbanded at Tengah, the aircraft flown to RAF Seletar and reduced to scrap. I enjoyed my three years working on the Javelin, the majority of which was as a linie, but all good things must come to an end."

AIR ELECTRICIAN – THE 'LECKY'

Having completed his trade training at 4 School of Technical Training (SofTT) at St. Athan in South Wales, **Ken Brereton** was posted to 29 Squadron at Leuchars. This would be his only tour on Javelins, although he came across them again when posted to the FEAF in 1963.

"I went to Leuchars as a boy entrant air electrician in July 1960, promoted to SAC in February 1961, and posted to 29 Squadron for approximately three years. We were operating FAW.6s, and the rumour at the time was that we were going to re-equip with FAW.9s, and after about six months we started to receive them.

"With the Mk.6s the worst job was changing the AI 22 radar inverter. They were in the forward part of the equipment/engine start and gearbox bay, an evil place in the belly. Another awkward job in the same bay was changing, or adjusting the generator control units (GCUs) when tackling a generator

Sqn Ldr Cameron's crash, Fg Off Cooper's catastrophe. The boss was not amused when his new jet XH721 MHM got scratched, 12 January 1966. Recovery underway. (60 Squadron)

fault, and then balancing the generators. The GCUs were very small relay boxes, so it wasn't the easiest of jobs to adjust the pull-in and drop-out voltages of the relays in the confined space. Add to this the noise level with two Sapphires thundering away and the noise of the gearbox, with no ear defenders, and you were deafened and roasted at the same time trying to set them up. The other thing was the weight of the engine-starter cartridges (bombs, as we used to call them). They were heavy lumps of metal, two for each engine. I was an electrician, but on operational turnrounds everyone mucked in.

"The rest of it, at that time, was just fun. We were just lads; the senior NCOs were only aged probably about 28-30. Fortunately, we had a good crowd of guys who really looked after us laddies and helped us to get on and learn.

"One of the awkward jobs on an engine change was disconnecting the electrical plugs. Unfortunately on one engine roll (the engines were rolled out backwards), the engine corporal in charge wouldn't listen to anyone when told that they hadn't been disconnected. He hooked up the tow bar to the rear of the engine and told the team to pull the engine out onto the stand. We tried to tell him that the engine wasn't unplugged, but he wouldn't listen. He told the team of four guys to extract the engine. As the engine came out, all the wires were pulled out of the plugs.

"We had occasions where someone would inadvertently release the ventral tanks in the hangar, so there was a splat and the hangar floor was full of fuel. I also recall one time when someone slipped and pulled an ejection seat face blind; fortunately the pins were in the back of the seat so no harm done, just an underwear change. The Mk.9 had an AVPIN engine-start system which was notorious for over-fuelling, causing either the start turbine to over-speed and shed turbine blades via the exhaust pipe, or catch fire.

"Whilst on a NATO exercise in Norway, during an operational turnround, an adjacent aircraft was scrambled. The first engine lit OK, but the start system on the second over-fuelled due to repeated attempts to start it. When the AVPIN finally ignited, the starter turbine over-sped and exploded sending turbine blades down the exhaust pipe. The pilot and navigator leaped out of the cockpit, ran down the wing, and off into the bundu. Everyone else from the other two aircraft were running and scattering. This thing was loaded, full of fuel and with live ammunition. A heroic armourer came running up the pan with a fire extinguisher; I don't think he realised you couldn't put AVPIN out.

"The aircraft were usually parked with the jet-pipes over long grass. During a before-flight inspection, an engine fitter who had gone up a jet-pipe to inspect the turbine blades, was heard to squawk like a strangled chicken. He emerged from the jet-pipe being chased by a large toad, resulting in his getting caught on the jet-pipe temperature thermocouples as he vacated – ouch! This caused a large amount of p*** taking.

"We were on a TACEVAL at Leuchars at about 2300 hours on a winter's night. The engines were usually started together but on this occasion, as often happened, one engine wouldn't start. They went through all the cartridges in the breech except that, on the last time they tried, the bottom of the starter cartridge box blew out; it was like a flame thrower. Believe it or not, the aircraft was repaired within 24 hours and flying again. That was caused by the AVPIN accumulating in the starter box, which was separated for the two breeches and the AVPIN had leaked into it. They were that hot that it just ignited and blew through the aircraft skin.

"We went to do a QRA down at Wattisham two or three times. The first QRA hangar we were located in was a large black tin shed (a Bellman hangar). We did QRA right out of the hangar, starting the Javelin up inside it. One night the lights went out as the fuses had blown, so some brave guy went in and put a six-inch nail across the fuse; that was a winter QRA. The summer time QRAs were done from the ORP at the end of the runway. The aircrew were changed every hour, the ground crew were changed whenever, or perhaps I should say, rather infrequently. We had a runway caravan which was just a wooden box with no heating. We had nothing except the NAAFI wagon in the morning. We did two weeks QRA at a time; everyone would rotate, so the aircrew took a couple of Javelins down to Wattisham and we drove down. They were scrambled quite often, but most of the time it was boring. It was the same when we went to Geilenkirchen, bored out of our tree except for daytime flying. We went there for six weeks to reinforce 2 TAF, and other deployments were to Sylt with the FAW.6s for air-firing practice. Back at Leuchars there are many other memories, such as our battles with the Dundee Water Guard (HM Customs and Excise) over smuggling fags, etc. on return from overseas.

"One of the stupid jokes with the Javelins was that the radar could sterilise you for a 'wee while' if you stood in front of it. Believe it or not, we had some idiots who stood in front of the aircraft when the radar boys were testing the radar. Another thing, which was equally daft, was that we spent Christmas and New Year in Geilenkirchen, where every squadron had its own bar. However, being visitors, we didn't have the same facilities – me and a couple of mates were in the NAAFI and 'borrowed' the jukebox. We actually got it onto the path outside before the manageress came out screaming at us; we had to put it back. However, there was a lad playing the piano in the bar, so we offered him free beer if he would play the thing for us in our hut. So that's what we did, we pinched the piano instead. One more adjunct to that is, the routine on the Christmas Day dinner, was that the officers served the airmen in the mess. Well, we'd all had lunch and were quite happily going back to the billet, where the duty fire crew were also going, so we hitched a lift on the fire engine. It looked a bit like a bunch of grapes, with all of us hanging off the ladders, and whatever else we could hang on to. The station commander drove up, wound down his window, lifted his hat, wished us a 'Merry Christmas' and went on his way.

"I enjoyed my time on 29 Squadron, I was a young man and we were getting to places we'd never been to before. The guys I worked with, and the NCOs, were a good squad and that made it. I was posted to 209 Squadron RAF Labuan, Sarawak in 1965. Javelin Mk.9Rs were operated by 60 and 64 Squadrons from Tengah. These were the remnants of 29 Squadron's aircraft and other FAW.9Rs which had had the in-flight refuelling probes fitted. We used to reckon there was a burned-out wreck on every airfield in North Borneo, I believe there was one at Kuching. We never had one at Labuan, but there was always an unserviceable one. FEAF made it a rule of 'one start', and if it didn't start you could not try again until you found the reason why it had not started the first time."

There was indeed a Javelin wreck at Kuching. As mentioned by Dave Curnock (page 130) FAW.9 XH874 H of 64 Squadron was badly damaged by fire there on 4 August 1964, declared beyond repair.

AIR RADAR – THE 'FAIRY'

Arguably the heart of the Javelin's systems, the AI 17 or AI 22 radar is the subject of much discussion by both air and ground crew. **John Augoustis** was another airman whose first tour out of training was to a Javelin squadron, in his case, No.72 at Leconfield in Yorkshire.

"I was a boy entrant. I joined up in 1959 and did my trade training on the AI 17 air radar at Cosford – including a week of endless wave guide films.

We had a nice comfortable seat to sleep in any way!

"I was posted to Leconfield but the airfield had no aircraft when I arrived. 72 Squadron was at Church Fenton as they were extending and resurfacing the runway at Leconfield; it was some time before they came back. While they were away, one of them crashed on the airfield because they'd left the crash barrier up at the wrong end of the runway. He came in and hit the barrier; the aircraft was written off anyway."

This happened on 2 March 1961 when XA752 F flown by Flt Lt Want and his navigator Flt Lt J Mitchell, hit the erroneously raised arrester barrier at Leeming, causing the undercarriage to partially collapse. **John Augoustis** again:

"Initially I worked in the air radar bay for some months. Not only did you service the radar, but I did wireless stuff and SARBE beacons as well. There was a SARBE cage in the workshop so that its signals didn't get out and set the air-sea rescue helicopters panicking, as they were just outside. Some of the black boxes wouldn't work in every aircraft and were labelled accordingly.

"I spent really only a few weeks on the squadron, on the line. Enough time to work on the aircraft and find out things about them. You could always tell a Javelin man by his black knees, where he had to check inside the starter panel for fire during a start-up. Fires didn't happen that often, they had it more on the Hunters (92 Squadron). You could always tell a Hunter man, because his beret had burn marks on it where he'd used it to put the starter exhaust fire out!

"Engine runs were conducted on the far side of the airfield at Leconfield. The aircraft were towed to the run-up area, and usually an engine fitter carried out the engine runs. On one night in particular, the fitter did the engine runs and then decided to taxi the aircraft. Unfortunately, this was observed by the control tower, which resulted in disciplinary action being taken on the fitter concerned. Then we had one chap who jumped off the wing and broke an ankle, he'd forgotten it was a concrete pan as previously he had worked where it was all sand.

"Sometimes the radar went on for a long time before anything needed doing to it, at other times it was just one or two sorties. You couldn't say it was really reliable, it was just the components they used in it, valves and so on. There was a complaint about a radar not being too good, so one of the radar mechanics went up on an air test, taking off from Leconfield and flying over Liverpool. He looked at the radar in the first five or ten minutes of flight and couldn't find anything wrong with it, so enjoyed the view. He checked it again and still couldn't find anything wrong with it – one of those 'gremlin' things they showed us in the training films. The Javelin didn't seem to me to go very fast on take-off, compared to Hunters or

Lightnings anyway. It seemed to trundle down the runway for quite some time before anything happened.

"I left the air force in 1970. I was a corporal then, it was a hard climb in those days; I was qualified for sergeant but didn't do the time."

Bryan 'Taff' Elliott looked after the AI 17 on 29 Squadron at both Leuchars and Akrotiri.

"I loved working on Javelins. They were an aircraft with bags of character, and those Sapphires made a lovely noise, the resonance when running up. It was not without its frustrations mind. One which easily springs to mind was the state of the Dzus fasteners on the panels either side of the nose, which we radar bods had to remove on each before-flight (B/F) to check the pressures on the AI 17 modulator and transmitter. Trying to get them done up was a real pain. I got so hacked off one day that I 'snagged' them in the F700. Boy-oh-boy did the wrath of the chief 'rigger' descend upon me! I never did that again, but I'd proved a point.

"I first worked on Javelins when I joined 29 Squadron at Leuchars in 1960. We were flying the Mk.9 having just converted from Mk.6s. The main difference as far as us 'fairies' were concerned was that the search radar reverted from AI 22 to AI 17. AI 22 was a bit of a pig to keep serviceable, although the concept was good. There was a large search scanner and, when you locked onto a target, the information was passed to a small track scanner which then followed the target, whilst the main scanner went back to searching for other targets. Air Radar Servicing Flight (ARSF) sweated blood trying to get the system to work, but they did manage to get one installed and working, however it came to a sorry end. It was installed in one of a pair flying over the North Sea just off the Yorkshire coast when they collided, in that the nose of one hit the tail of the other losing the radome and all inside [see Chapter Three]. There are no prizes for guessing which aircraft had the working radar installed! We were told that the pilot pointed it out to sea and ejected, whereupon the aircraft went

Bryan Elliott learning all about the AI 17 scanner at Yatesbury. (Doug Mansfield)

tearing about the sky doing things that a Javelin is not supposed to do. It then straightened up and flew between the pilot and navigator hanging in their 'chutes, before crashing just inland from the coast near Scarborough.

"Carrying out servicing on one of the black boxes that the Javelin carried was a bit of a trial for me. The IFF 10 was located in the top of the port-engine nacelle, and that's where it was lifted out from. However, all the connecting cables were on the underside and had to be accessed from another panel at the bottom of the nacelle. This panel was not that large, and this was my problem. I am somewhat broad of shoulder, which came in handy when playing in the front row, but not for getting into small panels to access the IFF connectors. It was painful and I lost much skin. I eventually came to an arrangement with the rest of the guys in the section, that if they would do my IFF changes, I would do all the scanner changes. For some reason they didn't like scanner changes, but I did. It took some hours to complete but it kept me out of harm's way and I could work at a steady pace.

"I always liked running the AI 17 upon the completion of any servicing, as it gave me a chance to see how it worked so I used to look for targets to track. One morning at Leuchars, around 3 o'clock, I was running an AI 17 that I'd been working on when I started to get interference on the search display; something we called 'spoking'. This could happen if two AI 17 radars were being run in the vicinity of each other, but I had the only radar running at that time. The interference kept coming and going, when suddenly I realised what it was. Every spring a Russian factory ship parked itself some three miles off the end of Leuchars' runway and stayed there until autumn. For a factory ship, they had a phenomenal array of aerials, and I reckoned that they were sweeping the frequency band to try and gauge the frequency that the AI 17 was transmitting on. I immediately shut down the transmitter and reported the situation.

"I was a member of the Leuchars Mountain Rescue Team when we had a sombre 'call out' one afternoon. The squadron had a singleton airborne carrying out an air test. The time came and went for his return and eventually we got to the point where we knew that his fuel would now have been spent; so we were ringing other stations to see if he had diverted for some reason or other. Naturally, word of his being missing went around the station like wildfire. Then the Tannoy broadcast a message asking for all mountain rescue personnel to report to the section – we all guessed why. It was the quickest I've ever experienced the team moving. From the Tannoy call to the trucks pulling out of the yard, no more than 15 minutes had passed. We were heading for the Moorfoot Hills south of Edinburgh. It was a fast run and going through Edinburgh we had a police escort. We went down Princes Street in the rush hour and hardly dropped below 60 mph, and that included two Bedford RLs in the convoy that had been 'de-governed'. Apparently, the Javelin had been doing a series of dives and the pilot had struck a hill at 1,800 feet. We parked up as near as we could to where we thought the aircraft had come down and went straight out onto the hill. We found the crash scene around midnight and started to recover the bodies; something that has lived with me ever since."

Flt Lt Victor Hill and Flt Lt John Knight were lost on 21 November 1960 when their FAW.6 XA825 K flew into Bowbeat Hill (elevation 2,054 feet) north-east of Peebles while descending in cloud, probably following an engine malfunction. Both crewmen ejected at high speed and low altitude but did not survive. **Bryan Elliott** continues:

"There was another near thing when I was on the squadron in the early 60s. This was in the days before QRA and was called Exercise Halyard. We were detached to Wattisham and had two aircraft at immediate readiness with the crew strapped into one. The aircrew changed every one hour and twenty minutes, and the ground crews around every two and a half hours. The replacement crew had to be strapped in and on line, prepared for a quick getaway, before the other crew was released. As it was winter, we had the two 'state' Javelins in a small hangar not far off the south end of the runway. We had just changed crews and I was clearing the access ladder away, when there was a panic shout from my associate. I spun around and was faced with a frightening scene; after settling himself into the cockpit, the pilot had reached above his head with both hands to slide the hood forward. Unfortunately, he had caught hold of the ejection seat face blind handle – it was pulled out to just above his eyes so he could see it! Luckily my associate was a 'plumber' (armourer) who ran to the pull-down step behind the wing trailing edge, got up to the cockpit in double quick time and stored the face blind safely. I dread to think what would have happened if my partner had not been so vigilant. As it was, he said that by the time he got to the cockpit the pilot was sweating profusely!

"In that era we used to have an annual exercise which lasted around two weeks when we were put on a war footing, all the available aircraft on standby, ground crews sleeping in the hangar etc. During Exercise Yeoman in the spring of 1961, our sister Javelin squadron at Leuchars (151 Squadron) were on state. Being spring, the grass on the airfield was growing well, and the contractors were out with their tractors towing triple-ganged mowers. Unfortunately, one of the drivers came down the rear of 151's aircraft and cut all the tele-brief 'phone lines. This was not noticed until a Canberra wandered across the airfield and declared Leuchars 'out of the war!' I think it was after this incident that they started playing music on the tele-brief lines to prove their integrity.

"I have never forgotten my time on Javelins. I worked on Lightnings after that, but I never had the close affinity with them that I had with the Javelin."

Doug Mansfield was also a 'fairy' on 72 Squadron, and like John Augoustis, he tended to spend a lot of his time on the line rather than in the air radar workshop.

> "Although I trained to work on the AI 17, I didn't have much to do with them. I was posted to a second-line shop and only had 'hands-on' experience after I'd retrained for AI 23 in Lightnings. Javelins would occasionally be part of duty crew activity, usually just marshalling in and out. Once, I had to change the pilot's radio lead by hanging over a running engine intake – scary to say the least!
>
> "I saw the first of two Javelins land with their port wheels locked up due to malfunctioning 'D' doors. I was up on a charge at the time, and was being torn off a strip by the CO, when I saw it coming into land via a window behind his desk. I think I just said 'Oh ****!' and pointed, to which he said, 'charge dismissed' and we all ran outside to see the 'plane slide gracefully down the runway resting on its Firestreak missiles. The story goes that when the pilot returned to his crewroom, some wag asked him if he needed clean underwear. At about 10 p.m. that same evening, the same thing happened to the wag pilot, but he didn't manage to keep the 'plane on the runway and it buried itself in the soft grass off the strip. We didn't get it out until the following day, and I believe all Javelins were grounded until modifications had been carried out.
>
> "There was an incident when a young 'erk' was going up for a joy ride and a fire started in one engine as the 'plane taxied out. Before abandoning the aircraft himself, the pilot told the erk to get out! But he couldn't get his seat belt undone, and the pilot had to clamber back up onto the wing and help him out. After that, no-one was allowed joy flights anymore."

Bill Ragg was another air radar man, working on Javelins at Middleton St. George.

> "I was on 33 Squadron with the Javelin Mk.7 and 9 as an SAC air radar mechanic. Compared to the nightmare Lightning (I also worked on Hunters), it was pleasant enough to work on for the air radar trades, although the AI 17 scanner looked like it had been made by the village blacksmith on an off day. The only problem was getting up to the FIS 2 kit which was perched atop the fin; FIS stood for fighter identification system. It was only ever fitted to the Javelin to prevent 'blue on blue' incidents at night and in bad weather. It never seemed to work and was little used. The receiver was on top of the tail and you needed a cherry picker to access it, so it was not a popular servicing job.
>
> "Centre-line closure was also a feature of the engine in the Javelin. A trick of the 33 Squadron engine fitters at Middleton St. George was to ground-run the engines just when the film was starting in the cinema. The

tin roof used to resonate in tune with the rumble and render the film almost inaudible. I left Middleton St. George to go on my fitter's course at Yatesbury. When I returned, 33 was no more. The squadron had gone to Germany and been renumbered."

GROUND PHOTOGRAPHER – THE 'PHOTOG'

Although not an aircraft trade, the ground photographer's role on a squadron included the loading, unloading and processing of cameras fitted to the Javelin to record both gun and missile firings. **Mick Speake** was posted to Cyprus where he supported 29 Squadron and found himself in the middle of a very troubled time on the island when civil war broke out (as also described by Brian Bullock in Chapter Four).

"Back in 1963 I was excited to get the news that I was posted from RAF Lindholme in Yorkshire, to RAF Nicosia, Cyprus. I arrived in September 1963 and initially worked in the ground section near the armoury and general office. The photo section had another smaller stone building located adjacent to the 29 Squadron line, where the processing of the 16mm GGSR (gyro gunsight recorder) and G90 cine camera films took place. The GGSR was mounted on top of the gunsight and recorded via a reflective glass plate mounted on top of the sight. The G90 was mounted in the starboard wing leading edge and was used to record the firing of the missiles, so was rarely used.

"The GGSR films recorded practice air-to-air combat between two aircraft, the aim of which was to get the gunsight circle of graticules ringing the opponent aircraft. Once the films were processed we delivered them to the squadron briefing room, where the aircrew had a cine projector to assess their air combat proficiency. Processing of black and white film has to be

Final 60 Squadron ground crew shot 1968. (60 Squadron)

done in complete darkness, but the roof of the 29 Squadron line photo section dark room was full of holes, so when you looked up in the dark it was like being in a mini planetarium.

"It was the first time that I had worked on aircraft (the squadron had 12 Javelins), and I helped out with the placing of the chocks on the main wheels when the aircraft arrived. Then I would download the GGSR film, replace it with another, run the camera to make sure the film transported and then sign for the turnround in the F700. One day I deeply scratched my back on one of the aerials on the underside of one of the Javelins, much to the amusement of my 'seeing-in' crew mates.

"The Javelin was a big lump of a fighter and was very noisy getting aloft, with its twin reheated engines incinerating the runway as it roared into the big blue skies. One day a Javelin was taxiing out when one of its Firestreak missiles began to smoke. We all ran for cover, but a fearless and obviously deranged armourer, SAC 'Dusty' Miller, ran up to the missile and struck its nose with the wooden handle of a large screwdriver. How this fixed it remains a mystery to me to this day. One of the pilots was a flight sergeant who was quite old compared to the other (commissioned) aircrew. He was a real gentleman and was well liked by the ground crew.

"When the first civil war broke out in December 1963, there was a lot of terrible blood-letting all over Nicosia, and fighting took place between the Greeks and Turks in Ayios Nikolaos (the nearest suburb to RAF Nicosia). Two 29 Squadron personnel who lived there in hirings, were wounded in the crossfire and were casevac'd back to the UK. Other RAF personnel were hastily evacuated from all the surrounding suburbs to the relative safety of the camp. We heard reports of many Cypriot dead lying in the streets, and of whole families being killed in their homes. The NEAF (Near East Air Force) Mountain Rescue Team and sick quarters' ambulances were escorted into Ayios Nikolaos to pick up the dead wherever they could; that must have been a terrible job. One RAF Police Land Rover was shot through the windscreen when it ventured into Ayios Nikolaos, wounding the RAF policeman in the face. We were placed on perimeter guard around the base with Lee-Enfield rifles and live rounds. There were both army and RAF Regiment personnel who got the defence of the base organised very quickly. However, the NAAFI remained open and there were many riotous nights in there.

"By this time, there were just three of us in the photo section, Cpl Jim Moore, LAC Rick Davies and me. Jim would invite us over to his on-base married quarter where we would have a couple of beers and a chat. One evening as we sat on Jim's verandah, two F-86 Sabres with drop tanks buzzed the airfield at very low level, and streaked around again for another beat-up. They then hastily withdrew. I think they were Greek aircraft, but they could have been Turkish.

> "Nicosia itself was known to us young airmen for its bars and restaurants, and we had many a good evening there, sometimes enjoying a kebab atop the Old City walls. Rickety tables lined the pavements, with waiters holding loaded trays aloft scurrying between the traffic to bring delicious food, all washed down with cheap Cypriot Kokinelli red wine or a frosty Keo lager. Our working hours were 0700 to 1300 hours, so a lot of afternoons were spent in the station swimming pool.
>
> "Most personnel were posted to Akrotiri and Episkopi in early 1964, with the mountain rescue team (and me) going to Akrotiri. What a wonderful posting. Here I worked in the ground photo section, so lost touch with 29 Squadron and, in any case, it was much more exciting to watch the Lightnings punching vertical holes in the blue Mediterranean skies. I eventually got a general service medal (GSM) for being in Cyprus during those times, 53 years after the event!"

All these different trades came together on the flight line, and there was a good deal of cross training in B/F, turnround, and after-flight (A/F) servicing. In a high pressure operational situation, there was the operational turnround (OTR), when aircraft taxied in to be refuelled, re-armed and sent on their way again in as short a time as possible. Experienced ground crew ran an OTR in a fashion akin to a Formula One pit crew, with their abilities frequently being tested in exercises.

An example of such tests came for the 60 Squadron and 64 Squadron engineers during Operation Angle Iron in June 1966, which was a test of the readiness of the two Tengah-based Javelin squadrons to provide an effective air defence. In the OTR stakes, it was 60 Squadron who came out on top with an impressive fastest time of eight minutes 55 seconds, with an average of ten minutes. Typical of inter-squadron rivalry was a comment recorded in 60 Squadron's photo album of the time.

> "Sixty provided nearly all of the airborne defence from Tengah. Rumour has it that 64 did manage two aircraft at some stage of the exercise."

NON-ENGINEERING SUPPORT

Apart from the aircraft engineers, there were, of course, many other trades involved in the day-to-day operation of an RAF station that were directly linked to the flying side. Not least of these was air traffic control (ATC) and controller **Piers Gardiner** saw much of the Javelins during his tour at Tengah, including a number of incidents.

> "Late in the Javelin's service life the main gear downlocks were a bit worn. These were large mechanical hooks which kept the main legs locked in the 'down' position. The effect of wear manifested itself during the landing roll, when one main leg would just retract, with the inevitable consequences ... mercifully non-fatal. I remember coming to work in ATC one morning to see a Javelin on

> the grass … during night flying the starboard leg had retracted on landing, the aircraft slewed off the runway at around the midpoint and hit the monsoon drain, causing it to rotate through nearly 180° in a flat turn and it ended up on its belly facing the way it had come. The crew were OK, if shaken. In the last few months it was not unusual to have almost one such incident a fortnight."

This was the very last Javelin to be written-off in RAF service. On 8 February 1968, Flt Lt Keith Fitchew was flying FAW.9 XH961 H on a night sortie with his navigator Flt Lt Holmes. On landing, the aircraft's port brake failed, resulting in it leaving the runway, crossing the grass and as Piers says, hitting a monsoon drain. It did indeed end up facing the other way, with bits of it scattered everywhere, but thankfully the crew were unhurt. Initially, the aircraft was assessed at Cat.3 (repairable), but given the short time left before the squadron was due to disband, it was not worth the effort and it was re-categorised as Cat.5, scrap. **Piers Gardiner** again:

> "On start-up the exhaust vents from the AVPIN starter used to get blocked somehow, so when the starter was fired up there would be a large explosion under the aircraft, which usually also caused the two large ventral slipper tanks to detach and crash onto the ground under the aircraft, with fuel spilling everywhere. This was a similarly frequent event, say every two to three weeks. I recall being told of one airframe which had been damaged following a down-lock failure. Following some weeks in the hangar being restored, it was pulled onto the line for an air test. On start-up, the bottom exploded! Reportedly the engineering chief tech burst into tears, although that may not be true.
>
> "After 64 Squadron had disbanded, its aircraft were towed away to F dispersal (below and in front of the officers' mess). From time to time, they would be exchanged for one of 60 Squadron's aircraft if they were in better condition, or needed less maintenance effort – obviously a quick paint job to ensure the correct squadron markings! At the end 60 Squadron just managed a diamond-nine flypast on disbandment. They were worrying about whether they could actually put up nine for their farewell flypast; they did actually manage it by using the 'T-birds' (T.3s). The aircraft were then broken up for scrap metal by local labourers using pick-axes and sledgehammers … in full view of the officers' mess, not a pretty sight. Mike Miller was the squadron CO at the time (with a three-character marking on his aircraft – MHM). Afterwards, he drove back to the UK from Singapore with his family in a Land Rover!"

When Piers completed his tour at Tengah, he was posted back to the UK to take up a post on Eastern Radar, at Watton in Norfolk. After finishing his long career with a tour at Port Stanley in the Falkland Islands, he retired from the service in 1994.

CHAPTER SIX

END OF THE LINE – SINGAPORE AND BOSCOMBE DOWN

THE BOYS

Wg Cdr Peter Day
Pilot. Trained 4 FTS Valley, Gnat. 228 OCU Leuchars. 60 Squadron Javelin Tengah '66-'68. CFS. RAFC Jet Provost. 'Red Arrows'. Hunter refresher. 6 and 14 Squadrons Jaguar. Jaguar staff officer. Staff College. Hawk refresher. TTTE Cottesmore Tornado. OC 617 Squadron Tornado '85-'88. Air Warfare College instructor.

With further contributions from **Eric Marsh** (Chapters One and Three), **Mel Evans** (Chapter Three) and **Brian Bullock** (Chapter Four).

FAR EAST AIR FORCE

Up until the early 1960s, no Javelin squadrons had been permanently stationed outside Europe. At the start of that decade, the air defence of the Federation of Malaysia rested primarily with the ageing Meteor NF.14s of 60 Squadron based at Tengah, Singapore as part of FEAF. The Meteor had long since been usurped in the UK and Germany and was really well past its 'sell-by' date.

60 Squadron had been based in South East Asia since the 1920s. It began wartime operations with Blenheims before having a brief and not very successful period flying the Brewster Buffalo. It then switched back to Blenheim IVs for a time, but in 1943 took up the fighter role once more with Hurricanes, followed by Thunderbolts. Post-war it changed to Spitfires and arrived at Tengah in 1949, later re-equipping with successively, the Vampire, Venom and in October 1959, the Meteor. On 13 July 1961 it began receiving Javelin FAW.9s, the last squadron to re-equip with the type. The Javelins were ferried out from the UK in batches, until the unit had its full establishment of 16 Mk.9s and a single T.3. The last Meteors left the squadron during August and with the exception of a single preserved example, were broken up in Singapore.

THE INDONESIAN CONFRONTATION

In September 1963 Malaysia invoked the Mutual Assistance Treaty, which called for Commonwealth support, in response to Indonesian aggression. The Indonesians opposed the newly-formed Malaysian Federation, made up of Malaya, Sabah (formerly known as British North Borneo), Sarawak and Singapore. The air defence response to the invocation of the treaty fell on the shoulders of 60 Squadron at

60 Squadron aircrew horsing around. (60 Squadron)

Tengah, plus RAAF Sabres based at Butterworth in Malaya. This meant the Javelins were kept very busy protecting a lot of airspace against intrusions by both sea and air, requiring deployments to Butterworth plus forward airfields at Kuching and Labuan in Borneo. Additional air defence back-up came from 20 Squadron Hunters at Tengah, and even on occasion, Meteor F(TT).8s from 1574 Flt at Changi, two of which were armed and stood some QRA duties. In late 1966 some Meteors were detached to Tawau Sabah in Borneo for the same purpose.

To relieve some of the pressure on 60 Squadron, it was decided to establish a second Javelin unit at Tengah, so 64 Squadron ('Firm of Purpose') was relocated from Binbrook in Lincolnshire, with effect from 1 April 1965. This squadron had flown Spitfires from April 1940 until re-equipping with Mustangs in late 1944, followed by Hornets and Meteors. It first received Javelins at Duxford in August 1958, moving to Waterbeach in 1961 and Binbrook in 1962.

Eric Marsh, having completed his first Javelin tour on 46 Squadron, was posted to 60 Squadron right at the start of its Javelin operations in August 1961.

> "After I left 46 Squadron, I went to 60 Squadron in Singapore at the time of the Indonesian Confrontation, where we had the FAW.9. I think it was a nicer and more balanced aeroplane to fly. Certainly you had more power, but of course we had the problems of the centre-line closure of the engines. Basically, the aeroplane sitting on the ground was in very high temperatures, but you got up to altitude very rapidly in a Mk.9 to very low temperatures, -40 or -50 °C even at 35,000 feet; this rapid change shrank the compressor casing onto the blades and of course they didn't like that. We had that a couple of times in Singapore. The first way of curing it was to grind down the blades so that it didn't shrink on to them, but then you lost power. One crew was involved while ferrying a Javelin out to Singapore. On 5 August 1961 his group of aircraft took off from Calcutta heading for Rangoon, and his aircraft had centre-line closure and they had to bail out. The pilot was killed, but the nav was in the jungle for three days before they picked him up with a helicopter.

"On 60 Squadron the day's work started with an 08:00 briefing, then night flying at 18:00 briefing, but you never had the two on the same day. You'd probably do two trips during the day, and when you were on night flying you'd do a couple of trips at night.

"We went to Butterworth in 1962 and if any Indonesian aircraft were coming across we went to have a look-see. We had a flight of Javelins there; subsequently a whole squadron went up there. After that, we sent a flight out to Borneo, probably the end of '63, something like that. Our sorties were usually about one hour 25 minutes, but there were some longer ones later, because they put additional fuel tanks on, but they hadn't done high-temperature take-offs with the extra fuel onboard. They claimed that, on paper, it would take off; so from the end of the runway I blasted off. I just about got airborne with 20 yards to spare, but it was touch and go. Our normal fit was two Firestreaks and two tanks, and it was all low level stuff, tree-top height, because we were looking for incursions. I came back with a bullet through the belly of the aeroplane on one occasion."

Echoing the low level nature of much of the Javelin squadrons' work, was the experience of Sqn Ldr Bob Lockhart of 60 Squadron who, in December 1964, used his reheat to convince a group of around 100 Indonesians surrounding a Gurkha platoon in the jungle, that they were being bombed. Unable to use his guns due to the close proximity of the Gurkhas to the enemy, he made five low passes over the area, each time engaging reheat which was accompanied by a double bang as they lit. The insurgents all disappeared back where they came from, even leaving all their ammunition behind!

Consideration of the possible threats from the Indonesian air force, included their use of Tupolev Tu.16 'Badger' bombers, for which the Javelin was well prepared. However, on the fighter side, although the Indonesians had MiG.15s, MiG.19s and MiG.21s, they also still flew somewhat aged P-51D Mustangs, so some thought needed to be given as to how these aircraft might be dealt with, if encountered in the air. The late **Gerry Shipley** was a 60 Squadron pilot and explained the thinking.

"Low level interceptions were our major commitment and we trained for it day and night. The standard night profile was

Indonesian air force Tu.16 intercepted at 12,000 ft by Flt Lt Baranowski, 60 Squadron 12 September 1965. (60 Squadron)

to have the target (another Javelin) over the sea not above 500 feet, evading and lights out, with the fighter requiring to close up to visual ident range, usually about 200 yards. This was before the development of night vision devices and so was a rather interesting exercise. The Javelin was quite a heavy aircraft for strenuous manoeuvring, but at low level it had enough thrust to make it useful and we thought we would be able to cope well enough with the Indonesian P-51 Mustangs.

"We didn't know (and sadly never had the opportunity to find out), whether our Firestreaks would be able to see the Merlin engine's exhaust. In the UK the AFDS did some trials with a Lightning versus a BBMF Spitfire PR.19 which showed it might work, given a small angle off the direct astern position. Air-to-air firing was a bit complicated, with the four wing-mounted guns being so far apart and harmonised to have a convergence range of about 400 yards. Trying to hit a banner target required very short bursts over a very small range bracket. For air-to-air, it helped to use the inboard Adens rather than the outboard, since they were, naturally, not quite so far apart."

Mel Evans left 23 Squadron to join 60 at Tengah in 1964 for a two-year tour. He left Leuchars on 23 January on FAW.9R XH955 with Fg Off Bill Meads in the back seat. They first routed to El Adem with two tankings en route, and the next day they flew to Muharraq, Bahrain. The 26th was Muharraq – Karachi, and the 27th Karachi – Gan. The 29th saw them into Butterworth, where the aircraft was reconfigured to an operational state with two Firestreaks and loaded guns. On the 30th they finally arrived at Tengah after a total flight time from the UK of 20 and a half hours.

"I was posted to C Flight of 60 Squadron based with the RAAF on their station at Butterworth. We were responsible for the night and all-weather defence of northern Malaysia but initially, we shared the task of defending Borneo with A and B Flights from Tengah. Later, 64 Squadron arrived at Tengah to take over our responsibility for Borneo, but not before Bill and I completed five detachments there. Our first detachment had been to the island of Labuan, where I had the privilege to meet a childhood hero, Ginger Lacey."

60 Squadron FAW.9 XH785 L rounding out at Butterworth. (60 Squadron)

Sqn Ldr James 'Ginger' Lacey DFM and bar was one of the RAF's top-scoring fighter pilots during the Second World War, ending the conflict with a total of 28 confirmed victories plus five probables and a further nine damaged. He flew Hurricanes with 501 Squadron during the Fall of France and the Battle of Britain. By 1944 he was flying Spitfires in Burma where he took command of 17 Squadron, and after the war he flew Vampires from Odiham. When Mel met him he was a fighter controller at Kuching and Labuan, retiring in March 1967. **Mel Evans** continues:

"The remainder of our Borneo experience was from the 'international airport' of Kuching. On arrival in Borneo, we had been briefed on the situation, and told that we were now in a 'war zone' and could fly at whatever height we felt was necessary to accomplish the task. Oh dear! The primary reason for our presence was deterrence by making our presence very obvious, visually and very noisily. Could this get better? The base commanders invited us to make low level attacks against their airfields to exercise their AAA guns by tracking our flight paths after take-off, and again before landing.

"In practice, our specific missions were either low level patrols along the shorelines, beaches and internal border, or as fighter escort to the many transport aircraft dropping supplies to the forts spaced along the border. We were now using an aircraft designed for high altitude operations in the very low level environment. To do this, the equipment of choice included two 230-gallon external tanks, two live Firestreak missiles and two loaded 30mm cannon. The operating range at low level was increased by flying much of the time on one engine. The Javelin's engines were first-generation axial-flow engines that worked most efficiently at 91% of their maximum rpm and at high altitude. We could do nothing about the altitude, but we could improve the rpm situation. Most of the patrols and escort missions would be flown at around 350 knots. At this speed on two, the engines would be out of the 'optimal' rpm range, but operating with one engine completely shut down, the operating engine would be at 91%. The Javelin would reach 400 knots on one engine, and it took 18 seconds to bring the unlit engine to full power. On reaching 300 feet after take-off, one engine would be closed down. To ensure that the fuel in the windmilling engine did not overheat, the engines were swopped every 30 minutes – starting the second before shutting down the first. After I left the Javelin, I sat down and calculated that in my Javelin time of over 1,200 hours I had made around 500 engine relights, without a single failure to relight. I had just one engine failure, due to a mild attack of centre-line closure. The phenomenon of centre-line closure, in which the engine casing would shrink more quickly than the compressor unit it housed, caused catastrophic failure of the compressor unit and scattered blades through the aircraft structure, as detailed earlier.

Remains of 60 Squadron XH785 L after engine explosion and loss of control, 4 April 1966. (60 Squadron)

"To me, it seemed an anomaly that this high altitude interceptor should be fitted with an extremely accurate radio altimeter that had two selectable operating ranges – 0 to 5,000 feet with intervals of 100 feet, or 0 to 500 feet with intervals of 10 feet. It was possible to select 10 feet and the 'traffic light' system on the navigator's panel indicated white when above the target height, green at the selected height, and red when below. The pilot also had the red warning light. Once again, there was a good case for good crew co-operation. We felt duty bound to regularly test the equipment, in case it became necessary to use it to achieve the heights briefed on day one in pursuit of our primary mission.

"The beach patrols were otherwise fairly uneventful, but the border patrols were much more interesting. On your first day in theatre, one of the experienced crews would lead you on a tour of the border and point out prominent features for you (your nav) to mark on your new map. This was quite easy as the existing map of Borneo was basically a blank sheet of white paper from the coastline back, with printed statements to the effect that the whole area was uncharted. Obvious features to add were the numerous individually shaped hills. However, there was a surprise waiting on the first day, in that you took off beneath a 1,000-feet cloud layer and found that all the hill tops were in cloud. During a mission, if at any time the weather conditions were unsuitable, the only options were to turn around (not always possible), or climb above the cloud before returning to the only let-down aid at Kuching to start all over again. One task included in the border patrols was the use of our VHF radio to contact the army personnel manning the numerous fortified positions along the border. While we circled overhead, they would pass a situation report, which the nav would write down and pass to the ground liaison officer after landing. We were their most direct link to the outside world. On more than one occasion, at the end of the report, the army guy would say, 'Oh, by the way, the Indons are firing at you, but don't worry, we have noted their position and we will sort them out tonight'. To my knowledge only one Javelin was actually hit by small-arms fire, and it was able to land safely. In fact, the crew were unaware of the fact until the ground crew made their post-flight inspection. On one sortie, in perfect weather, Bill and I were patrolling the border when something caught my eye. I turned my head round to look towards the tail of the aircraft, and was taken aback by a strange series of dashed lines in the sky behind us. I had started to say, 'what the hell...' when I realised that I was seeing, for the first time, tracer bullets from a twin-barreled anti-aircraft artillery. At this point I should mention that the rules of engagement for this little war allowed the enemy to fire at us, but we were not allowed to fire back. We ducked behind a small hill and discussed our response. Bill had not seen the incident, but we agreed that it was important to obtain an accurate position on this threat to future patrols. I knew the location of the gun because it was on a distinctive knoll. Out of sight, we increased speed and came out from behind the hill at considerable speed pointing directly at the gun position. We hoped that the enemy had time to reflect on the likely effect on his hill from our two 30mm cannon. We broke away just short of the border and left at speed.

"The other main task, escorting the transport aircraft dropping supplies to the forts right on the border, involved some very different challenges. To conserve fuel and give the transport (Hastings, Valetta, Beverley or Argosy) a head start, we would take off after them and build our speed to around 350 knots. The transport would normally be flying at 200 knots or thereabouts. We would fly a pattern, generally in the rear hemisphere of the transport, turning, climbing, descending and weaving to maintain a position from which we could protect the mother. This was fine over the lowlands near Kuching, but not so easy when the flight entered the valleys capped by a blanket of cloud, particularly when the leader realised that we were going down the wrong valley. I'm sure that their tight turn was pretty exciting for those inside, but not as exciting as in our cockpit. I positioned our aircraft high and wide on the one side of the valley, and then we held our breath as we flew the smallest possible radius of turn to miss the other side of the valley, and then set off in pursuit of the transport. On one occasion, the weather was good and we were following a Hastings to a border drop. Bill said, 'they've just crossed the border'. We decided to pull up to 3,000 feet to get a better check, before notifying the captain that we strongly recommended a turn through 180 degrees. The Hastings immediately 'stood on a wing' and reversed its course."

The transport force they were called upon to escort comprised 48 Squadron Hastings, 52 Squadron Valetta, 34 Squadron Beverley and 215 Squadron Argosy. **Mel Evans** again:

"On 15 December 1964, I was tasked to fly XH877 on an escort mission to protect a Valetta supply drop at Jambu. This was quite a long sortie, particularly at Valetta speed. The drop went without incident and we were on our way back, when the Valetta captain asked if I would like to stay with them all the way back to Kuching and do a 'run-in and break'. I knew that the captain had previously flown Brigands and was familiar with the procedure. My concerns were two-fold; did we have enough fuel to stay with the Valetta for the extended period – I was satisfied that we did – and would the Javelin be safe at Valetta speed? I asked what speed he would be able to give me, and he replied that he could make 180 knots. The Javelin pilot's notes recommended 200 knots as a minimum speed until the aircraft was in the landing phase. I interpreted the run-in and break as part of the landing phase, and said that I would give it a go. As we approached Kuching, I began to close in to an echelon position, deploying partial air brake to require more power and therefore better response from the engines. Although I was concentrating on maintaining my formation position, I recognised the terrain passing below as the approach to Kuching's runway. What I had forgotten was Kuching's elevated position. Suddenly, the Valetta's propellers were stirring up dust from the runway. As we passed the control tower, the Valetta 'broke' sharply up and to port. At this point, I remembered the briefing from the RAF operations officer the previous day, instructing all aircraft to cease over-flying the operations area at low level because of the noise. I gently eased up the power, assumed a gentle climb straight ahead and tip-toed away.

"In 1965, 64 Squadron took over responsibility for the detachments to Borneo and we returned to our primary area in northern Malaysia. From our arrival at RAAF Butterworth, C Flight had been responsible for the night defence of the area and providing a QRA aircraft. Living and working in the Malayan climate was very pleasant, but it did provide some challenges for air and ground crew. The main problems were heat, humidity and the power of the sun. There were no shelters for the aircraft, not even for the cockpit areas. The aircraft stood in the sun all day and became too hot to touch. The black seat cushion on the ejector seat became very hot and was painful to sit on when wearing a lightweight flying suit. During the brief period between leaving the air-conditioned crewroom and completing the external checks, it was possible to become saturated with perspiration. Relief was not available until the conditioning system kicked in on take-off. A small team of aviation doctors visited us, and established that we typically lost four pounds in body weight during a normal flight. Most of this was fluid loss that was soon replaced. There was an item of personal equipment in the Javelin that we tried; it was called the air ventilated suit. This one-piece undergarment had multiple fine tubes positioned to allow cool air from the aircraft's conditioning system to blow over the upper torso. Unfortunately, like the main system, it did not work until the aircraft was airborne, by which time the nylon garment was saturated. This proved to be a recipe for instant pneumonia and we quickly gave them up.

"When we arrived on their base, the Australian Sabre Wing greeted us with enthusiasm. They obviously saw these large delta fighters as good targets for their training. We were invited to participate in 'dissimilar type air combat training'. We accepted and, for a while, we put up one or two Javelins against their four-ship formations. It soon became evident that the Javelin could out-climb, and out-turn, the F-86 Sabre at any height. The Javelin had a powerful radar that enabled us to pick up the Sabres well before they could see us visually, and position for an attack from any chosen quarter to use our superior missile system. The invitations to fight suddenly stopped coming.

"On 5 May 1965, I was tasked to fly an air test on XH788. The unusual part of this flight was the lack of ventral tanks and any wing stores. This was a very 'clean' and lightweight Javelin. My brief was to see how high it would go. The take-off was shorter, the climbing angle was noticeably steeper and we were soon passing 40,000 feet. As the climb continued, I was able steadily to increase the climbing speed as we passed 50,000 feet. Up here, the reheat was increasing the engine's thrust by 20% and the reducing indicated airspeed was also reducing the drag. Eventually, when we were doing 0.96 Mach and the airspeed was down to 150 knots, I became aware of a rumbling sound similar to driving on cobble stones. The altimeter indicated 58,000 feet precisely. As I began the turn-about and started a gentle descent, I hoped the Indonesian radar unit in front of us at Medan had noted our height. Medan was the home of one of our main threat types – the MiG.21.

"On 5 November 1966, a small article appeared under the heading, 'Javelin Record'. It read, 'An RAF Javelin has clipped nearly three minutes off an unofficial speed record between Singapore and Butterworth, Malaya, set up only a few days before by a Sabre of the RAAF. On a routine flight from RAF Tengah the Javelin covered the 315 nautical miles to Butterworth in 32 minutes 38 secs, compared with 35 minutes 33.3 seconds taken by the Sabre [flown by Wg Cdr Ross Huggins Glassop DFC and bar, OC 77 Squadron]. The Javelin, from 60 Squadron, was flown by Flt Lt M N Evans, with Flt Lt C G Carter as navigator.' On 4 October 1966, my boss had approached me and said that I was tasked to go to Tengah and that, on the way back, I was to beat the record claimed by the RAAF Sabre Wing. At Tengah, we confirmed with the control tower that the necessary arrangements had been made with the tower at Butterworth before starting engines. After take-off, we completed an orbit to pass over the tower and start the clock. We maintained maximum speed in a shallow climb until Kuala Lumpur, then we began a shallow descent until we passed over the tower at Butterworth to stop the clock. Converting the distance to statute miles and our speed to mph, our average speed was 666.48 mph. I believe that 20 Squadron Hunters tried unsuccessfully to beat the record and that 74 Squadron's Lightnings did not have enough fuel to beat the record. It was eventually beaten when the RAAF received their new Mirage fighters. This had been a closing event to my time in Malaysia and with the Javelin. In just over five-and-a-half years I had flown 75 different Javelin airframes."

The Indonesian Confrontation ended on 11 August 1966 with the signing of the Bangkok Accord. Following the settlement it was decided to reduce the RAF's fighter force in the region, 64 Squadron being disbanded on 15 June 1967, the same month in which 74 Squadron arrived at Tengah with its Lightning F.6s to begin taking over the air defence duties. This period also saw some civil disturbance in Hong Kong and a fighter presence was deemed necessary. Operation Angle Iron I saw four 60 Squadron aircraft deployed to Kai Tak airport between 22 and 30 June, followed by Operation Gas Iron II from 11 July to 15 August. Flight operations there were severely restricted by the mountainous terrain and the small size of the colony.

Five days before 64 Squadron's disbandment day parade, both squadrons came together to produce a magnificent 19 aircraft formation on the occasion of the Queen's Birthday, comprising 17 FAW.9s and two T.3s, routing over the naval base,

10 June 1967, the Queen's birthday. 17 FAW.9s and two T.3s on the run-in to Tengah, ten from 64 Squadron and nine from 60 Squadron. (60 Squadron)

the airfields at Changi and Seletar, and finally over Tengah. The combined available fleet totalled 25 Mk.9s and two T.3s; ten in the flypast were drawn from 60 Squadron and nine from 64. The lead aircraft was flown by OC 60 Squadron Wg Cdr Mike Miller with OC 64 Squadron Wg Cdr Basil de Jongh as his navigator, who was simply "mentioning the odd heading and time". The remaining nine 60 Squadron aircraft comprising 'Markhor Section' (the head of a Markhor appearing on the squadron badge) were crewed by: Sqn Ldrs Don Cameron and Moores, Fg Offs Dave Sumner and Howard 'Gus' Geeve, Flt Lt Dave Bingham and Fg Off 'Jock' Turnbull, Fg Offs Peter Day and Dave Haslam-Eley, Flt Lt Alan Munro and Fg Off Chris Donovan, Flt Lts Sam St. Pierre and Robin Willis-Fleming, Fg Offs Gerald 'Gerry' Barnard and Geoff Clark, Fg Off Dave Binnie and Flt Lt Frank Chandler, Flt Lt Colin Holman and Sqn Ldr Jim Carter.

60 Squadron Mk.9 XH841 D and a pilot very proud of himself after aerobatics. (60 Squadron)

Following the flypast, Colin Holman gave a (very) low level aerobatics display over Tengah. With 64 gone the opportunity was taken for 60 Squadron to retain the best Javelins and, after 2,000 manhours of modification work, 12 of 60's existing fleet were parked for storage and eventual scrapping, with 12 of 64's coming the other way as replacements.

64 Squadron reappeared in May 1968 as a reserve squadron within 228 OCU at Coningsby, flying the Phantom, before disbanding again on 31 January 1991 when all Phantom training ceased. The remaining Javelin squadron was to soldier on for a further year. By this time, some impressive flying hours totals were being racked up by some of the aircrew, and the first man anywhere to reach 2,000 hours on Javelins, navigator Flt Lt Peter 'Dinger' Dell, did so on 20 December 1967 (and later achieved a unique double by being the first to reach 2,000 hours on Phantoms).

Peter Day arrived in Singapore in 1966 to join 60 Squadron, and stayed with it until the end.

> "We shut down 60 Squadron. I effectively did a full tour, but it was a last tour for the squadron, albeit my first. I went straight from Valley on Gnats to Leuchars on Javelins. As you can probably imagine, being with a back-seater was a bit of a culture shock for a 20 year old.

"It was an interesting time in advanced training, although there had been a little bit of ugliness with some postings and appointments. What actually happened was that the top of the course (and there was a fair amount of attrition on the Gnat courses early on), ended up trucking off to mainly Buccaneers (they didn't want many on Lightnings) and the occasional Hunter. What was left at the bottom mainly went off to the V Force. After a few years of this, the V Force were struggling to find any captains. The blokes at the bottom of the Gnat course, even though they'd done single-seat stuff, weren't exactly the sharpest tools in the drawer, and the V Force were saying, 'stop sending us the third-class people; competent, but third class'. There had been a bit of a volte face in the training system and a few people at the top of the class were frogmarched into the V Force. Believe you me, that did not go down well, and therefore it didn't last long. The Gnat had not necessarily been set up to develop V Force pilots. In fact, it was set up with the same instrument flying system as the Buccaneer and the Lightning. A slight attack of common sense there, so what they were doing was developing guys who were going to be, not necessarily single seat, but certainly to have an instrument flying system which they'd seen before. Ooh…marvellous.

"Suddenly they had a bit of a panic as the Indonesians started rattling their krises, and the East Africans their assegis. People were saying 'send in a gunboat', but no-one was going to send Hunters down there. We had Javelins hanging around in Cyprus so there was very obviously a case to rush down to Africa. We had some aircraft in position in the Far East, and there was a great 'shall we send down some more?' Everyone looked at the Javelins, which weren't expected to have a life expectancy of more than a few years, only to discover not necessarily that they were running out of pilots, but that some of them were actually about to retire! You know, not go off and do other things, but actually leave. There was a bit of a panic to find a dozen pilots. I don't know the precise figures, but something like a dozen first-tourist pilots were generated by the OCU. It might have been a few more, but a handful of us went to 60 and 64 Squadrons, and a few bods went to Cyprus. That might put a few things in context, like what the hell were we doing in Scotland?

"The OCU was regenerated, but had only a short life. It was alive and well at Middleton St. George, or had been for some time, with the famous George Beaton in charge, literally. Then there was an 'oh, we shan't need that anymore', so everyone was wandering off to CFS if they were a QFI, or were going to play golf or whatever and then they said 'Quick! We need half a dozen instructor crews in Scotland'. It was really a source of hilarious entertainment one way or another. The instructors really were extraordinarily good value. Ninety per cent of them were old enough to be my father, but a couple of them were in their mid-30s.

"I don't think there were very many crews, I think there were four on my course, and the OCU only did three courses. I ended up there in December '65 and I didn't see daylight for three months because it was a night/all-weather OCU and they meant that most sincerely. When I arrived I was 20 and three months. So there I was, in a moderately bleak place, and the interesting thing was that although in the case of the front-seaters (I don't think there were any re-treads), we all came from Valley. There might have been one guy who came from Meteors, a first-tourist, a very rare animal. They later went back to using Meteors at Strubby for the advanced course, because the Gnat early on went through some pretty serious technical issues.

"I was extraordinarily lucky and managed to get a Gnat course over the summer. I think I was on No.10 but certainly the first handful of courses, say 1 to 6, had desperate technical problems, which was when they were putting guys back. They were still trying to manage a front line that included Javelin, Hunter, Lightning, Buccaneer and the V Force, and they were trying to generate quite a few people.

"When I got to the Javelin I thought it had been in a museum. There weren't any of them in the UK, they were hiding in the Dominions. Nobody, let alone me, had known that there was a bunch of them in Cyprus, and a bunch in the Far East. You knew that there were Hunters in the Middle East, because there was a shooting war going on and you kept your eye on that

XH835 K heads the 60 Squadron line at Tengah. (60 Squadron)

because there might be a job there; but the Javelin wasn't shooting at anything. When they started the OCU at Leuchars the first questions were 'Where the hell is Leuchars? What's this Javelin thing? What's its life expectancy and what sort of a job are we going to get out of this?' – until somebody said all the Javelins were in hot places, and then we didn't feel quite so bad about it!

"The course was not very long because it was compressed. I went out to Tengah in April, so we were rushed through in four months. I did 60 hours, 15 in a T.3 and 45 in an FAW.9. It was my first front-line aeroplane, and the exciting thing was that it had four guns and potentially four missiles. That's quite a lot of clout, but it didn't have four guns and SNEB rocket pods or 60lb rockets like a Hunter, which you just pointed at the ground. We also always had a bloke in the back to carry the bags, this was quite new to me. If I wanted to know where I was I would look over the side, or pull out my map. If I wanted to know what was going on in front in the Hunter, you'd have a radar controller, but in the Javelin you'd have this bloke in the back with the radar. As the famous saying goes if you're in combat, 'kneel on your seat, face backwards and tell me what's coming'.

"The back-seater did have his uses and because the radar was useless, you had to treat your back-seater with care. We were not helped by the fact that the radar had been designed for high altitude, northern hemisphere interception of a moderately big target, i.e. Badger or Bear or similar. Luckily, on the OCU all the radar work we did was against a Javelin. That has to be, just short of a Vulcan, one of the world's easiest targets. But now if you take that to Cyprus or even Africa, where it is going to be almost useless I suspect, or to the Far East where you are going to be looking for the mad major flying his Mustang, at night, low level, in and around the fish traps in 40°C and humidity of around 99.9%, the radar struggles. In fairness, the blokes in the back seat did their very best to use either of its modes. We used an awful lot of pure scan as opposed to lock-on at low level because it would lock on to anything, flying fish, anything. They became very good at what was available to pick up. You might pick up anything on just one sweep; they'd pick up one bleep on one sweep and go from there. Any lock-on work, which could end up on my collimator (I wouldn't call it a head-up display), had to be medium level because we would otherwise get so much clutter from the ground; look-down was hopeless. It was designed for something specific and on the OCU and eventually in the Far East, we managed to use it quite well because it was simple. The guys learnt how to use it, but when you came to use it in anger it was a different matter.

"I had a first-tour nav. Crewing was hysterically funny as we were all sent down in the middle of December, in a coach, to North Luffenham in Rutland to do an aviation medicine course, and to be fitted with high-altitude pressure suits, would you believe? We were all stuffed on the bus by the team of instructors; five navs and five pilots, and told to come back as crews (it was very democratic). Having done the Gnat course, and the Jet Provost course at Church Fenton (which is extraordinarily close to the Tadcaster brewery), I was not a certified drunk but I did enjoy a beer. Being a slightly psychological beast, I worked on the principle that I would put myself in the bar at North Luffenham at whatever time it opened, and see who walked in. If it looked like a navigator I'd offer him a job. It worked very well and I connected up with Dave Ely; it was a nightmare but lovely to work with him.

"So in April '66 I made my way out to 60 Squadron on an Eagle Britannia. I was allowed two suitcases, and I sent my flying equipment via whatever passed for a logistics system in those days. We landed at Paya Lebar, which was a civil airfield in the middle of the country, because we were in a civil aircraft. They opened the door and I stepped into a sauna in the middle of the night. At about one o'clock in the morning and it was 35° C with a humidity of about a hundred per cent. It was a bit of a shock as we'd dug ourselves out of the snow in Leuchars to get an aeroplane out.

"The flying was very interesting. I was Singapore-based and we had effectively two thirds of the squadron (A and B Flights) based at Tengah, with the terrible C Flight up at Butterworth; what a wonderful job. I failed to get on C Flight, but I did get the replacement job there now and again, on the grounds that the odd bloke in C Flight wanted to get down to Singapore, so we'd swap over for a week or so. At Monday lunchtime, we'd pass at FL (flight level) 350 over Kuala Lumpur and wave to each other, with them going south and us going north. It gave our engineers a chance to look over their aeroplanes, and got them out of Butterworth for a week. The role there was northern defence. Butterworth is opposite Medan on the north Sumatran island and Kuala Lumpur is in the middle, so we had a system whereby if push came to shove, depending on an incursion or whatever of mainland Malaysia, Butterworth would send something down or we'd send something up to Kuala Lumpur. Meanwhile, Butterworth would look after the northern half of Malaysia where the threat was all from the Indonesian islands. They were partly worried about the fact that Medan had been known to host an Indonesian bomber now and again, so the potential threat was there. When you look back, that was a very sensible place to have a third of the outfit. Down in Singapore, we had air defence aeroplanes on QRA and we were holding a 24-hour Q seven days a week. Meanwhile, some guys were also covering a contingency in Borneo itself.

"You'd get practice scrambles now and again, that was also a source of great amusement. I was sent off after an airliner one night, which had decided not to fly down the airway on the Malaysian coast because of the cu-nims, (there were always cu-nims), but to fly down the middle of the

Malacca Straits. Wonderful, but that's also the route you'd take if you were getting airborne out of Medan in your retired Soviet bomber and pointing yourself at the centre of Singapore island which is, strangely enough, where the airliner was going to. That didn't look good on radar, so I was sent off after it. We came up behind what was very obviously an airborne Christmas tree, it was clearly not a covert Soviet bomber. We radioed the controller to tell him it was a commercial Christmas tree and came home. Back in 1964, long before I arrived, an Indonesian C-130 had crashed while being investigated by a Javelin. My understanding was that it was 'frightened to death'. I suspect the pilots had a loss of talent at a critical time, having discovered that a Javelin was in the vicinity, and flew into the sea in the Malacca Straits."

C-130B T-1307 of 31 Squadron Indonesian air force crashed into the Straits of Malacca on 3 September 1964 whilst attempting to evade a 60 Squadron Javelin. The five crew members all lost their lives. **Peter Day** continues:

"The Javelins were getting rather long in the tooth, but in reality they were extraordinarily simple. There were a few daft systems, but that was only as a result of the current engineering knowledge when they were designed. For example, who would have an electrically-fired cartridge-activated AVPIN starter motor? Was there any other choice in the matter? The T.3 was equally funny, because you would have to be standing up inside the belly of the beast, taking this 45lb shell canister and screwing it directly into the starter motor (I've done it many times). That was the most sensible system, because it had an extraordinarily large cartridge to directly start up your engine.

"Actually the Javelin was rather nice to handle; it wasn't an enormous beast. I wouldn't go along the line of the controls were 'light and well harmonised', I'm sick of the sound of that, but you didn't have to gorilla it too much because it had a fair amount of control authority. It had pretty big controls because they were designed to work in thin air, so when you were down in thick air there was lots of control authority and lots of bite. It had

60 Squadron Mk.9 XH793 J at Kai Tak, Hong Kong. (60 Squadron)

a mammoth tailplane of course. The only drawback was that it didn't have very much...what's the best way of describing it…travel? If they'd made the whole thing a little bit bigger it would have worked better, but it's a question of how fast do you want to go? You would run out of tailplane at higher speeds, some effects of which were quite exciting.

"If you got it up to around 550 knots it was extremely stable. It would still roll very happily. The problem was, it would fly itself out of its tailplane and, by that I mean you didn't have enough nose-down authority to keep it level. It wasn't going to break itself by going a bit faster. There was nothing that was going to fly off the aeroplane, but you could almost make the thing go supersonic if you took enough things off it. It did that reasonably well, but it preferred Mach number to indicated airspeed. It had a couple of very powerful engines because if you were going to make that beast do 550 knots at low level, you needed a lot of power – and there was. What you mustn't do is use the afterburner, because all you'll do is slow down. It had the most magnificent fuel-control system, along the lines of whatever happens, the priority is the afterburner. This meant that if you selected afterburner at low level, you got it, but at the cost of engine rpm – bizarre. Whereas above about 20,000 feet, it would maintain 100% engine rpm, and there would be enough spare to go to the burners. At low level the burners were used to dump fuel, or burn fuel prior to landing, or to frighten the locals. There was a landing weight issue, so if you were a bit high you could just pop it into burner in the circuit and get rid of some fuel.

"Aside from that, it handled quite well. It had a reasonable roll rate because it had monster ailerons and monster air brakes. You could stop it in the air like nobody's business, so you could do lots of things with it. It had barn door flaps, so it had quite sophisticated aerodynamics on finals. It really flew quite nicely on finals, but you could be quite slow and you'd get an awful lot of drag on the runway with big flaps and speed brakes out, so you could actually stop it aerodynamically. You could hold the nose up and it would wander along going ***'wong, wong, wong'***. Stopping was never a problem; it had socking great Dunlop tyres and it had an awful lot of things going for it.

"In 1966 I flew a dozen air-to-air gunnery cine sorties against a Meteor-towed flag, plus six live gunnery sorties. Then in 1967 I did a couple of cine sorties and six live gunnery, hence the old tug-pilot saying, 'I'm pulling this target not pushing it!' We also did some planned air-to-ground gunnery in 1967 and early 1968 on the Song Song range, but that was far too exciting with cross-harmonised guns. The main issues with operating a Javelin air to ground included the aircraft's performance envelope (angle of dive to avoid ricochet from targets on the beach at the sea's edge, the attack speed for gun harmonisation, and the recovery manoeuvre g available to recover safely from the dive). Then there was gun harmonisation, traditionally 400 to 600 yards cross arcs of fire for line-astern attack after radar interception, or visual tracking. All this on a very old airframe in some pretty hostile entropy. As was said at the time, if you hit the island and survived you'd done well. We rather hoped one gun would jam – our Adens never did – allowing you to snipe with the other one. Firing all four air to ground would just bring you to a halt, better than airbrakes, and they were good. I also fired one Firestreak on 16 November 1966. It flew off the rail and exploded in the proximity of the flare target from a co-operative (it cost beer), but fairly sceptical, Canberra.

"We went through a spate of exciting centre-line closures with the engines. It's also something the Sapphire had on the Victor B.1 because we had the same engines. Strangely enough, because it was an enormous fuselage, (it wasn't packed like a Lightning's), it didn't actually burn anything. You'd know when you got one and you'd just have to shut it down. What happened was that I was 'junior pilot' and as such, it was my duty to go up and do as much air testing as I could, because everyone else was off playing golf. So off I went to do a flight test on a new engine. This had been rolled into the Javelin because the previous one had suffered a centre-line closure. We knew what the potential centre-line closure entropy was, so even a junior pilot wasn't going to do a flight test of a new engine in a cumulonimbus. So I very carefully skirted round everything that needed to be avoided and the new engine performed beautifully, but the other one suffered a centre-line closure! I came back to Butterworth saying 'I like the new one, but sadly the old one's gone the same way', which caused some amusement. The back-seater wanted to know why I hadn't told him about the reason for the air test before the flight, and I said I didn't want to get him too excited.

"It was a wonderful aeroplane, but it did have a couple of issues. Gloster's, God bless them, having designed Meteors amongst other aircraft, never considered things like g limits and rolling g limits, partly because it wasn't in the spec, and partly because they had designed the Javelin to be a night, all-weather, high altitude bomber/interceptor. You would fire your 'Firewood' missile from two or three miles and, if that missed or didn't go bang (as it frequently didn't), you'd rush in to two or three hundred yards and gun it with your Adens. So there was no way you were going to get into a turning fight with anything. Unfortunately, no-one told the former Gnat pilots much about rolling g, or what the rolling g limit of the Javelin was. For instance, the limit was about half maximum aileron deflection which, at more than about 3g, would probably be too much for the aeroplane. So we did break the odd aeroplane and the odd crew in the process, sadly. There wasn't anything about that in the ops manual at all.

"If you're doing what is effectively colonial policing, either over the jungle hills or over the fish traps, or whatever, and turning corners with

64 Squadron FAW.9s XH708 P, XH763 C and XH892 E in April 1967. One month later XH708 was lost in a mid-air collision. (Alan Mudge)

the potential to meet the mad major in his Mustang, the lads are going to pull g, and rolling g is a very interesting animal. It's not fault free. You get fault-free flight nowadays with fly-by-wire, simply because the aeroplane knows what it can do, and it won't let you do any more than that, so you can put the stick in the corner and pull 9g and it will give you whatever it thinks the aeroplane will stand. We didn't have any of that but, in theory, we should have had a graph in our heads telling us that if we were going to have full-stick deflection, then the limit was 2g, half-stick 3g and if you're going to pull 6g, don't waggle the wings about at all. None of this was known – let alone what they did during the trials at Boscombe Down when they were considering whether it was going to be able to catch a Tupolev Tu.16 'Badger' at 40,000 feet.

"Anyway, I stayed with the squadron right to the end and we closed it down. 64 Squadron had been disbanded some while before us, and we inherited their junior pilots, mainly because they had plenty of spare capacity. By then, the majority of them had probably got about 400 hours on the aeroplane and, although they weren't up to being a deputy flight commander, they were good for what we were doing at that time, which was not terribly exciting stuff. At the beginning of 1968, we were down to flight commanders and authorisers only. There was the boss, flight commanders, QFIs, QWIs (qualified weapons instructors) and back-seat leaders; everybody else was a junior pilot or nav. We knew we were going soon, and it was going to be the end of the aeroplane. The Javelins were all going to be flown over to Seletar or somewhere, and be broken up, so we had a couple of months flying around, waving at everybody, which was entertaining. We didn't change the establishment of aeroplanes or crews very much in the last few weeks; I seem to remember that we hung on to about 12 aeroplanes to the end, and we certainly flew a diamond-nine farewell formation right at the end. I think we were about one and a half crews per aeroplane, so we must have hung on to about 16 crews; it was probably a mixture of around seven experienced and nine inexperienced crews. We had a two-month rundown, so everyone was having a good time and really doing whatever flying they were tasked with, knowing that we were going to wrap up at the end of April. I flew 12 times in April.

> "After I left Singapore I went straight to Central Flying School. I thought about going to the Middle East to have a war, and shoot at things, but I didn't do that. I went to CFS on Jet Provosts instead, which was probably the making of me, because I must have been a very 'gash' pilot in the Far East. At least I managed to fly fairly accurately thereafter."

During operations in FEAF, the two Javelin squadrons suffered quite a few accidents (see Appendix Three), and a number of them stand out as worthy of a more detailed description. On 3 December 1962, the dreaded Sapphire centre-line closure struck again. This time 60 Squadron's Mk.9 XH836 O suffered one in its starboard engine, which exploded at 36,000 feet, and the crew were forced to abandon the aircraft while it was in an inverted spin. The navigator, Sqn Ldr Frank Jolliffe, was the first to leave the aircraft, doing so while it was at 32,000 feet. Although he landed safely in the jungle, it was two days before he was found and rescued by helicopter. The pilot was the squadron boss, Wg Cdr Peter Smith, who ejected as the aircraft descended through 22,000 feet; he was picked up very quickly. Neither of them had any lasting injuries. The aircraft came down in the jungle 12 miles south of Mersing, Malaya.

On 10 February 1964, Mk.9 XH747 B of 60 Squadron suffered a structural failure and separation of the fin, causing loss of control and a crash into the sea off Singapore. This was witnessed by **Fred Butcher** in an accompanying Javelin.

> "I was to lead a formation of four Javelins, but one went u/s. We did our practice interceptions and then the usual tail-chase to finish up. Normally as leader, I would have led the chase, but I wanted some practice at following, so I became No.3. It was a beautiful morning and all was going well, smooth and gentle. We were about 17,000 feet in a dive, just starting to pull up. I was about 300 yards behind No.2 when I saw some glittering pieces of metal coming from the base of the fin. I started to tell my nav Paul Rundle, but before I could get the words out, the whole of the fin and tailplane broke away and disappeared under my nose (too close for comfort). There was no transmission from Gordon and Paul [Flt Lt Gordon Sykes and Flt Lt Paul Burns in XH747], so I flew alongside whilst making the Mayday call. We saw them both eject, and were relieved to see the 'chutes open. I circled them down to sea level and saw the dinghies in the water. It was only later that I found out that Paul was virtually unscathed, but Gordon had broken his back on ejection, and would remain paralysed for the rest of his life. Paul would eject again later at Akrotiri while on 29 Squadron [see Chapter Four]. He was so close to the ground that his 'chute did not have time to open and he hit the ground still in his seat. It was a miracle he survived."[7]

Top: Flt Lts Clive Stevens and 'Dinger' Dell in 60 Squadron FAW.9 XH787 G landing at Butterworth after the port leg refused to lower, 5 April 1967. (60 Squadron)

On 8 November 1965 Flt Lt Keith Fitchew and his navigator Flt Lt A Evans were forced to abandon 64 Squadron's XH887 B after it suffered an undercarriage jam during a night flight. They were both safe, but see page 97 for a disastrous consequence.

A mid-air collision on 30 May 1967 claimed the life of a ground crew engine man, Cpl Kenneth Ashbee after his aircraft, XH708 P and fellow 64 Squadron machine XH896 O came together during a formation join-up for a flypast rehearsal. Both aircraft were lost, but the other three crew members survived.

On 11 October 1967, 60 Squadron suffered another aircraft and crew loss. Fg Offs Gerry Barnard and Howard Geeve were killed, apparently during an attempted low level roll. The aircraft, XH788 E, was heavy with a full fuel load and this appeared to lead to a failure of the wing main spar and the aircraft broke up.

The height of the Javelin's tail meant that the ejection seats gave the crew a particularly powerful punch-out in order to ensure the height required to clear the tail. This almost always led to back injuries. As an example, there was a successful ejection from 60 Squadron's XH785 L shortly after take-off, following an engine explosion at 1,000 feet due to compressor blade root-end failure which caused the loss of hydraulic controls. The aircraft rolled inverted and dived into the jungle five miles north-west of Tengah. The pilot was Flt Lt Ted Rawcliffe who received a compound fracture of the 12th vertebrae but recovered normally. His navigator was Flt Lt Al Vasloo who similarly suffered a compound fracture of the 8th vertebrae, and a cracked coccyx. He too recovered normally, but was banned from ejection seats for six months, leading him to say, 'I just grit my teeth and think of beer'. The

7. www.ejection-history.org.uk

The final Javelin write-off, FAW.9 XH961 H. Keith Fitchew, no brakes, crossed the grass, leapt a monsoon drain, ended up facing the other way with bits everywhere, 8 February 1968. (60 Squadron)

Martin-Baker seat variant fitted to all production Javelins was the Mk.3. This was fitted with an ejection gun that provided an exit rate of 80 feet per second, thanks to one primary cartridge and two, later four, secondary cartridges, hence the preponderance of back issues on ejection.

The end came for Javelin flying in RAF service on 30 April 1968, with 60 Squadron formally disbanding the next day after 52 years of almost unbroken service, most of it in India and the Far East. The flying task had been completed by Easter, but not without some very impressive flying totals, including having all ten remaining Javelins airborne simultaneously on two separate occasions during April. On 25 April, the squadron provided a dawn flypast over the ANZAC memorial at Kranji, with seven aircraft led by Sqn Ldr Jim Carter (OC A Flight) with Flt Lt 'Dicky' Derbyshire in the back seat. The formation flew over in vic formation before executing a steep climb and a 'Prince of Wales Feathers' break. On Friday 26 April, Wg Cdr Mike Miller with navigator Sqn Ldr Geoff O'Brien (OC B Flight) led a diamond-nine formation over the principal military bases in Singapore as a final salute. The weather was abysmal, but all the points were overflown on the estimated times. The disbandment parade was held on 30 April at 18:30 hours, and again was accompanied by a diamond-nine formation, this time led by Jim Carter and Dicky Derbyshire. The finale came at dusk over the ceremonial parade, with a night formation flypast by a box of four Javelins with their engines in reheat, with the same crew in the lead. The remaining five aircraft landed at one-mile intervals as the final four came in for the run in and break, still in reheat. All nine aircraft then taxied in together and formed up before the reviewing officer. Engines and lights were extinguished together, and a spotlight was played on the ensign at it was lowered to the sounds of 'the Last Post'.

On Thursday 2 May, six Javelins made their final flights to nearby Seletar for disposal. These were XH777 R, XH793 J, XH839 W, XH872 MHM (the boss's aircraft), XH893 V and XH895 G. The Javelins' 12 years of RAF service were over.

'Thank goodness that's over, now for a smoke' after a 60 Squadron flypast. (60 Squadron)

Although the original plan had been to re-equip 60 Squadron with Lightnings, the decision to gradually withdraw all UK forces from east of Suez caused that idea to be abandoned. When the squadron closed down, most of the Javelins were unceremoniously dumped and broken up for scrap, with a few being passed on to the nascent Singapore Air Defence Command for use as ground-training aids. On 3 February 1969 60 Squadron was reformed at Wildenrath, Germany by renaming the RAF Communications Squadron flying a mixture of Andovers, Herons and Pembrokes, until disbanding again on 1 April 1992. Two months later, it became a Wessex helicopter unit at Benson, Oxfordshire. In 1997 it became part of the Defence Helicopter Flying School at Shawbury, where the squadron remains intensely proud of its fighter heritage.

The final aircrew shot, 60 Squadron May 1968. (60 Squadron)

BOSCOMBE DOWN – THE LAST OF THE JAVELINS

Although the Javelin had disappeared from the RAF inventory in May 1968, that did not quite mark the end for its flying career as the A&AEE at Boscombe Down continued to fly a single FAW.9 for a further seven years. Previously flown by 25, 33 and 5 Squadrons, XH897 went to Bristol Siddeley at Filton before moving to Boscombe Down on 19 January 1967. **Brian Bullock** finally got his dream posting and flew this aeroplane a good deal.

"A Squadron was established for one navigator and eight to 12 ETPS (Empire Test Pilots' School) graduate pilots. I was told my main task would be as the RAF Phantom project nav/rad, not the clever chap in navigation division, but the chap who did the nuts and bolts flying. I then attended numerous Phantom project meetings, but never saw a Phantom. MoD decided to fit the Spey engines with reheat for the first time, and this together with additional problems, put the aircraft's introduction into RAF and Royal Navy service back by some three or four years.

"I had very few additional trials, for example checking out the VOR (VHF omni-directional radio range) fit for the Army Air Corp's de Havilland Beavers so they could fly in the airways in Germany. Lots of flights in the Jet Provost T.3 to trial the new mini oxygen regulator – unusual attitudes and lots of positive and negative g, but on the plus side I got up to solo standard, flying aerobatics, spinning and plenty of GCAs. I got myself a target of flying in all the aircraft at Boscombe Down that had two seats, with the exclusion of helicopters, and eventually got about 25 different types in my logbook.

"The Javelin pacer aircraft on A Squadron XA778, was a Mk.2 airframe fitted with the uprated Sapphire engines of the Mk.7 with 11,000lb thrust. A lot of heavy equipment, radar, guns, etc., had been removed and much lighter specialised equipment fitted – this aircraft went like manure off a shovel! It was used primarily to establish pressure error (PE) correction factors for new military and civilian aircraft, having itself been set up as an accurate data. It was flown in fairly close formation with the new aircraft, whilst its numerous cameras took photographs, and the photographs and telemetry were analysed on the ground to establish the PE corrections for the new aircraft. Switches for the cameras and the other recording equipment were shared between the cockpits.

"The civilian observer was often not available, so I got myself checked out and flew quite a lot of these sorties. XA778 was also used in a photographic chase role, its many cameras being ideal for recording unusual activities, i.e. gun firing, flap and undercarriage raising and lowering, etc. Eventually it had to be retired, and a Mk.9 XH897 formerly with 5 Squadron, arrived in May 1967, still in its full squadron fit. The civilian boffins in Performance Division wanted to strip it down immediately, but the new instrumentation wasn't available and, with OC A Squadron's backing the AI 17 radar remained in situ. For a couple of months I got back behind the scopes and flew about 20 sorties of PIs. There was no shortage of targets, mostly aircraft based at Boscombe Down, and most of the A Squadron pilots were eager to participate. I'd left A Squadron before XH897 re-appeared as the new pacer, but I did re-acquaint with it after it had gone to Duxford for preservation.

"A Squadron were the handling squadron, and occasionally another Javelin would arrive for trials or investigation. Unfortunately, mostly their AIs were u/s and no facilities to fix it were available. When I arrived in June 1965, a Mk.5 XA711 was on the line. It was with A Squadron for an 'MDI' (meaning unknown) trial involving air-to-sea gun firing in Lyme Bay range to assess gun and ammunition temperatures. I flew in the rear seat for all the flights, but not all were trial flights. The aircraft stayed with us until April '66.

"Many of the test pilots wanted to try out the Javelin, including the superintendent of flying, one Gp Capt David Dick who, as a squadron leader at Boscombe Down, had carried out the initial Javelin spinning trials in December 1955. I was able to listen to a recording of his fascinating commentary, about the time when he successfully ejected, after numerous spin recovery attempts from about 40,000 feet down to about 10,000 feet, which all failed. His calm, methodical activities were being described in an amazingly unhurried manner.

"When XH897, the new pacer arrived, I had it in my logbook for a few days for nozzle trials, which we flew out of Filton near Bristol. Later that year in September/October, XH849 – a Mk.9R – flew into Boscombe for handling trials at the handling squadron. I filled my boots, but again no radar. I left Boscombe Down in March 1968 at the end of my three-year tour with a heavy heart. Other nav/rads were queueing up to take my place and I then moved to Bentley Priory, just before Fighter Command became Strike Command. When I retired, my final total was 2,756 hours including 1,210 hours on various Javelins.

"I retired in the big RAF contraction in late 1970, when quite a few of the squadrons disbanded. I was told you can do anything you like but fly and that really p****d me off. Initially I thought to hell with it, but as I got to know quite a few of the civilian test pilots, people like Jimmy Dell at BAC Warton, I wrote to them all and asked if there was any chance of filling an observer slot with BAC or Hawker-Siddeley, or whatever. I found it was dead man's shoes and no-one was about to retire. I wasn't interested in going into civilian flying, as navigators were clearly on the way out, so in the end I took up air traffic control as the nearest thing to flying. I did that from 1970 to 1987, when I retired. I went through the mill at airfields and air radar units, and I had an interesting tour as a liaison officer with

> the German air force at Frankfurt, which made it all bearable. I came out in December 1987 at the age of 55 as a squadron leader."

Time finally ran out for the last flying Javelin in 1975, one of its final duties being as a calibration aircraft on the MRCA (multi-role combat aircraft) programme, which emerged as the Tornado. On 24 January 1975 it was flown to Duxford to join the Imperial War Museum collection.

Thus ended the Javelin's flying career, one which had not been without its challenges. Despite that, it came to be well-liked by most of the aircrew who encountered it, while the ground crew tended to have a love/hate relationship with it – as ground crew usually do.

APPENDIX ONE

OPERATING UNITS

SQUADRONS

3 –'The third shall be first'. Geilenkirchen Jan '59 FAW.4, T.3 Sep '59, disbanded 4 Jan '61.

5 – 'Thou mayest break but shall not bend me'. Laarbruch Jan '60 FAW.5, FAW.9, Nov '62 – Oct '65, T.3 Dec '59 – Sep '65, Geilenkirchen 11 Dec '62.

11 – 'Swifter and keener than eagles'. Geilenkirchen Oct '59 FAW.4 – Mar '62, FAW.5, T.3 Jan '61– Jan '66, FAW.9 Dec '62, disbanded 11 Jan '66 and number allocated to 228 OCU Leuchars as a shadow squadron until the OCU disbanded Dec '66.

23 – 'Always on the attack'. Horsham St. Faith Mar '57 FAW.4 – Jul '59. Coltishall 28 May '57, Horsham St. Faith 7 Sep '58, FAW.7 Apr '59 – Jul '60, T.3 Apr '59 – Aug '64, Coltishall 5 Jun '59, Horsham St.Faith 31 Mar '60, FAW.9R Apr '60 – Oct '64, Coltishall 11 Jul '60, FAW.7 Apr '62 – Sep '62, Leuchars 9 Mar '63, Lightning F.3 Aug '64.

25 – 'Striking I defend'. Waterbeach Dec '58 FAW.7 – Jan '61, T.3 Jul '59 – Nov '62, FAW.9 Dec '59 – Dec '62, Leuchars 30 Oct '61, FAW.7 Apr '62 – Sep '62, disbanded 31 Dec '62.

29 –'Energetic and keen'. Acklington Nov '57 FAW.6 – Aug '61, Leuchars Jul '58, FAW.9, T.3 Jun '59 – May '67, Nicosia 1 Mar '63, Akrotiri 16 Mar '64, Ndola 3 Dec '65 detachment at Lusaka, Akrotiri 3 Sep '66, Wattisham and Lightning F.3 10 May '67.

Final 72 Squadron start-up before disbandment 29 July 1961. (John Augoustis)

33 –'Loyalty'. Leeming Jul '58 FAW.7 – Jan '62, Middleton St. George 30 Sep '58, T.3 Aug '59 – Dec '62, FAW.9 Oct '60, disbanded 31 Dec '62 by re-numbering as 5 Squadron.

41 –'Seek and destroy'. Coltishall 1 Feb '58 FAW.4 – Feb '60, Wattisham 5 Jul '58, FAW.6 Aug '58 – Feb '60, T.3 Apr '59 – Dec '63, FAW.8 Nov '59, disbanded 31 Dec '63.

46 – 'We rise to conquer'. Odiham Feb '56 FAW.1 – Oct '57, FAW.2 Aug '57 – Jun '61, FAW.6 May '58 – Oct '58, T.3 Mar '59 – Mar '61, Waterbeach 17 Jul '59, disbanded 30 Jun '61.

60 – 'I strive through difficulties to the sky'. Tengah Jul '61 FAW.9, T.3 Nov '61 – May '68, detachments at Butterworth, Kai Tak, Kuching, Labuan, disbanded 1 May '68.

64 –'Firm of purpose'. Duxford Aug '58 FAW.7 – Oct '60, T.3 Sep '59 – Jul '66, FAW.9 Jul '60, Waterbeach 17 Jul '61, Binbrook 24 Aug '62, Tengah 1 Apr '65 detachments at Kuching, Labuan, disbanded 15 Jun '67.

72 – 'Swift'. Church Fenton Apr '59 FAW.4 – Jun '61, FAW.5 Jun '59, Leconfield 28 Jun '59, T.3 Aug '59 – Jun '61, disbanded 30 Jun '61.

85 – 'We hunt by day and night'. Stradishall 30 Nov '58 FAW.2 – Mar '60, FAW.6 Nov '58 – Jun '60, T.3 May '59 – Mar '63, West Malling 5 Jun '59, FAW.8 Mar '60, West Raynham 6 Sep '60, disbanded 31 Mar '63.

87 –'The most powerful fear me'. Brüggen 2 Jul '57 FAW.1 – Jan '61, FAW.5 Sep '58 – Oct '60, FAW.4, T.3 Nov '59 – Jan '61, disbanded 3 Jan '61.

89 – 'By the help of God, with my own weapons'. Stradishall Sep '57 FAW.6 – Nov '58, FAW.2 Oct '57, renumbered 85 Squadron 30 Nov '58.

96 – 'We stalk by night'. Geilenkirchen Sep '58 FAW.4, renumbered 3 Squadron 21 Jan '59.

137 – 'Do right – fear naught'. Not an operational Javelin unit. A shadow (reserve) squadron as part of 228 OCU.

141 –'We stay by night'. Horsham St. Faith Feb '57 FAW.4, Coltishall 28 May '57, renumbered 41 Squadron 1 Feb '58.

151 – 'Fidelity into duty'. Turnhouse Jun '57 FAW.5, Leuchars 15 Nov '57, T.3 May '59 – Sep '61, disbanded 19 Sep '61.

219 – 'From dusk till dawn'. Not an operational Javelin unit. A shadow (reserve) squadron as part of AWFCS.

SQUADRON PERIODS OF SERVICE

Squadron	1956	1957	1958	1959	1960	1961	1962	1963	1964	1965	1966	1967	1968
3				■	■								
5					■	■	■	■	■	■			
11					■	■	■	■	■	■			
23				■	■	■	■	■	■				
25				■	■	■	■						
29			■	■	■	■	■	■	■	■	■	■	
33			■	■	■	■	■						
41			■	■	■	■	■	■					
46	■	■	■	■	■	■							
60						■	■	■	■	■	■	■	■
64			■	■	■	■	■	■	■	■	■	■	
72				■	■	■							
85				■	■	■	■	■					
87		■	■	■	■								
89		■	■										
96			■										
141		■											
151		■	■	■	■	■							

CONVERSION UNITS

228 OCU Leeming, Jun '57 FAW.5, FAW.7, T.3 Feb '59, disbanded 15 Sep '61, reformed Leuchars 1 May '65 T.3, FAW.9, disbanded 23 Dec '66.

All Weather Development Squadron. Part of Central Fighter Establishment (CFE) West Raynham. Mar '57 FAW.5.

All Weather Fighter Combat School. Part of CFE. West Raynham '58 FAW.5. Renamed Javelin Operational Conversion Squadron 1 Jul '62. Disbanded end 1962.

Javelin Mobile Conversion Unit. Part of 228 OCU Leeming Feb '57, disbanded 1959.

Javelin Operational Conversion Squadron. Part of CFE West Raynham 1 Jul '62 FAW.5, disbanded 12 Oct '62. Allocated shadow squadron number 219.

Night Fighter Leader School. Part of CFE. West Raynham. Oct '57 FAW.5. Renamed All Weather Fighter Combat School 1958.

OTHER UNITS/OPERATORS

Aeroplane and Armament Experimental Establishment. Boscombe Down, prototypes, Jun '54, Jul '55 – Mar '56 FAW.1, May '56 – '58, Mar '61 – '69 FAW.2, '61 – '62 T.3, Jun '56 – '58 FAW.4, '58, '60 – '62 FAW.5, '59 FAW.6, May '57 – '63 FAW.7, '59-'60 FAW.8, '60 – 24 Jan '75 FAW.9.

Air Fighting Development Squadron. Coltishall 1 Sep '59 FAW.1, FAW.2, FAW.4, FAW.5, FAW.6, FAW.7, Oct '59 FAW.8, Binbrook 5 Oct '62 and absorbed into CFE.

All Weather Development Squadron. Part of CFE. West Raynham Feb '56 FAW.1, FAW.2, FAW.5, Mar '58 FAW.7, absorbed into AFDS Aug '59.

Armstrong Siddeley. Bitteswell Feb '56 – Dec '60 FAW.1, Apr '56 – Jul '59 FAW.4, '57 – Jul '58 FAW.2, Jul '57 – Feb '58 FAW.5, Jan '58 – Oct '61 FAW.7, Apr '59 – Aug '59 FAW.8.

Boulton Paul Aircraft. Defford Aug '55 – Dec '57 FAW.1.

Bristol Aeroplane Company. Filton Oct '55 – Jul '57 FAW.1.

Bristol Siddeley Engines. Filton Jun '62 – Apr '63 FAW.1.

College of Aeronautics, Cranfield May '59 – Dec '64 FAW.1.

De Havilland. Hatfield Dec '56 – Jun '62 FAW.1, Feb '58 – Aug '59 FAW.7.

Ferry Training Unit. Benson FAW.1, FAW.4, FAW.6 Jun '58 – Apr '59, disbanded '61.

Fighter Command Ferry Squadron. Leuchars Oct '64 – Dec '64 T.3, FAW.9.

Fighter Command Instrument Rating Flt/Squadron. Part of CFE. West Raynham 29 Dec '59 T.3, Middleton St. George 3 Aug '61, Javelin Flight renamed Javelin Instrument Rating Squadron Apr '63.

Fighter Command Missile Practice Camp. Valley 1 Jun '62 FAW.7.

Flight Refuelling. Tarrant Rushton Mar '59 – Dec '59 FAW.7.

Guided Weapons Development Squadron. Valley FAW.7, renamed Guided Weapons Trials Squadron 31 Dec '58.

Guided Weapons Trials Squadron. Valley 31 Dec '58 FAW.7, renamed Fighter Command Missile Practice Camp 1 Jun '62.

Handling Squadron. Part of A&AEE. Boscombe Down Oct '56 – Jun '57 FAW.4, Mar '57 – Jan '59 FAW.5, Jul '63 – Aug '63 FAW.7.

Javelin Instrument Rating Squadron. Middleton St.George T.3 Apr '63, downgraded to Flight status as part of 228 OCU at Leuchars and disbanded 31 Dec '66.

Rolls-Royce. Hucknall Jan '58 – Aug '62 FAW.1.

Royal Aircraft Establishment. Bedford, prototype. Farnborough '54 – '61 FAW.1, Jun '58 – Nov '59 FAW.7.

BOYS AND THEIR TOYS

Following a long-standing tradition, a number of squadron and other unit commanding officers chose to embellish 'the boss's Javelin' with their initials, in addition to the usual practice of carrying the CO's pennant under the cockpit. Known examples are listed below.

Sqn Ldr George H Beaton, OC 228 OCU 1966; FAW.9 XH898 marked GHB (also stripped of camouflage and flown in bare metal).

Wg Cdr J Fraser AFC, OC 60 Squadron '64-'65; FAW.9 XH846 marked JF.

Wg Cdr David Leonard Hughes DFC AFC, OC 33 Squadron '60-'62; FAW.7 XH835 then FAW.9 XH773 marked DH.

Wg Cdr Michael Horace Miller, OC 60 Squadron '65-'68; FAW.9 XH839, XH721 then XH872 marked MHM.

Wg Cdr Norman Poole, OC 33 Squadron '58-'59; FAW.9 XH853 marked NP. Unusually, a navigator as OC a fighter squadron.

Wg Cdr Peter Smith, OC 60 Squadron '61-'62; FAW.9 XH722 marked PS.

Wg Cdr James H Walton AFC (nav/radar), OC 25 Squadron '60-'62; FAW.9 XH880 then XH883 marked JHW.

Wg Cdr P D Wright, OC 64 Squadron '65-'66; FAW.9 XH834 marked PDW.

APPENDIX TWO

PRODUCTION LIST

Prototypes (5)
WD804, WD808, WT827, WT830, WT836

FAW.1 (40)
XA544-XA572, XA618-XA628

FAW.2 (31)
XD158, XA768-XA781, XA799-XA814

T.3 (23)
WT841, XH390-XH397, XH432-XH438, XH443-XH447, XK577, XM336
A further five aircraft cancelled, XM337-XM341.

FAW.4 (50)
XA629-XA640, XA644, XA720-XA737, XA749-XA767
Note: XA720-XA737 and XA749-XA762 built by Armstrong Whitworth.

FAW.5 (63)
XA641-XA643, XA645-XA667, XA688-XA719, XH687-XH692
Note: XA654-XA660, XA662-XA667 and XA688-XA719 built by Armstrong Whitworth.

FAW.6 (33)
XA815-XA836, XH693-XH703

29 Squadron FAW.6s, XH700 A and XH699 L, starting up at Sylt. (Ken Brereton)

FAW.7 (142)
XH704-XH725, XH746-XH795, XH833-XH849, XH871-XH912, XH955-XH965
Note: XH785-XH795, XH833-XH849 and XH871-XH899 built by Armstrong Whitworth. 118 conversions to FAW.9.

FAW.8 (47)
XH966-XH993, XJ112-XJ130, XJ165
XJ112 was a static test airframe only. A further 13 aircraft XJ166-XJ178, were cancelled in August 1960 during final assembly and broken up for spares.

FAW.9 (118)
All conversions from FAW.7

Total built 434

Production by Gloster Aircraft except where stated otherwise.

APPENDIX THREE

ACCIDENTS

29 Jun '52 WD804
Glosters. Elevators fluttered at high speed and broke-off near Brize Norton. Struck the ground on final approach at Boscombe Down. Sqn Ldr Bill Waterton.

11 Jun '53 WD808
Glosters. Stalled on test flight and spun in at Flax Bourton near Bristol. Deputy CTP Lt Peter Lawrence MBE unsuccessfully ejected too low.

21 Oct '54 XA546
Glosters. Spun into Bristol Channel on test flight. Flt Lt Robert Ross killed.

8 Dec '55 XA561
A Squadron A&AEE. Abandoned in a flat spin, crashed Ashey, Isle of Wight. Sqn Ldr David Dick.

12 Jun '56 XA570/B
46 Squadron. Flew into ground near Odiham on a night GCA. Pilot and Squadron CO Wg Cdr Frank Birchfield OBE AFC and Fg Off Brian Chambers killed.

24 Aug '56 XA644
Glosters. Collided with CFS Hunter F.4 XF980 and crashed Wotton-under-Edge, Glos. Pilot E B Smith killed, navigator Flt Lt R E Jeffries survived.

25 May '57 XA732
23 Squadron. Ventral tank detached while taxiing at Horsham St. Faith, caught fire.

6 Dec '57 XA642/H
AWDS. Both engines flamed-out on air test following an engine change. Crashed into the sea 10m east of Skegness. Flt Lt Arthur Wright and Flt Lt Reginald Ashworth killed.

11 Feb '58 XA734
23 Squadron. Abandoned near Wymondham, Norfolk after starboard engine flame tube casing failure and fire in rear fuselage. Fg Off F Hugh Stark and Fg Off Peter Baigent.

26 Feb '58 XH714
A Squadron A&AEE. Pilot Flt Lt Richard May ejected at 5,000 ft due to seat malfunction. Crashed Sandford in the New Forest. Navigator Fg Off John Coates ejected at 2,000 ft but both were killed.

12 May '58 XA625/L
87 Squadron. Caught fire and burnt out in refuelling accident at Brüggen.

5 Jun '58 XA558/A
87 Squadron. Abandoned after double-engine flame-out on approach, crashed near Brüggen. Pilot Flt Lt James Breakwell killed, navigator Fg Off J Jackson survived.

11 Jul '58 XA751
41 Squadron. Abandoned in a flat spin during aerobatics and crashed at Moat Farm, north of Wattisham airfield. Pilot Capt Earl Taylor USAF exchange officer killed, navigator Flt Lt Brian Bedford survived.

19 Sep '58 XA779/M
89 Squadron. Stalled and spun in on approach Stradishall. Flt Lt Derek Kenney and Fg Off Gordon Lewis killed.

20 Sep '58 XA648/M
AWDS. Stalled recovering from dive during aerobatics and abandoned 3m WSW of Fakenham, Norfolk. Sqn Ldr G P Kingston and Flt Lt A T Morgan.

18 Feb '59 XA569/M
87 Squadron. Pilot Flt Lt R A V 'Dick' Carey ejected due to seat fault, crashed at Katwyck-aan-Zee Netherlands. Navigator Flt Lt Alec Cooper killed when his parachute failed to open.

9 Mar '59 XA802/D
46 Squadron. Starter exploded on start-up at Sylt, caught fire.

20 Jun '59 XA750/A
3 Squadron. Attempted roll after take-off, stalled and spun in 1½ m NW of Norvenich, West Germany. Flt Lt Wilfred Jacques and Fg Off David Ritchie killed.

7 Jul '59 XA722
72 Squadron. Engine failed and disintegrated after take-off at Church Fenton, landed safely but not repaired and SOC as Cat.5 27 Oct '60.

9 Jul '59 XH750/R
33 Squadron. Lightning strike, possible centre-line closure, hydraulic failure and fire, abandoned near Horsham St. Faith. Flt Lt Jack Buckley and Sgt D U Epe.

30 Jul '59 XH789/G
64 Squadron. Hydraulic pumps 1 and 2 failure leading to loss of flaps and airbrakes. Engines cut on touchdown, overshot emergency landing at Akrotiri. Flt Lt Grindley and Sgt Steve Sanders uninjured.

1 Sep '59 XH775/E
23 Squadron. Collided with XH781 during night interception and abandoned, crashed Brundell, Norfolk. Fg Off F Hugh B Stark and Fg Off Peter Baigent.

1 Sep '59 XH781/J
23 Squadron. Collided with XH775 during night interception, crashed Brundell, Norfolk. Flt Lt Christopher Brooksbank and Sgt Graham Spriggs killed.

29 Sep '59 XA662/N
228 OCU. Starboard engine caught fire at 30,000 ft after turbine failure and second shut down after fire warning. Abandoned and crashed Leyburn, Yorkshire. Fg Off Christopher Cowper and Capt Robert Nietz (USAF).

14 Oct '59 XH720/G
33 Squadron. Brake locked, swung on landing at Akrotiri and undercarriage collapsed.

22 Oct '59 XH761
Glosters. Abandoned take-off at Moreton Valance after hydraulic warning lights came on. Overshot runway and crossed a road breaking off the undercarriage, declared Cat.5 and SOC 27 Oct '60.

9 Mar '60 XH988/X
41 Squadron. Double generator failure. Out of fuel while trying to find airfield and abandoned, crashed Crownstone Farm, Durdar, Cumberland. Flt Lt Mike Gill and Sgt Bob Lydall.

8 Apr '60 XA640/A
3 Squadron. Nose wheel jammed up, overshot runway and ran into wood, Geilenkirchen, West Germany.

21 May '60 XA823/P
29 Squadron. Collided with XA835 at 42,000 ft, abandoned and dived into sea NE of Scarborough, Yorkshire. Flt Lt J S Wilson and Fg Off E Wood.

21 May '60 XA835/Z
29 Squadron. Collided with XA823 at 42,000 ft, abandoned on reaching coast 4m NW of West Hartlepool, Durham. Flt Lt D J Wyborn and Flt Lt J S Clark.

29 Jun '60 XA706/C
228 OCU. Jet-pipe failed and heat damage to rear fuselage caused electrical failure. Force-landed at Leeming but not repaired and re-cat Cat.5 for ground display and later fire practice.

20 Sep '60 XH838/F
33 Squadron. Tyre burst on take-off Middleton St. George, swung and undercarriage leg collapsed. Used for fire practice at Catterick.

27 Oct '60 XA754/D
72 Squadron. Damaged by heat during ground run at Leconfield with split jet-pipe, not repaired. SOC 18 Nov '60 for fire practice at Catterick.

21 Nov '60 XA825/K
29 Squadron. Flew into Bowbeat Hill 4m NE of Peebles while descending in cloud, probably following an engine malfunction. Crew ejected at high speed and low altitude but did not survive. Flt Lt Victor Hill and Flt Lt John Knight killed.

2 Mar '61 XA752/F
72 Squadron. Hit arrester barrier raised in error and undercarriage leg collapsed on touchdown at Leeming. Flt Lt Want and Flt Lt J Mitchell.

12 Apr '61 XA813/U
46 Squadron. Jet-pipe fractured and aircraft damaged by heat. Not repaired and SOC 17 Apr '61.

4 May '61 XH692/K
228 OCU. Starter cartridge fired after landing at Leeming and aircraft caught fire. Not repaired.

31 May '61 XH875/L
64 Squadron. Engine exploded on start-up at Nicosia, not repaired.

5 Aug '61 XH791
12 Group Ferry Unit. Engine blew up on delivery flight to 60 Squadron, abandoned in a spin and crashed Manga river, Ganges delta, East Pakistan. Flt Lt Edward Owens killed, master nav Tony Melton survived.

29 Aug '61 XH971/A
41 Squadron. Broke up due to excess g at Geilenkirchen during run-in and break. Flt Lt John Hatch and Flt Lt John Nothall killed.

27 Sep '61 XH840
OFU. Damaged at Luqa during refuelling on delivery flight to 60 Squadron. Allocated for fire practice.

26 Oct '61 XH906/Q
25 Squadron. Collided with 32 Squadron Canberra B.2 WD995 N of Akrotiri on practice night interception and abandoned. Pilot Flt Lt John Morris killed, navigator Plt Off Roger Lloyd survived.

27 Nov '61 XH878/R
64 Squadron. Hydraulics failed leading to loss of control. Abandoned and crashed 11½ m SE of Waterbeach. Sqn Ldr D A P Saunders-Davies and Flt Lt P Dougherty.

9 Mar '62 XH794/X
33 Squadron. Hydraulic failure on approach to Wildenrath during air test, overshot and undercarriage collapsed. Pilot Sqn Ldr S Burrows.

13 Apr '62 XH844/L
64 Squadron. Starter exploded on start-up at Waterbeach, burnt out.

18 May '62 XH755/Y
33 Squadron. Control lost, abandoned in a spin and crashed 7m E of Tynemouth, Northumberland. Master Pilot J Crowther survived, navigator John 'Bert' Farey killed.

7 Jun '62 XA645/M
5 Squadron. Port engine turbine blade failure, rear fuselage caught fire, abandoned and crashed 4m NW of Wesel, West Germany. Flt Lt J H Adam and Flt Lt C M Pinker.

12 Jul '62 XJ128/H
85 Squadron. Engine caught fire on start-up at West Raynham, burnt out.

25 Jul '62 XA646/S
AWFCS. Engine caught fire on start-up at West Raynham. Cat.5 17 Sep '62 and allocated for fire practice at Manston.

4 Oct '62 XA701/X
AWFCS. Starter explosion at West Raynham and aircraft caught fire. Cat.5 for ground instruction at Bicester.

29 Oct '62 XA661/F
11 Squadron. Engine exploded on start-up at Geilenkirchen and aircraft caught fire. SOC 13 Nov '62.

3 Dec '62 XH836/O
60 Squadron. Starboard centre-line closure, abandoned in a spin and crashed Mersing, Malaya. Pilot Wg Cdr Peter Smith, navigator Sqn Ldr Frank Jolliffe, both ejected when inverted.

27 Jun '63 XH962/C
29 Squadron. Swung on take-off at Akrotiri and undercarriage collapsed. Pilot Jim Froud and his navigator unhurt.

2 Aug '63 XH990/Z
41 Squadron. Undercarriage leg jammed up, swing off runway on landing at Marham.

11 Sep '63 XJ113/X
41 Squadron. Failure of starboard engine compressor blades during take-off at Wattisham cutting fuel and hydraulic lines and starting a fire. Left runway and burnt out.

17 Oct '63 XH758/R
5 Squadron. Starboard engine centre-line closure leading to control failure, crashed Dutch-German border. Flt Lt R Boulton and Flt Lt L P Morley.

5 Nov '63 XM336/B
FCIRS. Double engine failure due to centre-line closure, crashed on houses near Saujac, France. Flt Lt Colin Holman, Flt Lt D E Berks. This accident resulted in a two-week grounding of the Javelin fleet.

5 Nov '63 XH765/A
64 Squadron. Overshot aborted take-off at Kalaikunda, India.

30 Jan '64 XH723/R
29 Squadron. Starboard engine compressor blade failure during take-off at Nicosia causing a fire. To 103 MU 10 Feb '64 and SOC 18 Aug '64.

10 Feb '64 XH747/B
60 Squadron. Crashed into sea off Singapore after structural failure and separation of the tail. Flt Lt Gordon Sykes and Flt Lt Paul Burns.

20 Mar '64 XH443/C
228 OCU. Found to have twisted fuselage after heavy landing at Leuchars. Cat.5(C) 14 Apr '66 as rogue aircraft.

29 Mar '64 XH955/T
60 Squadron. Cat.3 damage in heavy landing Labuan. Re-cat 5(C) 5 Aug '64.

3 Apr '64 XH724/F
60 Squadron. Ran off runway at Tengah and SOC the next day as Cat.5(C).

14 May '64 XH436/C
Javelin Instrument Rating Flight. Cat.4 after starter explosion at Leuchars. SOC 21 May '64 as Cat.5(C) and allocated for fire-fighting practice.

20 May '64 XH774/B
29 Squadron. Engine failed on take-off at Akrotiri and caught fire, probably due to centre-line closure. Pilot Flt Lt Forbes Pearson.

4 Aug '64 XH874/H
64 Squadron. Ground fire at Kuching, Sarawak. Provisionally Cat.4 but re-cat 5(C) 27 Aug '64.

19 Aug '64 XH437/X
23 Squadron. Starter explosion at Leuchars. SOC as Cat.5(C) 24 Aug '64 and allocated for fire-fighting practice at Leuchars.

28 Aug '64 XH845/N
23 Squadron. Starter fire at Leuchars. SOC as Cat.5(C) 1 Sep '64 and allocated for fire-fighting practice at Leuchars.

3 Mar '65 XH833/I
60 Squadron. First stage compressor failure on take-off at Butterworth, starboard ventral tank caught fire, aircraft burnt out.

22 Jun '65 XH877/W
64 Squadron. Port engine compressor failure, control lost, abandoned and crashed NE of Taiwau. Flt Lt P J Hart and Flt Lt P E 'Dinger' Dell.

3 Sep '65 XH911/J
5 Squadron. Caught fire on start-up at Geilenkirchen. Not repaired.

8 Nov '65 XH887/B
64 Squadron. Undercarriage jammed on night flight, abandoned off Changi, Singapore. Flt Lt Keith Fitchew and Flt Lt A Evans.

8 Nov '65 XH959/U
64 Squadron. Lost horizon and hit sea on night ASR search for XH887. Pilot Flt Lt Peter Poppe killed, navigator Flt Lt Bruce Unsted survived.

17 Nov '65 XH749/Q
60 Squadron. Tyre burst on landing at Butterworth, Malaysia, swung off runway and ground-looped. Not repaired.

4 Apr '66 XH785/L
60 Squadron. Crew ejected after loss of control following engine explosion 5 miles north-west of Tengah. Flt Lt Ted Rawcliffe and Flt Lt Al Vasloo.

26 Apr '66 XH6/C
60 Squadron. Declared Cat.3 after starboard engine exploded on start at Butterworth. Re-cat 5(C) 28 Apr '66.

2 Jun '66 XH890/M
29 Squadron. Skidded on landing at Ndola, Zambia, causing undercarriage to collapse. SOC as Cat 5(C) the next day and abandoned when RAF detachment left, hulk being extant in '74.

14 Jun '66 XH709/K

64 Squadron. Abandoned after controls jammed, crashed Senai, South Johore, Malaysia. Fg Off South and Flt Lt A Johnson.

27 Jun '66 XH847/G

29 Squadron. Wheel locked on landing at Khormaksar, Aden, swung off runway and undercarriage leg torn off.

11 Jul '66 XH445/Z

64 Squadron. Swung off runway at Tengah after landing and ran into monsoon drain, losing its undercarriage. Cat.5 and SOC 16 Aug '66.

25 Aug '66 XH876/N

64 Squadron. Throttles jammed in the closed position downwind to land at Tengah, the crew ejected and the aircraft crashed in the grounds of Radio Singapore. Flt Lt Pete Hart and Flt Lt Jim Jackson.

11 Oct '66 XH958/N

228 OCU. Swing off runway during emergency landing at Leuchars after one undercarriage leg failed to lower. Declared Cat.5(C) and SOC 31 Oct '66.

20 Oct '66 XH909/J

228 OCU. Declared Cat.5(C) with over-stressed airframe. SOC 31 Oct '66 and later to 27 MU Shawbury for scrapping.

15 Nov '66 XH885/R

64 Squadron. Cat.3 after starter fire at Tengah. Re-cat.5(C) 2 Dec '66.

14 Dec '66 XH848/L

29 Squadron. Stalled in another aircraft's slipstream on approach to Akrotiri and crashed near the bomb dump after the crew ejected. Fg Off J W Pierce and Flt Lt Paul Burns.

18 Jan '67 XH888/S

29 Squadron. Nose wheel collapsed on landing at Akrotiri. Cat 3 but re-cat.5(C) 25 Jan '67.

5 Apr '67 XH787/G

60 Squadron. One undercarriage leg failed to lower and swung off runway at Butterworth causing Cat.3 damage. SOC as Cat 5(C) 20 Jul '67.

11 May '67 XH764/C

29 Squadron. Damaged on landing while staging through Manston en route from Akrotiri after unit disbanded. Damage minor but allocated for display at Manston and declared Cat.5 with maintenance serial 7972M.

30 May '67 XH708/P
64 Squadron. Collided with XH896 during formation join-up for rehearsal of a six-ship flypast and dived 10 miles north-west of Tengah. Fg Off William Kay and Cpl Kenneth Ashbee (engine ground crew) killed.

30 May '67 XH896/O
64 Squadron. Abandoned after being struck from below by XH708 and crashed 10 miles north-west of Tengah. Fg Off P McKellar and SAC M Lokanadan.

12 Sep '67 XH891
A&AEE. Declared Cat.5(C) after AVPIN fire on start-up at Boscombe Down. Allocated to Chivenor for fire practice 12 Oct '67 and arrived there 13 Dec '67.

11 Oct '67 XH788/E
60 Squadron. Crashed Johore after main spar failure and breaking-up in mid-air. Pilot attempted a roll at low level when full of fuel. Fg Off Gerald Barnard and Fg Off Howard Geeve killed.

8 Feb '68 XH961/H
60 Squadron. Ran off runway at Tengah after port brake failure and hit storm drain causing Cat.3 damage, but SOC as Cat.5(C) the same day. Flt Lt Keith Fitchew and Flt Lt Holmes. The last Javelin of 93 to be written-off.

Some information taken from http://www.ejection-history.org.uk

ABBREVIATIONS

AAA	Anti-Aircraft Artillery
A&AEE	Aeroplane and Armament Experimental Establishment
AAFCE	Allied Air Forces Central Europe
ACF	Air Camera Fitter
Aden	Armament Development Enfield
ADIZ	Air Defence Identification Zone
AEO	Air Electronics Officer
AEW	Airborne Early Warning
AF	Air Force
A/F	After Flight servicing
AFC	Air Force Cross
AFDS	Air Fighting Development Squadron
AFS	Advanced Flying School
AI	Air(borne) Interception
AIDEX	Air Defence Exercise
AIDU	Aeronautical Information Documents Unit
Air Cdre	Air Commodore
AM	Air Marshal
ANS	Air Navigation School
ANZAC	Australia and New Zealand Army Corps
AOC	Air Officer Commanding
APC	Armament Practice Camp
ARSF	Air Radar Servicing Flight
ASP	Aircraft Servicing Platform
ASR	Air-Sea Rescue
AST	Air Service Training
ASTOR	Airborne Stand-off Radar
ASV	Air-to-Surface Vessel
ATAF	Allied Tactical Air Force
ATC	Air Traffic Control
AVM	Air Vice-Marshal
AVPIN	Isopropyl Nitrate
AWDS	All Weather Development Squadron
AWFCS	All Weather Fighter Combat School
B	Bomber
BAC	British Aircraft Corporation
BBMF	Battle of Britain Memorial Flight
B/F	Before Flight servicing
BFPO	British Forces Posted Overseas
B(I)	Bomber Interdictor
BJF	Borneo Jet Force
BOAC	British Overseas Airways Corporation
Cat	Category
CFE	Central Fighter Establishment
CFS	Central Flying School
Chf Tech	Chief Technician
CO	Commanding Officer
COMBRITZAM	Commander British Forces in Zambia
Cpl	Corporal
CTTO	Central Trials and Tactics Organisation
CU	Conversion Unit
DFC	Distinguished Flying Cross
DFLS	Day Fighter Leaders' School
DFM	Distinguished Flying Medal

DSO	Distinguished Service Order
Elint	Electronic Intelligence
Esc	Escadrille
ETPS	Empire Test Pilots' School
F	Fighter
FAW	Fighter All-Weather
FCMPC	Fighter Command Missile Practice Camp
FEAF	Far East Air Force
Fg Off	Flying Officer
FIMgt	Fellow of the Institute of Management
FIS	Fighter Identification System
FL	Flight Level
Flt	Flight
Flt Cdr	Flight Commander
Flt Lt	Flight Lieutenant
FTS	Flying Training School
F(TT)	Fighter (Target Tug)
GCA	Ground Controlled Approach
GCF	Group Communications Flight
GCI	Ground Controlled Interception
GCU	Generator Control Unit
GEE	Radio navigation system (from 'Grid')
GGSR	Gyro Gun Sight Recorder
Gp Capt	Group Captain
GS	General Service
GSM	General Service Medal
HP	High Pressure
HQ	Headquarters
IFF	Identification Friend or Foe
IFT	Intensive Flying Trial
IRF	Instrument Rating Flight
JMCU	Javelin Mobile Conversion Unit
JOCS	Javelin Operational Conversion Squadron
J/T	Junior Technician
KD	Khaki Drill
Kgs	Kilograms
LAC	Leading Aircraftman
LATCC	London Air Traffic Control Centre
LP	Low Pressure
Lt Cdr	Lieutenant Commander
MARDET	Maritime Reconnaissance Detachment
MATO	Military Air Traffic Operations
MEAF	Middle East Air Force
MFPU	Mobile Film Processing Unit
MoD	Ministry of Defence
Mph	Miles per hour
MT	Motor Transport
MU	Maintenance Unit
NAAFI	Navy Army and Air Forces Institute
NATO	North Atlantic Treaty Organisation
NATS	National Air Traffic System
Nav	Navigator
Nav/rad	Navigator/Radar
NCO	Non Commissioned Officer
NEAF	Near East Air Force
NF	Night Fighter
NOTAM	Notice to Airmen
OASC	Officer and Aircrew Selection Centre
OBE	Order of the British Empire
OC	Officer Commanding

OCTU	Officer Cadet Training Unit
OCU	Operational Conversion Unit
OR	Operational Requirement
ORB	Operations Record Book
ORP	Operational Readiness Platform
OTR	Operational Turn Round
PAI	Pilot Attack Instructor
PE	Pressure Error
PI	Practice Interception
Plt Off	Pilot Officer
PPI	Plan Position Indicator
PR	Photographic Reconnaissance
PR	Public Relations
PSP	Pierced Steel Planking
QFI	Qualified Flying Instructor
QRA	Quick Reaction Alert
QWI	Qualified Weapons Instructor
RAAF	Royal Australian Air Force
RAF	Royal Air Force
RAFC	Royal Air Force College
RAFG	Royal Air Force Germany
RAuxAF	Royal Auxiliary Air Force
RCAF	Royal Canadian Air Force
RO	Radar Operator
RPM	Revolutions Per Minute
R/T	Radio Telephony
SAC	Senior Aircraftman
SARBE	Search and Rescue Beacon
SATCO	Senior Air Traffic Control Officer
SBAC	Society of British Aircraft Constructors
Sgt	Sergeant
SHAPE	Supreme Headquarters Allied Powers Europe
SHQ	Station Headquarters
SNCO	Senior Non-Commissioned Officer
SNEB	Societe Nouvelle des Etablissements Edgar Brandt
SOC	Struck Off Charge
SofTT	School of Technical Training
SOP	Standard Operating Procedure
Sqn	Squadron
Sqn Ldr	Squadron Ldr
Stn Cdr	Station Commander
T	Trainer
TACEVAL	Tactical Evaluation
TAF	Tactical Air Force
TFF	Target Facilities Flight
THUM	Temperature and Humidity
TTTE	Tri-national Tornado Training Establishment
TWU	Tactical Weapons Unit
UAS	University Air Squadron
UDI	Unilateral Declaration of Independence
U/S	Unserviceable
USAF	United States Air Force
USS	United States Ship
U/V	Ultra-violet
VHF	Very High Frequency
VID	Visual Identification
VIP	Very Important Person
VOR	VHF Omni-Directional Radio Range
Wg Cdr	Wing Commander
WO	Warrant Officer

SELECT BIBLIOGRAPHY

Caygill, Peter, *Javelin from the Cockpit – Britain's First Delta Wing Fighter*, Pen and Sword, 2011.

Docherty, Tom, *Swift to Battle – No.72 Fighter Squadron RAF in action*, Pen and Sword, 2010.

Flintham, Vic and Thomas, Andrew, *Combat Codes*, Pen and Sword, 2008.

Halley, James J, *Broken Wings – Post-War Royal Air Force Accidents*, Air Britain, 1999.

Jefford, Wg Cdr C G, *RAF Squadrons*, Airlife, 1988.

Lindsay, Roger, *Service History of the Gloster Javelin*, Roger Lindsay, 1975.

Meekcoms, K J and Morgan, E B, *The British Aircraft Specifications File*, Air Britain, 1994.

Napier, Michael, *Gloster Javelin an Operational History*, Pen and Sword, 2016.

Palmer, Kel, *A Roving Commission*, iUniverse, 2007.

Sturtivant, Ray and Hamlin, John, *RAF Flying Training and Support Units since 1912*, Air Britain, 2007.

INDEX

PLACES

PERSONNEL

MILITARY ORGANISATIONS

French Air Force

Royal Air Force

OTHER UNITS

MISCELLANEOUS